The Life and Times of Ollie Barney

An Arizona Native Son

**An Autobiography By
Ollie O. Barney**

THE LIFE AND TIMES OF

OLLIE BARNEY

AN ARIZONA NATIVE SON

Written By

Ollie O. Barney

ISBN 978-0-7414-3609-2

Published by:

INFI∞ITY
PUBLISHING.COM

1094 New DeHaven Street, Suite 100
West Conshohocken, PA 19428-2713
Info@buybooksontheweb.com
www.buybooksontheweb.com
Toll-free (877) BUY BOOK
Local Phone (610) 941-9999
Fax (610) 941-9959

Printed in the United States of America

Published February 2014

N E

Dedication

This book is dedicated to my late wife, Beryl Barney, for her love and understanding during the years of our marriage.

There are many family members and friends to thank for helping me along the way, but there are two that I owe very special thanks: Layne Brandt and my daughter, Sherry Caldwell.

Thanks to Layne for the encouragement to start and finish this project, and for the patience to listen to my stories, *one more time*, while he was recording them. And thanks to Sherry for typing the stories and then making them into this book. I couldn't a-done without you.

Table of Contents

Chapter Five: The Army Years

Chapter Six: Family and Other Interesting People

Chapter Seven: Construction Companies

Chapter Eight: Hunting in Arizona and Mexico

Chapter Nine: International Hunts

Chapter Ten: Later Years

Introduction

Hello. My name is Layne Brandt. The date is October 2002, and we are beginning the collection of stories defining the life and times of Ollie O. Barney of Rio Rico, Arizona. Ollie was born and raised in Arizona and was 84 years young in January 2003. He has lived all of his life in Arizona, excepting his years in the Army, and has spent a lifetime hunting in Arizona and around the world. He is considered by many to be one of the best mountain lion hunters Arizona has ever seen. Ollie and I have been friends and lion-hunting partners for many years and I invite you to sit back, pour yourself a drink, light up a cigar and enjoy some of the best stories ever recorded.

Hello from me, too. I'm Sherry Caldwell, Ollie's daughter. I have transcribed the tape recordings Ollie has made over the past several years. From the beginning in October 2002 to the last tape made in August 2006, I have tried to capture the flavor and spirit of his stories. To set the background a little more than the above from Layne, I wanted to add the following:

Ollie O. Barney II is a second-generation Arizonan. He was born in Phoenix on January 23, 1919, the eldest of four sons born to Ollie and Hazel Barney. Ollie Senior was born in Camp Verde, just south of Flagstaff, on August 20, 1879, and moved to Southern Arizona about the turn of the 20th Century. He and his Uncle Jim settled in the Rincon Mountains east of Tucson and raised goats, then cattle, on ranches that were homesteaded when Arizona became a state in 1912.

Ollie was raised and lived primarily on the ranch until being drafted into the Army in January 1941. He served in the Pacific Theater from the beginning of World War II until it was nearly over in August 1945. The following years were full of working, raising a family, and hunting until he was able to retire and devote his time to guiding and hunting.

He has been a ranch kid, a cowboy (his discharge papers list his occupation as "cowpuncher"), a warrior, a rancher, a builder and a hunter. But during most of his adult life he has been, and still is, a very special dad. These are the stories of his life and accomplishments.

Chapter One   The Barney Family

Roots

I don't know a whole lot about my family, but I do know a little bit. My dad's father was a full-blooded Irishman. His mother was full-blooded English. On my mother's side, her father was half Irish and half Cherokee Indian. Her mother, I think, was first generation and she was Scots-Irish. That kinda explains what kind of blood I got, but I never figured it out and I probably never will.

My dad was born in 1879 in Oak Creek Canyon. His dad came from the Cherokee Nation, which is Oklahoma and they came to Arizona in 1873. He went to work up there in Camp Verde as kind of a half-assed carpenter and blacksmith for the Army, shoein' horses and workin' on their wagons. He told me back in those days, they had to make their own horseshoes. And they made their own nails. He told me they used to like to make the nails out of old gun barrels. They were steel and made pretty good horseshoe nails.

He told me about this one horse that his uncle gave 'im. He was a little horse; Dad called him "Chino." The following year, when they gathered up the horses, Uncle Jim said to Dad, "I gave you that little horse. This cowboy we had here breakin' these horses told me I stole that horse when we branded 'im. He said there's another one in there we stole, but I'm only gonna give you the one!" Dad said he rode that little horse down to this country when he came with Jim and 30 head of horses. One day, after they were here, he rode Chino from Benson to Bisbee for some reason – about 50 miles. The next morning at the table, there was some guy talkin' about this guy who rode his horse 50 miles the day before and the horse was in just a hell of a shape. My dad said, "God, I don't know how that could be my horse 'cause he was in good shape." He went down to the stable and checked 'im out and it was some other horse – it wasn't his.

3

Dad had a half-brother from his second step-dad, the one he called a "tinhorn gambler" and when the brother got up to 18, 19 years old, he joined the Army. He didn't like the Army so he deserted! He stole a horse and a posse trailed 'im up and their story was they'd found where he'd hung himself in a tree! They brought 'im back, and that's the story they told his mother. But Dad told me, "Back in those days, they hung horse thieves! And that's what happened to my half-brother!"

Back to my mother's side of the family: I already told that my Granddad Owens was half Irish and half Cherokee Indian. He was a fairly well-educated man. He had an aunt that raised him up that was pretty well educated. I guess she educated him at home. He got to where he worked in the mines and the smelters as an engineer. He was down in Nacacera, Mexico, workin' there in the mine and it was durin' one of the Mexican revolutions. My granddad and a couple of other mining men were comin' back and had a little river or somethin' there to cross and these Rurales opened fire on 'em! They killed one of the guys and Granddad got back to his house where he had a .30-.30 and two boxes of shells hid. He claimed he broke the revolution up! He found the Rurales, shot up his two boxes of shells and then he left! This Dr. Blodsoe, who worked later in Tucson, was sent to check on any of the wounded guys. He said that they'd packed part of 'em off when he got there, but there were still 21 dead Mexicans!

Granddad gathered up my grandmother and two or three kids and come out to Bisbee. My mother said there was a bridge there and when they'd go into town she'd run ahead to see how many dead Mexicans was layin' under the bridge. There was generally one or two of 'em! After he was back in Bisbee for six months or so, he went back to Nacacera to get 'im a job. He went to the mill foreman; he hired 'im, put 'im back to work. He said there was an old Mexican cop that he used to drink with. They called 'im "Buckskin." And ol' Buckskin come to 'im and give 'im a paper. Granddad talked Spanish, but he didn't read it. So he took this paper to the foreman and gave it to him and he read it. "Hell," he said, "this is a goddamn warrant for your arrest, dead or alive!" Well, he went back up there where he had this rifle hid, got that .30-.30 and went down to the railroad track. There was an engine hooked up to some cars so he climbed up in the cab and stuck that .30-.30 in this engineer's side, told him to unhook that train and head for the American side! That's the way he come out and I'll tell you, he never went back to Mexico!

My grandmother was one of the old pioneer women, you know. Her mother was first generation in the new world – half Irish and half Scottish. My granddad and grandmother got together over in New Mexico, some mining town and got married. They moved to Arizona and that's where my mother was conceived. Granddad was sent up to Colorado Springs and that's where she was born, but was raised in Arizona. My dad had had one or two wives before her, no, one wife, and he and my mother were married when she was about 17. They didn't get along too well and she give 'im a lot of hell and when I was maybe 18, 19 years old, they divorced. She moved down to Phoenix and remarried down there. My youngest brothers, Dick, Homer, and Alvin, went with her. I stayed with my dad, helped him run the ranch. Then I went into the Army and after I'd been out a couple of years, I bought the ranch from my dad. My step-mother was a good 'ol pioneer lady and she was real good to my dad and to us boys when we were around. I went down and bought the ranch, visited with him when I bought it, and told him that I'd pay him $7,500 that I'd won playin' poker in the Army. Then I'd pay so much a year, so much interest, and I had a date with him to go down to Bisbee and make out all the papers for the ranch. When I got there, my dad got me off to the side and said, "Elsie's raisin' hell about me sellin' this here ranch! She said we're not sellin' that ranch unless Junior can come up with a $5,000 down payment!" Of course, she'd never saw $5,000 in her life! So dad said, "Now what I want you to pay is like this: just $5,000, you can use that $2,500 for other things you've probably needed!" So that's the way I bought the ranch! Elsie was wantin' to sell it to her daughter and son-in-law and hell, they couldn't a-come up with $50! She really thought she'd kill the deal.

Ollie Barney, Senior

My dad was pretty much raised up there in the Flagstaff area. His mother had been married three times and back in those days, you know, a lady that'd been married three times was looked at kinda suspicious-like by the upper crust. She apparently had a business mind, hell, at one time she owned a whole city block there in Flagstaff. She's buried there in Flagstaff and I went and saw the cemetery. There's a lady in Flagstaff who's wrote a couple of books and she was real interested in my grandmother. She actually measured all the tall headstones in the cemetery and she claims that my grandmother has the tallest headstone in the place. I saw a picture of it in her book and, Christ, it's up there eight, nine foot high! After she died, this Woody, that the Woody Mountain is named after, got her the nice headstone.

Dad's other step-dad was a black cowboy and Dad always referred to him as a "tin-horn gambler." He said that his step-dad had a racehorse that he matched against another horse there in Flagstaff but got worried that maybe he didn't have the fastest horse. They had already put up the money and set a date for the race. So one moonlit night they sneaked both horses out and ran a race and sure enough, he found out that the other horse could beat his pretty easy! He knew he had to do something to call the race off, so he put the horses back, then ran a needle through the fetlock of his horse and pulled a horsehair in it and clipped it off on both sides. Of course, his horse came up lame, so they had to cancel the race and he got his money back! After the race was off, he pulled the hair out and the horse got well again.

My dad had a little cash saved up because he figured that he was leavin'. He had an old .38-.55 single shot rifle and his step-dad had a good Colt single action .45. Dad decided that, since he was leavin', he'd just steal that .45. His step-dad was off on a round-up somewhere so he hid that gun out in the barn. There were two bales of hay in there and he hid the pistol under one of the bales. Dad came back from work one evening and saw his step-dad's horse in the corral – he'd come home two or three days early. So he slipped in the barn to see what bale of hay was used and it was the one the pistol was under! Dad had already made up his mind that he's runnin' away to his uncle down on the Barney Pasture south of Flagstaff so he went and gathered up his little camp outfit and headed out for his Uncle Jim Barney. He was with Uncle Jim for eight years.

At that time, Uncle Jim went out on all the neighboring round-ups to look after his own cattle and horses and he'd leave my dad in their camp to take care of things while he was gone. And in the spring when they were brandin' and startin' to break the colts, Uncle Jim would hire a bronc rider to ride the four year-olds. Dad said that when the horses were two years old, they'd gather 'em up and castrate and halter break 'em, then turn 'em out again. At four years old, they'd start to break 'em to ride. The bronc buster would ride 'em for the first ten saddles and then Dad and Uncle Jim would take over. When the horses were bridle-wise, they'd sell 'em to the ranchers around there. They got good prices for 'em; they had good horses. He had 200 mares, so he raised quite a few horses.

Uncle Jim was quite a trader. Dad said they'd be in camp and they'd pretty much run outta groceries and money so Jim would get the sorriest damn horse they had for a packhorse and he'd go to Flagstaff. He'd stop around and visit and trade horses all the way into Flagstaff and trade horses all the way back. And when he got home, he'd have a lot better packhorse, a pack load of groceries and have money in his pocket, too!

Dad's Uncle Jim had a big ol' hound he called "Blutch." He was kind of a blue tick hound and according to Uncle Jim, the dog was absolutely worthless. Dad made up his mind one time that the next time Uncle Jim went out on a round-up and left that dog for him to take care of, he'd just kill 'im. But he figured that he wasn't worth the cartridge it'd take to kill 'im, so he was gonna tie the dog up and stab him with his Bowie knife! And when it came time for Uncle Jim to go on a round-up, he got all packed up with his bedroll and extra clothes on his packhorse and got on his horse. Then he whistled for ol' Blutch! He said to Dad, "I'm just gonna take ol' Blutch with me – if anybody's gonna have the pleasure of killin' him, I'll do it myself!" And Dad said that he never knew if his uncle was clairvoyant or maybe he'd been talkin' in his sleep!

Dad and his Uncle Jim moved to Southern Arizona when copper went to $.22 per pound. Jim sold his ranch and most of the livestock and brought 30 head of young horses with 'em. They ended up in Happy Valley (on the east side of the Rincon Mountains east of Tucson) and had a copper claim or two. Dad said that they worked there for about a year and a half before he went broke. A couple of the Purdyman boys had come down with 'em and they were broke. So they quit and went back to Flagstaff. Dad went back to the Barney pasture area and for two years he made his living huntin' bear and lion for the bounty money. The government was paying $20 for a lion and $10 for a bear.

He'd killed five grizzly bears up in Northern Arizona, in Sycamore Canyon. When he went back up and was huntin' bears and lion for the bounties, he had a partner. My dad had trapped one a-these grizzly bears and he'd broke the drag on the trap and he was just draggin' this trap. So they're trailin' this bear up a big canyon and the bear charged 'em! And this huntin' buddy had a .30-.30 and he fired one shot and he broke to run. My dad's first shot, it broke the bear's shoulder. On his second shot, after he'd hit that shoulder and the bear went down, he just cut a furrow right down on top a-that bear's back. The third shot, the bear was right on 'im and he shot 'im in the head and the bear fell right beside 'im. And he jumped off to the side and fell and hit his knee on a rock and he was crippled up for several days. He went along and a month or so later his partner trapped a bear and it broke the drag off. They was trailin' it along and my dad says, 'Well, what are you gonna do when we find this bear?" He says, "I'm gonna do just like I did last time – I'm gonna take my one shot and run!" My dad says, "Well, you just track this bear up and take your one shot and run. I'm goin' to camp! I'm not trackin' this bear up with you for one shot and run!"

It went along there for about three or four months and one a-
these black cowboys come into camp. He'd found this bear,
dead in a water hole. He said there was seven head of
livestock layin' out in front a-that water hole, that this bear'd
run out and killed before he died. So you can get an idea,
you know, they charged with a little goddamned enthusiasm!
If they can catch healthy cattle and kill 'em! I understand
why my dad didn't go back for seconds with this partner
takin' one shot and run!

And then he told about a trick he played on this here partner
a-his. One mornin' it was his time to wrangle the horses and
he got out there and in a couple a-places he made some 18-
inch bear tracks where this guy would see 'em on the trail.
And the next mornin' it was this guy's time to wrangle and
he come back and boy, he was excited, tellin' my dad about
these bear tracks! 18 Inches long! My dad says, "Aw hell,
you never saw anything like that! Hell, there isn't any bear
with 18 inch tracks." And this guy swore to Christ that he'd
saw 'em and he'd measured 'em out and they were about 18
inches long! My dad told me, "I never even bothered to go
look at 'em. Hell, I just told the guy he was just wrong. He
was just imaginin' things!"

While Dad was huntin' in the north, Uncle Jim had gone to
Texas and bought a bunch of Angora goats. He bought
goats because out in that country, the Heart Cattle
Company had the place overgrazed with cattle but there
was a lot of browse for goats. After a couple of years, he
wrote my dad a letter and said that if Dad would go down
there and help him with the goats for five years, they would
divide 'em and Dad could take his half and move over to a
place of his own. It turned out that after three years they had
more goats than they could run, so they divided 'em up then.

But in the meantime, Uncle Jim was always busy herdin'
goats. He owned a two-gallon canteen and he told my dad,
"Ollie, the next time one of us goes to Benson, I want to get
a one-gallon canteen. This two-gallon canteen is too heavy
to pack!" So Dad said, "Why don't you just fill it half-full?" "By

9

God, Ollie," Jim said, "I never thought of that!" And he never did buy a smaller canteen.

From time-to-time, Dad would hire somebody to help herd the goats. This goatherder kept seein' a nice buck or two and he wanted to take a day off and go huntin'. My dad said that he finally caved in and loaned him his .30-.30 and a box a-shells. Dad took the goats out and the goatherder took the .30-.30 and the shells and he went out and he hunted all morning. It got along about lunch time so he got up on a big rock on the edge of a canyon. He's finished his lunch and gettin' ready to leave and a nice buck, a real nice one, jumped up out from under this rock and run off down into canyon and climbed out on the other side. He shot the whole box of .30-.30 shells at 'im and never touched 'im! He told dad, "It made me so damn mad I just jacked off!"

After Dad moved to his own place, just a few miles away, Jim got his brother, Dad's father, to come down there and help him. And a lion came into the goat pen, killed a goat and packed it off about a quarter-mile from the corrals. They tracked it and found the carcass and then took a couple-a Number 150 bear traps – they have about a ten-inch jaw spread with big teeth – and set them up near the dead goat. They had one covered up and were coverin' the second one when Uncle Jim reached over near the first one to get a handful of stuff and got caught in the trap! In the excitement, while Granddad was tryin' to help Jim out, he stepped in the other trap! Now they're both caught in the traps! But they finally got their clamps and got Jim out first and then got the second one off Granddad's foot. *That* would've made a movie!

The Jess Howard Stories

A good friend of Dad's Uncle Jim was named Jess Howard – and he was a friend of mine, too. If you read about him in Arizona history, they refer to him as "Bear" Howard. He hunted and killed a lot of bears and he'd bring the meat into Flagstaff and sell it. Back in those days it was legal and folks really liked that bear fat to make piecrusts. My dad did quite a lot a-huntin' with his uncle. Jess was an old-timer who'd come from California, but before that he'd fought in the Mexican War. He'd been wounded; got a mini-ball through one lung and it had lodged somewhere in his back. He told my dad that when he got wounded he went up into some shelving rocks and got back into a place where he was out of the fire. He was pretty sick and had lost a lot of blood but he still had his rifle with the bayonet on it. A Mexican came up on him and stuck his head into the hiding place, so Jess stuck the bayonet in the guy's head but was too weak to pull it out!

Jess finally lived through the wound and the war and got moved out to California but got into trouble there! I've read in Arizona history about "Bear" Howard getting into some kind of a jackpot in California and had to leave. They didn't expound on the story, but Jess told my dad what had happened. He had had a nice wheat field growin' and one day he went into town in his wagon and when he came back there's a Mexican sheepherder out in the middle of his wheat field sitting on a stump. And there's about 2000 sheep just ruinin' his field! So he got off his wagon and took a rest on the wagon wheel and killed that Mexican! They put him in jail and were going to hang him! His daughter made him a cake and hid a hacksaw blade in it so he sawed through a couple of window bars and got out. He left California; he told my dad, "I just tore their goddamn jail down, shit on it and walked off!" And that was his version of the problem in California.

My dad told me about a time he was huntin' with Jess Howard and his Uncle Jim. They were comin' back into camp one evening, comin' down a canyon and a little black bear jumped up and started runnin' down the canyon. Jess had an old .45-.70 single-shot, his uncle had .45-.70 single-shot and he had a .38-.55 single-shot and they all took a shot at the bear. The bear ran up a tree and then fell out – dead! Uncle Jim and Jess got into a big argument about who killed the bear; both claimed they'd killed it. When they got into camp and skinned the bear out they found this .38-

.55 bullet in him! Dad said, "That settled the argument!" And that was the first bear Dad ever killed.

There were a lot of bear around back then, in fact Dad claimed that he had killed five grizzles in the eight years he was in Sycamore Canyon. One story he told was about a big bear that had a crippled foot or something; they called him "Old Dad." When they finally caught the bear with the dogs, they were all in there shooting and finally killed it. Ol' Jess Howard took it into town and they estimated it weighed 800 pounds. He sold the meat and the fat for lard.

Another story Dad told on this Jess Howard was about the time they were walkin' down in a brushy canyon and Jess told Dad that he had wounded a bear in that canyon with his single-shot rifle. The bear had turned and charged him so Jess ran for a tree that had a fairly low limb. He was able to jump up high enough to catch it and pull himself up into the tree. Then he stayed there until the bear died. For several years after that, whenever he was in that canyon, he would make a run at that tree and jump at the limb but he never could catch it again! That bear on his ass inspired him to jump a little higher than he thought he could!

Sometime after that, Dad and Jess Howard were out huntin' one morning and then came back to the house for lunch. Ol' Jess was telling 'em, "By God, I shot the biggest ol' pinto bear I ever saw, but I just wounded 'im!" So after lunch they all went back out to track this big pinto bear and found 'im – but he was one of the Black Angus bulls Uncle Jim had just bought; the one with some white spots on him! Luckily, it was just a flesh wound and the bull got over it.

Dad and Uncle Jim went by Jess Howard's camp one morning and Jess was in the corral butchering a steer. And it was one of Uncle Jim's steers! And he said to Jess, "Goddamn it, what are you doing killin' and butcherin' one of my steers!" "Aw, hell," said Jess, "I didn't know it was your steer! One of the black cowboys drove it into the corral and said to butcher it! And I butchered it!" Dad said that after that, every time they rode by Jess' camp, they drove one of the black cowboy's steers or calves into the corral and would tell Jess to butcher it! The Old Man said that Jess used quite a bit of meat because he had eight or ten damn hounds around there he was feedin'.

When they were out ridin', goin' down a trail off into a big canyon, Jess looked across and said, "By God, Ollie, there's a damn lion!" Dad looked over there and saw one of Jess' hound dogs that was colored about the same as a lion. So Jess got off his horse, got his gun out and went to aimin' at it. Pretty soon he dropped his gun and said, "By God, that's not a lion! That's one of my dogs!" Hell, Dad was going to let him shoot it!

Figure 1. Ollie Sr. in Front of the Original Ranch House (About 1925)

Chapter Two   Early Ranch Years

School Years

When I was about six years old, my mother and dad decided that I needed a little education. We lived on a ranch in Happy Valley and there were no schools. So they sent me to Superior, Arizona, with my grandparents on my mother's side, Alvin and Rachel Owens. I went into school there in Superior and I remember one girl there who had my name, Ollie. I have no recollection whatsoever of what she looked like, but I do remember that. I also remember when they dumped the slag from the smelter at night – they'd come out with the little mine cars loaded with this slag and dump it and I could see the fire still in it.

I probably went to school there for a couple a-months when the teacher wrote a letter to my mother. She didn't think my grades was what they should be, so my mother come up and took me outta school. And apparently she had overstayed her time a day or two and we rode the bus back to Tucson. I remember the streetcars runnin' up and down there and after a few minutes, seein' my dad come a-walkin' down the street, packin' his .30-.30. Course, he saw my mother there, and me, and a couple of the younger boys and he got on the bus with us, with his .30-.30. And I remember comin' back on the bus to Benson, all dirt road and there was some of 'em talkin' on the bus about gradin' that road and figured they was gonna wear it out because they was cuttin' off a few inches of the surface ever time.

We got back to Benson and course my dad had his wagon and team there at his dad's place. We went back to the ranch and it was several years after that before I got back to school. They moved us down on the San Pedro River. My mother was camped in a couple of tents; one she lived in it and cooked in it and one was for us boys – my younger brothers and me. My dad, he brought us down a bag of apples – a gunnysack, probably 50 or 100 pounds. That day the wind blew the tent down. And this Soco Farm that was there, they had hogs and I remember the hogs come in and tore that tent up gettin' to those apples. So my dad, he got back and got the tent back up and sewed some kinda patch on it – it wasn't too good. That was down at the old Soco School where we spent a couple a-terms. Then they moved the school up to Cascabel. This Cascabel was a little store run by the Harens, and they had the Post Office there. And how the Post Office got its name; they was a-thinkin' and a-tryin' to figure out a name for it when a Mexican come in with a big pair of rattlesnake rattles. Mrs. Harens asked what they called rattles in Spanish and he said, "Cascabels." And that's how Cascabel come to get its name.

We went to school there at this Cascabel School for a couple of years during the Depression times. There was this Mrs. Kane – she taught there for two years. The next two years of schooling was at the ranch. The county paid so much, you know, to take children away from the ranch and board 'em. The county paid this Mrs. Kane that money they would a-paid my folks to take us to Benson or back down to Cascabel to school us at home. After two years, I graduated from the eighth grade there at the ranch. And that's all the formal education I ever had. I've had to pick up a few little things since then. I was always good at math and reasonably good at history, but I've always had problems with language. I didn't rate very high; I always got poor grades on that all the time, but the rest of the stuff, I got good grades on. Really, even today, I don't talk the best English in the world.

Along about that time, it was mostly Mexicans; all the ranches and businesses in town hired Mexicans – it was probably 80% Mexicans in Southern Arizona then. My folks was both bilingual and they'd go and spend the night on a visit with Mexican families and never a word of English spoken. Mexicans at that time didn't talk any English. Us kids would play and we never had a language problem – it wasn't that I was bilingual, but kids can play and their vocabulary's not very big.

Along about that time when I was goin' to school, the Okies started comin' into the country and a lotta Texans. These old maid schoolteachers, they wouldn't allow a word of Mexican bein' spoken on the school grounds or in the school. These teachers was bilingual and could instruct their pupils in Mexican if needed and they done a real good job a-teachin' the kids English. Nowadays, these Mexicans, they all talk better English than I do.

Havin' grown up with Mexicans, I've always had kind of a soft place in my heart for 'em. I really like the Mexican people and I like some of their forms a-livin'. One thing I like is that they're all strong family. And another thing I like about 'em: if you've got a Mexican friend, you've got a loyal friend! No ifs and ands about how you stand with 'em. If they like you, they like you and they're friends for life.

I used to work with Mexicans and I kinda felt sorry for 'em, havin' liked 'em, and they always havin' the shitty end of the jobs. After bein' around 'em more and seein' their wives and girlfriends, all nice-lookin' women, hell, I quit feelin' sorry for 'em!

First Deer Hunt

A young fellow was in Benson at the same time my dad was, gettin' on towards October. This guy, if I recall, his name was Max True, told my dad, "Mr. Barney, would it be all right if I come out to your ranch and deer hunted; rough it a little bit?" Dad says, "Well, you just come right on out and we'll rough it a little." Come the day before deer season, he drove in there with a friend in a wagon and he had a whole wagonload a-groceries. You know, back in those days you could buy a wagonload of groceries for $15 or $20, if you had the $20.

I went with 'em and I don't know how old I was then, but I couldn't a-been over seven, probably at the most. We headed out huntin'; they had their guns and everything and my dad, he was a-runnin' the operation. He'd tell these guys

16

where to go and where we'd meet, you know, pointin' out the landmarks. Along about 2:00 o'clock, this young feller said to Dad, "Mr. Barney, it's startin' to get late. Don't you think we should start headin' towards the ranch?" My dad says, "Well, we're not a-goin' into the ranch; we're gonna lay out tonight." The guy says, "We gotta! I'm getting' hungry!" Dad says, "You're gettin' hungry? With all these acorns layin' around under these oak trees? And these juniper berries? If you're hungry, you can eat some of them. Remember, we're roughin' it!" And we just kept on a-goin' until late. Then we camped, built a big campfire and we laid around this campfire. My dad, he'd put a few pieces of jerky in his pocket so he slipped me a couple of pieces – one for the evening meal and another piece for morning meal. But these two guys, they didn't get anything.

We went on huntin' the next morning and dad told 'em, "Hell, you can do a lot better huntin' when you're hungry than when you just got a full stomach." We hunted back towards the ranch that day, got 'em in about sundown, and I'll tell you, right away, they broke into their groceries! They had 'em a campfire a-goin' and they was a-cookin'!

For several years after that he come back out there and we went huntin'. I had my uncle's .25-.20, my dad had his .30-.30 and the same two guys had whatever they always used. We got up there on what we called Fox Mountain and a little ol' whitetail buck jumped up and run off towards some brush. I was the only one who got a shot at 'im and he never did come outta that brush. These two guys was wonderin' why that deer didn't show up again, come out. My dad said, "Well, Junior probably killed that deer!" We went up and sure enough, it was lyin' there in the brush. I got the first deer on that hunt and it was the second deer I ever killed in my life.

When I come back from the Army in 1945, I run onto this guy and he was tellin' me about my dad and this hunt. He says, "I told 'im that I wanted to rough it and he took me at my word!!! We roughed it for two days. And I never did tell that ol' man Barney I wanted to come out and rough it again!"

Life in the 1930s

This happened back in the Depression days. We were camped down on the San Pedro River by the schoolhouse. They had this Post Office: the Ahren's, in conjunction with the grocery store, ran the Post Office. My mother give me a one-dollar bill to walk up to the store and get three pounds of salt pork. I bought the three pounds of salt pork and it was ten cents a pound. I got the seventy cents change and come back and give the seventy cents change to Mother and she asked, "What did you have to pay for that salt pork?" I said, "Well, it was ten cents a pound." "Oh," she says, "that's outrageous! That's way too high! You shouldn't a-bought it!" And you know what salt pork is now, over $2.00 a pound!

I remember about Levi's, too. When I got up in my early teens, I was buyin' my own clothes and I could buy a pair of Levi's at Porter's for $2.00. And they paid the postage! My dad said that when he was 15, 16 years old, he went to work up in Flagstaff in the box factory. He said Levi's then was costin' a dollar a pair. Now, they're about $23 or more and I don't wear 'em.

Roping Wild Burros

I was boardin' with the Glenns for a month or so and Christmas come along. Comin' down the San Pedro River road there was an old man and his wife by the name of McCluskey. They was in a covered wagon pulled by burros. They'd built some fence for my dad a year or two before so I knew who they were. I was only about eight and Rex Glenn, he was a couple a-years older than I was, so he couldn't a-been over 12. We struck up a conversation with this McClusky and his wife about their covered wagon and their burros. Mr. McCluskey said he needed another burro. Rex

18

says, "Well, what would you pay for another burro?" "Oh," he says, "I'd gladly give five dollars for one." Rex informed 'im, he says, "We'll have you a burro here tomorrow mornin'!"

So we went home and saddled up and went lookin' for the wild burros that come down to the San Pedro every evening to water. When they come in to water, we charged 'em and Rex roped one of these wild Jacks; he was a stud burro. Between the two of us, we got him into the corral and tied him to a log overnight with a hackamore we'd rigged up. The next morning we worked 'im a little while and got him to lead and we led 'im over to where the McCluskeys was camped across the river, about a mile away. So we delivered our burro and collected our five dollars. As far as I know, they went on down the river with their extra burro and no problems.

This is just an example of what kids would do 70 or 75 years ago. Now, you know, I don't think you could find eight or ten-year-old kids who could go out and rope a wild burro and tie 'im to a log with a rigged-up hackamore and then deliver him and collect five dollars.

The Rooster

One day at the ranch – I don't know where my mother was; she was gone a lot of the time – us boys was a-batchin' there at the ranch with our dad. On this particular day, he decided to ride down to the post office at Cascabel. It was about a ten-mile horseback ride down to the San Pedro River where the post office was. He had some chickens and among these chickens was a big ol' Rhode Island Red rooster. Now this ol' rooster was a kind of a feisty rooster and sometimes he'd charge one of us boys.

My dad, he always kept a little bootleg whiskey 'cause he liked to have a toddy in the mornings; it was the only time he drank. He didn't drink coffee, he drank tea, and he would have this toddy with his tea at breakfast. We got to thinkin' how fun it would be to get this rooster drunk – I guess we were a little bored there by ourselves. Course, we had a little problem figurin' out how we was gonna get the rooster drunk 'cause he wouldn't drink it and we didn't know how to mix it in with his food. But we found a little rubber tube that we could slip down his throat. So I got my dad's jug of whiskey and took a big mouthful of this bootleg whiskey and I force-fed this poor ol' rooster – I put that tube in his mouth and pushed this whiskey down in 'im. We pulled out the tube and turned 'im loose and the ol' rooster, he's walkin' around there. Pretty soon, he's startin' to get a little more lively! He strutted across the pen, threw his head up in the air and crowed real loud three times. Then he spied a hen out there among all these other chickens and he run out there and "flopped her" and wandered around some more. By now, he's gettin' a little wobbly and pretty soon he's down and out! We figured he's dead, so we chopped his head off, plucked all his feathers out of 'im, quartered him all up and got him all ready to eat. I knew, since I was the oldest, that I'd have to 'fess up to my dad when he got back. (Now that I'm grown up and drank a little whiskey myself, I wonder if maybe that rooster wasn't dead, he was just passed out!)

By the time my dad got home it was after dark and I got right on down there where he was unsaddlin' his horse and told him that we'd killed his rooster. He wanted to know how so I told him the whole story. He was quiet a bit and then asked, "What did you do with the rooster?" Well, I told him how we had chopped off the head, boiled up some water and plucked out the feathers, then quartered him up. "We got the meat," I said. My dad finally said, real serious like, "Well, you know we haven't had any chicken and dumplings for a long time, so that's what we'll do with that rooster." He never scolded or corrected me for that and the next day we had the biggest pot of chicken and dumplings I've ever seen!

Making Jerky

One day at the ranch, our mother was still gone and dad was off somewhere, and a couple of us boys were out ridin', checkin' the water holes. We found this cow that had run her hind leg under a root and broke the leg up in the thigh. We really didn't know what to do, but we did know that she couldn't live with her leg broke up in there. So we went back to the ranch and got an axe and knives and one of the other

Figure 2. Ollie (right) and Brothers Ready for Anything (About 1932)

boys and we went up and chopped this root in two and got the cow out. I shot her, then we skinned her out and started makin' jerky. We had a wire corral there and we had jerky all over this wire corral. We ended up with four gunnysacks full of jerky.

When dad come back we had to tell him what happened; we said we got her out, but with her leg broke way up in the thigh there was no way of savin' 'er, so we butchered her out and got four sacks of jerky. He asked, "What did you do with the calf?" We said that we had brought it back and got it on one of the milk cows. He figured that was the best we could do. Later on, we went over to see Alvin Owens who was runnin' that Agua Caliente Ranch at that time, and took him a sack of the jerky. He was real glad to get the jerky.

Another one of our escapades that we never told Dad about was tryin' to ride the milk cows with our saddles on 'em. We had a lot of trouble keepin' the saddles on, but we rigged up the britchin' and rode all the cows. I know now that he knew that somethin' went on because we'd left a lot of tracks around there. He never said anything – he never put a lot of restrictions on us boys, he was real tolerant. He could be firm with us – he was a great dad!

Figure 3. The Barney Family: Homer, Dick, Alvin, Hazel, Ollie Sr., Ollie Jr. (About 1935)

Chapter Three   Neighbors

Dan Allen

My dad preached to us boys: he'd say, "If you wanna have good friends, you gotta be a good friend. If you wanna have good neighbors, you gotta be a good neighbor. And there'll be people you'll run on to that you absolutely can't get along with. So you hafta stay away from 'em because it's agin the law to kill 'em!" My dad had good neighbors; he had one that was kinda little bit "iffy". They'd had a dispute a time or two in their life and one of 'em, the most serious one, was in the early 1940s.

Durin' World War II, they was a-trainin' these pilots here in Tucson and accordin' to my dad, they was flyin' all over that country. My dad's fence come up there and cornered. Right there in the corner, ol' Dan had a water tank and he had some horses and cattle waterin' there. Accordin' to my dad, he figures that one a-these pilots saw those horses and he buzzed 'em and run 'em over the fence. It knocked the fence down and the horses run over the fence but after they were over it, the fence jumped back up! The damn horses – there was 11 of 'em there and when ol' Dan found 'em, 10 had already died from lack of water. One was still alive and they saved him. Dan come over and looked my dad up and he was out on the range a-ridin and ol' Dan found 'im. He told my dad that these horses was lost and he wanted my dad to pay for 'em! And my dad told 'im, "I can't pay you for all those horses; you should a-been watchin' your water and it would a-never happened! I got cattle in there but they're all waterin' at the ranch and I see 'em ever day when they come in and water. But I'll pay you for half of 'em." "Nope," says Dan, "By god, you gotta pay for all of 'em!" My dad just wasn't gonna do it.

My dad was down workin', he had a garden there below the house, and ol' Dan come over there one day and he jumped my dad again about gettin' paid for them horses. Dad had his rifle leanin' up agin a tree there...Dad never went anywhere without a gun! Hell, he wouldn't go to the bathroom – it was outside – without a gun a-some kind! My dad says, "You know, Dan, I tried to pay you for half of 'em but you made such an ass of yourself I'm not a-gonna pay you a damn thing! It's your responsibility to take care of your horses and you let 'em die from neglectin' your work." Dan got his rope down and said, "Mr. Barney, I'm just gonna whup you over your old grey head with this doubled rope!" My dad says, "Dan, you're a goddamn coward and a son-of-a-bitch to boot! You don't have the goddamn nerve to hit me over the goddamn head with a double rope!" And he had that .22 leanin' there agin the tree where he'd been shootin' birds that'd been peckin' around his garden. Ol' Dan says, "Mr. Barney, you're gettin' mad. I'm goin' home!"

That would a-been a hell of a mistake of his part – he wouldn't a-hit my dad over the head with a double rope and lived to tell about it! And I think he realized it, too!

Clinton Allen

Here in the past week we had company, an ol' kid that we grew up with that had a ranch – his folks had the ranch just north of us. His dad was Dan Allen.

Years earlier, when I got back from the Army – I'd got back in August – this was up in, probably, November and the nights was terrible cold and we had to move some cattle to the shippin' pens. We got over to the Heart; that was the first drive 'cause we had to go on out to the railroad at Miramonte and that was a two-and-a-half-day drive. We stayed at the Heart this first night and Dan Allen had this Clinton; he was a 16-year-old kid. Hell of a good kid. In fact, he turned into a pretty good man. This morning there when we saddled up to start these cattle out, his dad had him on a big, stout horse, a sorrel. The ol' horse was all humped up and the kid got on 'im and it pitched and threw 'im off out there in the corral. Christ, he hit out there on his back and his butt and it ripped the seam in the seat of his pants up through the crotch. The kid finally got up and he's not cryin' but he's whimperin'. His dad caught the horse and brought it up and told him to get back on it. This kid, I could see that he didn't wanna get on it and I didn't wanna see 'im get on it. I told his dad, I says, "You're not puttin' that kid back on that horse! Hell, he's already thrown 'im real hard and he could hurt 'im! This ground's frozen! I'm gonna put my saddle on 'im and I'll ride the bastard. The bastard needs a little education."

So we changed horses and saddles and I got 'im and the bastard's tryin' to pitch. I was strong enough that I could hold his head up. Then we got the cattle to goin' and I told his dad, "I'm goin' up to the head of 'em." When I got up to the head – they'd been through here before and they knew how to go. So I got on up about a quarter mile ahead of 'em and I jumped off quick and took my lariat, pulled a loop out and put it around his nose just above the bridle bit. I got back on 'im and while I was off, I'd cut me a whippin' stick about three foot long. Out at the end of it, it was about the size of my thumb and a little bigger back on the end I got. I pulled his head around right up as far as I could get and dallied the rope around the saddle horn and just reached up and spurred him in the shoulder and hard as I could. Christ, I really worked the shoulder over! He's jumpin' around and I'm beatin' 'im with this stick; I'm makin' some damn welts on his goddamn rear end! Well, I got that shoulder cut up pretty good so I just whipped my rope around and pulled it up the other side and I worked that shoulder over real good! I worked his other side over pretty good with that stick. Hell, he'd worked up a pretty good damn sweat! And a little froth around on that bastard where he's sweatin'! Bastard was hurtin'!

I took my rope off and curled it back up and got around back up to the head of the cattle. Along about an hour of so, his dad come up. He saw that horse's shoulder all worked over and these big welts on his goddamn butt and I still got the stick. He asked, "What happened?" I said, "He just tried to do the same damn thing with me that he did with Clinton! I think I took all the goddamn buck outta him for awhile." He looked at those shoulders and said, "Did he pitch with you?" I said, "Jesus Christ, what do you think I was spurrin' 'im in the damn shoulder for if you didn't think he pitched? Of course he pitched! He won't pitch anymore today and I don't think he'll pitch anymore on this trip." And Clinton, he told me as far as he knows that horse never did pitch with anybody after that.

Course, while they were here in the area, they come out; they wanted to see the trophy room. His sister lives over in Sonoita and he lives down in Missouri. When he got outta college, he went to college with Dick, and somewhere along he bought 'im a little airplane. And he went to work there at FICO for Keith Walden when they was plantin' their trees in there at first. He said he worked for Keith, I think he said three years, when they got all the pecans planted. He had this little airplane and he said he fooled around leavin' there and saw a ditch that was overflowin'. So he flew back around to land in the river there and let the irrigator know that this ditch was broke. He said he come in there too close to some ranch that had a phone line goin' into it and he took a big section outta it! This thing is draggin' all that damn wire and he landed in the river and got the wire all strung out that was tangled up in the plane. A wrangler rode down there a-horseback and asked, "Why did you land here in the creek?" He said, "I had to tell this irrigator that the ditch was broken." The wrangler didn't know he'd wiped out his goddamn phone line!

When the trees was all planted, he quit. Keith told him, he says, "Young man, I want you to come into the office with me." He went in with ol' Keith and they just visited there awhile and that Keith, he could fly over his new trees in his twin airplane and land and come up there and tell 'em ever mistake they were makin'! Anyway, Keith told him, "Young man, if you ever come back and you wanna go to work here on this farm, you've got a job!" Then Keith gave him a month's paycheck, sayin', "This money might come in handy, you know, before you get lined out on another job." He told me all the good things about Keith! He was impressed with that old man.

From there, he went down on the Texas coast somewhere and learned to fly helicopters. For years there, until he retired, that's all he done, he flew helicopters out supplyin' these offshore drillin' rigs. He said that was a good job; they had a lot of fun in doin' it (and got in trouble a few times). He survived it and he was back out here about five years ago, after he'd retired. He's the same age as Dick, maybe 75 or 76 years old now. He had a helicopter then. This trip, he'd traded his helicopter off and had an airplane, a four-seater of some kind. He said he was flyin' out here and got over by Lordsburg and there was two big storm clouds a-beatin' right up in front. He landed in Lordsburg right quick! When the storm kinda passed over, he got back in his airplane, got airborne and here come another damn storm! He landed again and called his sister to come and get him – and his airplane was still parked over in Lordsburg!

Another story about Clinton: just after I got outta the Army, Clinton told me about this A20 airplane that crashed into the Rincons, over by Vail. Him and another ol' kid walked up there and apparently the crew had bailed out or something, there wasn't anybody killed. But they had two .50 caliber machine guns on this plane. They was kinda banged up but these two boys, they packed one of 'em apiece off the mountain and hid 'em! He was tellin' me about it and he had some .50 caliber ammunition he'd got somewhere – he might of got it off that airplane! But he had 20 or 30 rounds of the stuff, some singles and some in the clips, and he said the guns were pretty banged up and one of 'em, the barrel was bent. I says, "Hell, bring 'em out here. We'll strip 'em down and maybe we'll get enough good pieces; we'll put one back together!" So this one Saturday, he come back from high school and he had these two blamed .50 caliber machine guns. We took 'em out on the workbench – you know I had a machine gun section at one time there when I was a corporal – and I knew how to strip these here Browning machine guns. The .30's anyway and the .50's was made the same way, only bigger. We stripped both down and I got enough good parts, I put one of 'em back together. The sear fired electrical but we didn't have any 24 volts or whatever it took to work the sear, but you could cock it and you could take a rod and poke the sear and shoot it!

We had it out there on the workbench, clamped in a vise, and we moved it around it and had a outhouse out there about 50, 60 yards. We aimed it at that and this damned ol' hound dog; he's a layin' there under the workbench. I put one of these shells in there and poked it and Christ, that thing went off and knocked a lotta the stuff off the workbench! And that damn hound, outta there he leapt with his tail between his legs just a-hollerin' like he was shot! Well, that worked pretty good, so we put a clip in. Touched it off and fired about eight or ten rounds through that thing before the rod got off the sear and got it to stop shootin'. Christ, I had Clinton and his mother Elizabeth all excited about shootin' that damn machine gun! We got some hits on their outhouse, too! Then his mother got real excited, thinkin', hell, we'd get in trouble for stealin' that damn machine gun off the airplane!

I took the bad parts and took 'em over to the ranch and they was just sittin' there in an empty room there in the house and a deputy sheriff called me up, wantin' to know about that machine gun. I said, "Hell, I picked it up there on the mountain, off a damn wrecked airplane. They'd left it there." And he said, "I would sure like to have it." I asked, "You didn't take it did you?" He says, "No, I didn't take it." I says, "Well, if you're not gonna put me in jail over havin' it, you can have the bastard." And he went back and got it. And ol' Clinton, he took that damn one he had and he hid it somewhere there on the ranch. There was some rocks up there and he said he was gonna bury it up there in a crevice. This is years ago. I looked for it but I never could find it. This last trip he told me he'd buried it where no one would ever find it.

It's out there buried somewhere. He knows where it is but whether he could find it or not I don't know. Hell, that thing would of sold pretty good down there in Mexico when they was havin' a revolution.

Anyway, while he was there in the trophy room, he saw a pair of his dad's spurs that my dad had traded him out of when this kid was about two or three years old. My dad had told me this kid, this Clinton, this little kid, was wild! He said, "God, what a noisy little devil! I nicknamed him 'Hyena'!" I showed Clinton these spurs and I told 'im the story about how my dad had traded his dad for 'em. They'd been used a lot. I told 'im, "You know, you can have these spurs if you want 'em. They don't mean much to me." He said, "What can I do for you?" I said, "All you can do for me: if you want those spurs, take 'em! They just don't mean a lot to me and they might mean something to you." Boy, he was really beamin'! He was hangin' onto those spurs when he left! He had no idea that I had those spurs. He asked if I still had a huntin' knife that his dad had made for me when I was in the Army – give it to me when I got back – but I didn't. I was pretty sure one of my wetbacks had packed it off, 'cause it just disappeared one day. I remember that knife. His dad, Dan Allen, was pretty handy at makin' things.

AB Carey

I've had some real interestin' friends and neighbors in my lifetime and one I recall is this AB Carey, a little ol' dried-up guy, had a whinin' voice. AB was a real good friend of my dad's and ever time Dad and his wife would go into Benson, they'd stop and spend the night with AB and his wife. Everbody called him AB because his initials were ABC. They was good friends. Anyway, both of 'em did a lotta readin' and they had things to talk about. The one time they had a little "discussion" – it didn't ruin their friendship or anything – but it was when they was dividin' up the forest allotments.

I remember that him and my dad – the Forest Service had to fence their allotments off, you know, put the partition fences in. My dad, he made a deal with this AB Carey and his Mexicans to put the division fence in between us. There was a long ridge that come up through, and up on the main mountain there, the Rincons, was some big bluffs up there.

Their agreement was to run this fence pretty well on up this ridge and tie into these bluffs on the mountain and that would separate the ranches. My dad and I were ridin' one day and we run onto ol' AB and his fence crew and he had the fence clear down in this Deer Creek. He was goin' across to another bluff and the way he was puttin' the fence in, it was gonna cut my dad off of quite a chunk of his Forest land and one of the best waters he had! He had this fence down into the creek pretty well built, he hadn't put stays on it or anything. My dad reminded 'im, he said, "AB, you know in our agreement, you was supposed to stay on top of the ridge there and run into the mountain bluffs up on the Rincons, not over here where you're goin'. You're cuttin' me off from my water and I'm not a-gonna let you do it!" And ol' AB give 'im a little problem. Finally, my dad said, "AB, you can either roll this fence up or leave it, I don't care what you do, but you're gonna stay up on that ridge!" Then we left. That was the end of the argument 'cause ol' AB knew he wasn't gettin' away with it.

Later I heard he was tellin' one a-my other neighbors, he says, "That Ollie Barney made me so *goddamn* mad I just wanted to hit 'im...but I was afraid to!"

Another time this Rex Glenn that I grew up with, we went down there to AB's ranch to help 'im round-up. He had a little Briggs and Stratton engine that he was workin' on – it pumped water from the well down in the corrals up to a holdin' tank for the house. Hell, we sit there for 15 minutes, it seemed like, might not a-been but five, no one spoke a word and ol' AB, he's a-tinkerin' with this motor. Finally he got up and he says, "Boys, if one a-these goddamn little Briggs and Stratton engines won't drive you crazy, just get yourself two of 'em!"

On this same trip, his wife had a little feisty lapdog a-some kind that she called "Leppie". And Leppie was in heat and she got outta the house. His wife sent AB out lookin' for this dog with a flashlight in the dark. God, he was gone for 10 or 15 minutes and pretty soon he come in and just went over and sit down in his chair and jerked his hat down, kinda sullen-like. His wife come out and says, "AB, didn't you find Leppie?" "Goddamn, no!" he says, "Anyone that'd own a damn bitch dog, they oughta be happy, 'cause they haven't got sense to be any other way! Besides that, Jesus Christ couldn't find 'er with a search warrant!"

Another time we was helpin' him, this was at his upper ranch there, and he gathered a big heifer, she was 10, 11 months old, and she wasn't branded. This was durin' the screwworm time of year. Ol' AB said, "We better brand that heifer even though we might have problems with screwworms. You know I trust my neighbors, but I don't wanna tempt 'em!"

AB shipped most of his cattle over to the Washburn and Condon Auction in Los Angles to be sold. If you had a couple a-carloads they'd let you ride in the caboose over to see about sellin' your cattle. So he's ridin' over there in the caboose and I don't know what brought the subject up, but him and the conductor got in an argument. AB's a little bastard, and this conductor got upset with 'im and he grabbed AB by the nape of the neck and the collar and the seat of his britches and rubbed his nose on the floor of the caboose! And then turned 'im loose. Goddamn, he headed for his satchel and the conductor probably knew what he was lookin' for so he went up the ladder to the top of the train. By the time AB got up there with his six-shooter, all he could see was a light runnin' down there, so he emptied his six-shooter at it, at the light, tryin' to kill 'im!! First stop, this conductor, he run into the depot and latched the screen door. Ol' AB Carey's not far behind 'im with his six-shooter and he took out his pocketknife, ripped the screen open and reached in and unlatched the door. He come in there where the people are waitin' and they collared 'im and took 'im back out and put 'im in the caboose with a new conductor!

AB had an ol' pet horse he called "Silver". I know one time we was down at the Watkins' ranch, helpin' 'em round up. It's a frosty morning, ol' Silver was feelin' pretty frisky, and the old man was havin' a little trouble keepin' 'im under control. He yelled at us, "Goddamn, boys, I just wish I could reach up and spur this goddamn horse in both shoulders, but I can't. I'm too goddamn old to get bucked off. I'm not a-gonna do it!" Later he said, "I don't know what would happen to me if I lose this horse!" Silver was just about the only horse he rode. And he was particular about how that horse was shod, too. I knew how he liked to have horses shod 'cause I'd seen his horses shod and seen people shoe 'em. He asked me one day, "Boy, you think you could shoe ol' Silver for me?" I said, "Yeah, he's gentle, it'll be no problem. I can shoe 'im." I shod the ol' horse and he went around, walkin' around us, watchin', and finally said, "Boy, you know I think I could teach you how to shoe horses! You done a good job."

AB had a stiff neck. He had to turn his shoulders around to look backwards. They claim it happened down there in Douglas in his younger days. He got drunk in the bar and he went out in the back, sittin' there on a stump, tryin' to sober up when someone shot 'im off the stump! Shot 'im in the neck! It didn't kill him, but it left his neck stiff.

Another good friend of mine, Mac MacKenzie, Malcolm's father, went to work for AB. It was durin' the war when labor was short and they'd made some kind of an agreement, you know, plus his wages. It went along there for about a year, year and a half, and ol' AB wasn't livin' up to his part of the agreement. There was beginnin' to be a little friction there. Mac knew my dad knew AB real well so he rode over to see my dad and, hell, that's a half a day's ride. He was tellin' my dad about his problems and he asked my dad, "How in the hell am I gonna handle this situation?" Dad told him, "Hell, just buy him out!" And that's what he did! He went back and made a deal with ol' AB to buy his ranch. He had $20,000 or $30,000 cash he paid down and they had lawyers draw up the agreement. Ol' AB didn't think Mac could make the payments, so he told it around town that "when the year's up and he can't make the payments, I'll just haul him and his family out over on the road and turn 'em loose." Course, this MacKenzie, now, goddamn, he's a businessman himself; he'd went and made a deal with the Land Bank to finance the ranch. When it come time for his money, AB told Mac, "You're gotta make that first payment or I'm gonna hafta turn

33

you loose out on the highway!" So MacKenzie, he went into his desk drawer, drug out his checkbook and give it to 'im! Mac, he bought that ranch and a couple more and ended up, he owned most of the damn country around there.

AB, he's the one got out on the road, but he did leave with his money!

Bill Allen

Another neighbor we had to the north was Bill Allen. Dad had several stories about him that were hilarious. Some were about the years before when Bill had worked on a ranch that had cattle and guests. They all eat together in a big dining area, a big table. The cowboys and the guests all eat there together. Ol' Bill, he's wound up on one a-his long-winded stories and he picked up his coffee. He took a big swig a-that and it was just *scaldin'* hot! And he just spit it out all over the goddamn livin' room table! You would a-thought he'd been real embarrassed and everthing but his comment was, "You know, a lotta damn fools would a-tried to swallow that coffee!"

Another day they was out workin' cattle in the corral and for some reason or other, they was workin' 'em afoot. There was this one ol' cow there, she got on the hook! She'd run several cowboys up on the fence and ol' Bill, he's still down. One a-these ol' dude gals kinda took a shine to ol' Bill Allen. Pretty soon she says, "Bill, aren't you afraid a-that ol' mean cow?" This Bill, you know, he was about 6'4" or 6'5" and skin and bones. "No ma'am," he says, "if she charges me, I'll just lift my leg and she'll think I clumb a pole!"

Another story they tell on 'im – he'd been out ridin' all day and his wife had an Eastern friend where she'd went to some kind of a girls' school sometime in her life for a little higher education. This ol' gal come out to see her. They was livin' out on this ranch in a ol' frame house and it was propped up on rocks and a post or two there and there was quite a area under this house there. She's a-sittin' there on the porch there in a kinda rockin' chair visitin' with his wife. She was on the wood pile, choppin' some wood to prepare the evenin' meal. Bill comes a-ridin' in and his ol' horse is all tired and sweaty. He rode right up to the porch where he could talk to this friend of his wife and while they're there a-talkin', this ol' dog come a-crawlin' out from under the house. The wife's still a-choppin' wood. Ol' Bill says, "Lady, what do you think of the West?" She looked at him, she looked at the horse, she looked at this dog and says, "Bill, I think it's Heaven for men and dogs and Hell for women and horses!"

Another time he was workin' for this Hooker Ranch outta Wilcox, this is years ago. The cowboys was out workin' the cattle and they jumped about a two-year-old grizzly bear! And ol' Bill Allen roped 'im! He was havin' a little trouble with that bear and finally one a-the Mexican cowboys heeled it and then one of 'em got off and killed it with his six-shooter. He actually roped a grizzly bear!

Ol' Bill, he finally died and they say he died of malnutrition. All he was livin' on, from what they tell us, he was batchin' out there with the wife in town with the kids in school, he was just livin' on cornflakes! Finally done 'im in.

John Glen

John was a rancher there, another neighbor of my dad. One time John sold 'im a bull and I went along with him to bring the bull back to our ranch. My dad paid him in cash. John patted his six-shooter and said, "I'm gonna sleep tonight with this money in my mouth! Nobody's gonna get it!" What brought on that conversation, I don't know, but it was quite a little cash back durin' the Depression.

Guy Cates

I hadn't been out of the Army very long when Dad wrote me a letter tellin' me about the problems he was havin' with Dan Allen, so I wrote Dan a letter. I told 'im, "Now listen! My dad tells me you guys is havin' trouble and I'm advisin' you to stay off 'im 'cause you're gonna have me to contend with!" He was in the process of sellin' his place then and this Guy Cates (the buyer) was with 'im when he got this letter. He read it about twice and handed it to this here Guy Cates and says, "Read this! What do you think about it?" Ol' Guy read it and said, "I think you'd better leave the old man alone!"

Guy Cates, he was kind of a character himself. I got real well acquainted with him and we were good neighbors. We helped one another. I remember one time when we were gatherin' up my side of the fence and we found a bull yearling that had never been branded. It was a Hereford and I had a few Herefords. Neither one of us knew the thing, but it was on my side of the fence so course, I claimed it. Cates, he claimed it 'cause he had more Herefords that I did. And we discussed the situation all the way back to the ranch. We put my cattle in the pasture; I'm a-stayin' with him, so I rode over with him. On the way over to his place, we decided the only fair thing to do is just to butcher this animal and divide the meat up!

We had a couple of wetbacks there, workin' for us, cowboys. Guy's wife, Grace, was off in Tucson and we were batchin' together there. We'd had a few head of his cattle when we come down but we cut 'em out on his fence and we picked 'em up and had this bull yearlin' there. So we butchered it and Guy told these Mexicans to save the guts – we was gonna make some menudo. "Clean 'em up good," he told 'em. Then we give them a hindquarter of beef. And the head, you know, we kept the head 'cause we was gonna barbeque this head. These Mexicans, they got this here hindquarter of beef on their back and they're walkin' outta there and I hear 'em say in Spanish, "These gringo ranchers is loco." Ever ranch they've been workin', they got the heads and the guts. These gringos are gonna eat the head and guts and they give us a hindquarter of the meat! They're loco!

Later, Guy told me about the way him and Grace got married. There never was no courtship to it. He went up into Montana and got a job on a ranch. Grace was already there, a-helpin' in the kitchen, cookin' and waitin' tables and stuff. It turned cold! He said at the breakfast table, he announced to everbody, "It's too cold up here. I'm quittin' and I'm goin' back to Arizona." Grace spoke up, "You goin' to Arizona for sure? Yes? Then I'm goin' with you!" When he got packed up, he come around, picked her up, and they're drivin' outta town. Then he says, "You know Grace, if we're gonna be travelin' together for a couple of days, I think we oughta get married." And she agreed to it! So they looked up the JP and got married! Never had a date in her life and he says, "We're still married some 45 or 50 years later! And we get along better than most married couples, but that once in awhile we have a little problem." He told me, "I wasn't married too long, we had a problem. We had this guy workin' on the same ranch and all three of us went to this country dance at the schoolhouse. We drank a little bootleg whiskey and I was feelin' pretty good. The guy I was workin' with was good, so we just loaded up and went back to the ranch. It's about 10, 12 miles. We got back and Christ, we forgot Grace! We had to drive all the way back to pick up Grace and by then she's as mad as a wet hen!"

He said, "The next time I kinda upset her, we was stayin' in a little board house, made out of 1x12's and 2x4's. Over by my bed there, there was a knothole. Grace, she had to leave for a few days, so I got a funnel and a piece of garden hose and run it through this knothole and put the funnel on it. I never used it, but it looked like it could be used!" And when Grace come back and saw it she told him, "Why, you lazy damn thing! You can't even go outside to take a leak?" He said that he never told her any different.

I was over helpin' Guy, he was doin' some round-up, brandin' calves and what-not. There was a survey crew comin' through the country puttin' in benchmarks. And a-course, we run onto 'em and we had to stop. I'm a-visitin' with the head honcho there and ol' Guy Cates he went over and he got to foolin' around with their transit they had set up.

And there was a mountain over there about a half a mile and there was an Oak tree out by itself. He says, "How far do you think it is over to that Oak tree?" The guy says, "Hell, I don't know; Christ, probably six hundred yards." "Nah," he says, "You're wrong." And he told 'em exactly, right down to the damn foot, how far it was!

The survey man who was runnin' the transit says, "Shit, that's not right!" Guy says, "What the hell makes you think it's not right?" The man went over and got on it and looked and, "Christ," he says, "You're right! Where did you learn how to run a transit?" Guy says, "Oh, you know, bein' a cowpuncher, you gotta know things!" What he didn't tell 'im is that he'd worked over 20 years on the Highway Department survey crew!

Another time, he were roundin' up and he had this river Mexican, this Chico, that had worked cattle all of his life and he had 'im up a-helpin' and we had a good wetback there, workin', helpin' us. We got through early one day and Christ, ol' Chico took the ranch Jeep and the wetback and they went to town! Long about 2:00 o'clock, I hear this wetback in there talkin' to Guy Cates. He said that Chico had run off the road back there a couple of miles. Ol' Guy, he was talkin' Mexican but I could understand 'im, he says, "Well, how come Chico to run off a-the road unless he's drunk?" "No, no," he says, "Chico was talkin' with both hands!" Guy says, Well, goddamn, I'm not a-goin' over there and pull 'im out tonight! I'll do it in the mornin'!"

Come mornin', ol' Chico, he was kinda tired a-waitin' and he'd walked over. We went down there and hooked onto the Jeep and pulled it out.

Another story is about Guy Cates' dad. He'd worked all a-his adult life in Southern Arizona as a deputy sheriff in different towns. He was tellin' me they had these fast-draw guys, but he says, "When there was trouble in town, I never walked down the sidewalk. I walked right down the middle of the street with a sawed-off shotgun. Never had any problems!" And my dad told me that about the turn of the century these arguments, most of 'em was settled with sawed-off shotguns! Wasn't much of this fast-draw stuff a-goin' on!

When Guy's dad was in Casa Grande, he was runnin' cattle out in the desert with Papago Indians. Guy Cates was a young man, I guess he might a-still been in his teens, and he'd represent his dad and ride with the round-up with the Indians. This one cold mornin', this one buck Indian got on his horse and the horse threw 'im off! And his other cowboys, you know, they come there to his rescue and got 'im up on his feet and he had his one finger broke, runnin' off at an angle. They pulled on that finger and straightened it up and got 'im back on his horse. That night they treated that finger. They got bailin' wire and cut it in about two foot lengths and put it in the campfire and then about four a-them big, stout buck Indians got this one with this broken finger and got 'im down! Holdin' 'im! And then another one started gettin' these hot wires outta the fire and they just burned two circles clear to the bone all the way around his finger! It was swelled up pretty bad but the next morning it was swelled up a lot worse! God, he rode around there for 10 days, two weeks with his finger up in the air. Guy said when the finger got well from the burn, the bone was all knitted and hell, it was a good patch job! They knew somethin' about what they were doin'.

One time, when Guy's dad was a deputy sheriff in Casa Grande, the Indians called 'im up; they had a problem out there with a white man. So he went out and when he got there, they had this white man a-sittin' down with his back agin a post and his hands tied behind him, behind the post. And he had a big, heavy, black mustache and they'd pulled out, on one side of this mustache, they'd pulled it all out! The ol' lip was swellin' up and it was bleedin' and Guy Cates' dad turned the guy loose. He wandered off but the Indians, they got upset about turnin' the guy loose! One says, "That white man was botherin' us Indians!" Cates told 'em, "I don't think that white man's gonna bother you Indians any more!"

Malcolm's Bull Calf

This happened back years ago when I was neighborin' with my good friend, Malcolm MacKenzie. I was out ridin' and I saw a bull calf that I'd never seen before, nearly a yearling, runnin' with some of my cows. I told 'im, "Malcolm, he's old enough to brand, isn't he? I think he's past old enough to brand." He says, 'If he was on my place, I'd brand 'im!" So the next time I was out I jumped 'im and I branded 'im. And when I branded 'im, he didn't look like a calf that should of belonged to me, but as Malcolm said, he was old enough to brand. He was around a year old.

The next time I saw Malcolm it was the following week and I said, "Malcolm, I branded that calf." He says, "Yeah, I know it. I saw him following one of my cows the other day!" "Well," I says, "Maybe I owe you for a calf then." He says, "Nah, forget about it. I told you that if it was old enough to brand, brand it. But I didn't think you could!" I had a couple of good cow dogs then!

Hell, it went on close to six or eight months and I was throwin' trash out one afternoon when I saw this Wilcox Auction letter in there and it hadn't been opened. I opened it and it was a past-yearling steer that Malcolm had sold for me and there's a check in there for right at $400. This was way back there when $400 was $400! I never said anything to Beryl about throwin' this money away – I just cashed it and put it in my pocket! And it went on then with winter comin', along about February, and I went out and Christ, there's horse tracks all over the place. Two horses. That morning, I discovered there'd been a calf butchered in my corral! I saw some car tracks comin' in and trailer tracks and several of 'em! I pretty well figured out what had happened then. I'd stopped the night before and visited with Malcolm before I'd come on over to the ranch. I rode Saturday and Sunday and Christ, there's horse tracks – I said before – everwhere! Whoever was ridin' in there knew the country because they hit all the trails right and everthing.

Sunday evening I stopped by Malcolm's and we're visitin' and pretty soon he asks, "How'd things go up at the ranch?"

I says, "There's horse tracks all over the damn place where someone's been ridin', two people. And their trailer tracks comin' in and out." He asks, "All those horse tracks – you see anything else?" I said, "I saw where a calf's been butchered in the corral." "You did?" he said, "someone butchered a calf?" I said, "Yeah." He asked, "What are you gonna do about it?" I said, "I'm not gonna do anything about it! I know who did it." He said, "You do?" I says, "Yeah, it was you and Guillermo. I thought it all over and I pretty much know why it was done. You remember this big bull calf I branded and I got a check for it. At the time you said it was your calf and it wasn't anything to worry about. You needed meat and it looks to me like you just went over and butchered a calf. Puts us pretty much even, don't it?" "No," he says, "I saved half of it for you and you can take your half back!" I said, "Malcolm, I got plenty of meat so you just keep all of it!"

He apparently didn't know how I was gonna take it. He told me, "Hell, I knew when we missed a couple of calves out there that they'd be fat and I didn't have anything fat and I needed a beef. I got to thinkin' about them two big heifers I knew we missed. I liked to never found the damn thing! We finally found one and drove her down to the corral and butchered her! Hell, I think we're even now on this *one* thing!"

41

Chapter Four   Ranch Stories

Cowboys

Back in those days, when I was growin' up, they had a few cowboys around in the country. One of 'em, one a-the best cowboys I ever worked with, was Malcolm MacKenzie. He not only was a good cowboy, he was a hell of a good roper; best roper I ever saw out on the range. He was one a-these guys that was always in the right place at the right time. I think Malcolm wouldn't ride a damn mule but if he was forced to, he could make a hand on one.

Figure 4. Ollie as a Young Cowboy (About 1940)

Another one I met was before I went in the Army. There was this Bar L Y Ranch; they called it the Barley. They probably run 1,000 head of cattle and they was wild cattle! They had a guy outta New Mexico, livin' in Arizona at that time, by the name of Jip Clute. He was not only a cowboy; he was a good lion hunter. I worked with 'im a couple of seasons on that Barley Ranch and he was one hell of a cowboy! Even with wild cattle, he didn't care where he was at or what happened, he was always in the right place at the right time! How he got there, I don't know, but he was always there! And he wasn't ridin' the best horses on the ranch, either. This ranch foreman, this Mahlan Pettit, he knew 'im well and he knew he didn't have to ride the best horses to make a hand. He had one ol' skinny sorrel horse and this Clute had named 'im "Streamline". I'll tell you what: him and Streamline always managed to get where they was supposed to be and be there at the right time. And if somethin' needed to be roped, by god, he could rope it on Streamline, too!

I haven't done much cowboyin' in the past 20 years but what I've seen on these ranches from lion huntin', they don't have the quality of cowboys now that we used to have. A lotta these cowboys they got, they do more cowboyin' in an ol' beat-up pickup than go a-horseback!

I don't wanna say much more – some of these modern cowboys read this, they might get upset with me, but facts is facts and the truth's the truth!

Ranch Horses

First thing I can tell you – when you're ranchin', you gotta have horses. There's no gettin' around this rough country without horses. My good friend, Malcolm MacKenzie, when he got married, his daddy-in-law over in New Mexico give Malcolm and his wife a quarter horse colt. It was about a three year-old; it was a weddin' present. I don't know what experience Malcolm had with 'im, but I come out one weekend and he was all ready to sell this horse to me or trade 'im to me. I didn't have anything to trade, but I had the $250 he wanted for 'im.

So I bought the horse. And then he tells me, "Better be careful how you ride 'im because he bucks real hard." I said, "You should a-told me this before you sold this horse to me!" Over to the ranch north of me is Gavin's place. And he had a big ol' husky boy. I bought a whole bunch of horseshoes, used, in Tucson; I had about 1,000, 1,200 pounds of 'em. Horseshoes is pretty expensive, you know, if you're runnin' a ranch, makin' payments. I told this kid, I says, "See that pile of horseshoes? If you'll take this horse and ride 'im for four or five months, you can have half of those horseshoes." And I'd bought 'em for $30. So I'm gettin' my horse rode out pretty cheap. He took the horse and hell, he was gettin' along with 'im fine and he and his dad went down on the San Pedro to help someone gather his cows. This cattle inspector, he starts to admirin' this horse. Because he was a pretty nice lookin' quarter horse. And the kid says, "I'm breakin' 'im for Ollie Barney." "You are," he says, "have you got haulin' papers to bring 'im down here?" And of course, he didn't!

Figure 5. Ollie with One of His Horses (About 1945)

The first thing I know, I get a letter from the cattle inspector wantin' to know where I got that horse and where the haulin' papers were on 'im. Haulin' papers back then was just about like a bill of sale. And I didn't have any! So I told Malcolm my problem and he says, "Hell, I don't have any haulin' papers for 'im either! But I'll talk to Jack (the inspector) and tell 'im I raised this horse right there on the ranch." When he talked to Jack, he told 'im, "Ollie and I made a trade and I never thought anything about gettin' 'im inspected. Now, ever time Ollie and I make a trade, if you wanna come out and inspect, I'll call ya. Ever week we trade. We might trade a bull, we might trade horses, or if nothin' else, we trade pocket knives!" So he took it to Jack that this horse was legal and he would give me haulin' papers for 'im, which was a title to 'im. So he done that and ol' Jack signed 'em. So we're in real good shape then.

I started ridin' this horse but somewhere along the damn line, that colt, he'd been loco'd 'cause when he got hot, hell, goin' up a hill, he's just liable to rear up and fall over backwards! 'Bout half dangerous! I come out this one time to round-up and Malcolm had been over the day before and shod the horses, with my Mexican. This horse had really been out on green grass and he was pretty frisky and Malcolm told me, "Ollie, don't ride that damn horse tomorrow!" Well, next morning, I saddled the bastard up! He was all humped up, but we got off on a good start. I got up on what we call Fox Mountain to make a drive up there. Over across the fence, down there about a half a mile, this Jesus, the Mexican who was a-workin' for me, could see by the color of the cattle that they was probably mine. So we went on up the fence line about a quarter mile to a gate and we get off down there. These cattle made a run and course we had to whip up a little bit to get around in front of the cattle. This quarter horse I'm a-ridin', he run over a dead manzanita and that thing rolled under his belly and Christ, he went into orbit! I tell ya, pitchin' off the damn hill. No way I could tell ya how high he was a-gettin' but I'm lookin' out over the tops of some pretty good-sized little oaks! And he changed direction and I went down and I went down on the down-hill side and Christ! I thought for awhile I was in orbit!

But finally, I hit. I had on a heavy down jacket, zipped up about halfway and I hit the ground! Christ, it knocked all the damn wind outta me and I'm a little while a-gettin' up. Ol' Jesus, he come back and he says, "Are you all right?" in Spanish. I told 'im, "Yeah, I'm OK. I just gotta get my breath." So he went and caught my horse and come back and by that time I'm on my feet. Where this jacket was zipped up, it broke the zipper – when I hit, I hit hard! So I got back on the horse and we went on around and got the cattle and brought 'em through the gate.

The next morning Malcolm, he come over to help me and he sees me a-limpin' around and says, "I see you rode the quarter horse." I said, "I rode 'im for awhile, probably three or four good jumps! Then he lost me!" He says, "Goddamnit Ollie, I told you not to ride that bastard; he's gonna throw ya off! I guess you believe me now." I says, "I believe ya!" Then he goes on, he says, "Ollie, I think we oughta trade that horse off." I says, "You got my permission! But, by god, at least I wanna get what I've got in 'im out! Hell, I've got $15 worth of horseshoes in 'im and I paid you $250 for 'im." So we let it go at that. I'm a-stayin' over in Happy Valley with him at night and Jesus was stayin' there at the ranch. On the way out who should we meet but Bob, the game warden. He'd been admirin' this horse for some time or another. He's got a little grey horse in his trailer. Course we both got out; Bob got out and Malcolm, he went around and looked in the trailer, looked at this little grey horse. He said, "Goddamn, I sure like that grey horse." "Well," Bob says, "He don't belong to me. He belongs to another game warden." Malcolm asks, "You still wantin' to buy or trade for Ollie's bay horse?" "Oh yeah," he says, "I'd sure love to have 'im! He's a fine-lookin' horse." Malcolm says, "Well, he's a good horse, hell of a nice horse. How about we just trade horses?" The warden says, "Well, he don't belong to me." Then Malcolm tells 'im, "Ollie told me if I got a chance to sell that horse for a pretty good price, sell it! But you know, I'd trade 'im for that grey horse." "Yeah, I'll trade," he says, "He's not mine, but I'll trade!" So they traded horses! And then ol' Bob turns to me and says, "Ollie, can Malcolm trade your horse off that way?" I said, "Hell, it sounds to me like he already did it! A done deal!"

So we go on over and spend the night at Malcolm's place. Next morning, it was a cold morning, Betty Sue (Malcolm's wife) said that after we left, the mercury got down to six! We got up to the ranch and this goddamn ground is froze hard! Bob, he's come outta the house and Jesus come out. He had this horse, his new horse with a halter on and tied to his trailer. So he goes in the saddle compartment on the trailer and drug out his saddle and blankets. He's standin' between the horse and the trailer, on the wrong side of the horse to saddle 'im, puts his blankets on 'im, put the saddle on the wrong side, walked right around behind his damn heels, and cinched 'im all up. Boy! He's admirin' – that damn horse looks pretty good under his saddle! Anyhow, he put his bridle on and unhaltered 'im and led 'im out in front of the house and barn and got on 'im. The ol' horse is humped up a little. I can see his front legs and joints are all swelled up from this pitchin' he done the other day. And he's a little bit ouchy in his walkin'. Malcolm and I are both a-hopin' that this goddamn horse'd throw 'im off on this frozen ground, but he didn't! And he went out and rode 'im all day and come back and unsaddled 'im and went in the house and eat a bite. We had some whiskey before we eat and quite a little bit more afterwards. Ol' Bob's a-braggin' on his new horse. Then he gets to tellin' us how fast this grey horse is. "Aw hell," Malcolm says, "He's not that goddamn fast!" Malcolm's a-ridin' a young horse and he says, "Hell, I can beat 'im on my horse!" I said, "Hell, Bob, I can take your quarter horse and out run both a-you!" Course, the ol' horse is all limbered up by then. Down below the house, there's a grade that goes up the hill and it's probably 400 yards or maybe a little farther or a little less. So that's what we was gonna do, run from the front of the barn down to the foot of this grade, turn and come back. That's agreeable to everbody. And we went and I'm a-lettin' both of 'em outrun us 'cause I had the damn speed to get up and get ahead of 'em. Anyway, I kinda held back and when I got to the grade, I turned and I come back. That's where the damn horse race started. When I got to the barn I was at least 300 foot ahead of the goddamn grey horse and about 50 yards ahead of Malcolm! We'd had a bet there. I was bettin' a half a gallon of whiskey to both of 'em and Bob and Malcolm, they was bettin' a half a gallon of whiskey to a case of beer. Well, I ended up, I'd won two goddamn half gallons of whiskey on Bob's horse. Boy! I'll tell ya then, ol' Bob, he's really blowed up on his horse even if he lost a case of beer and a half gallon of whiskey! He's still braggin' on 'im!

Then Malcolm, he gets real cocky. He says, "Bob, you don't have any business ownin' that horse. He's gonna throw you off!" "Oh no," he says, "I can ride 'im." Malcolm says, "I don't know whether you can ride 'im or not but I'll bet you a half a gallon of whiskey against another case of beer that in 30 days, he throws you off." Bob, he took that bet! It wasn't two weeks, he come out and give Malcolm his case of beer. But he's still got the horse and I don't know how many times he got throwed off. He had one of these town ferriers a-shoein' 'im and he's settin' down the back of the heel too much. His ankles was swellin' up and his muscles comin' up the forelegs was swelled up. Damn, it hurt the horse to travel and by god, that broke 'im from pitchin'!

Ranch Pets

I had a Mexican kid there at the ranch; he must a-been 20 years old or so when he started workin' for me. He was a wetback – a hell of a good kid. Bright. He worked there for me; he'd stay out there at the ranch a lot a-times by himself. I come out there one day and he's got a young javelina there runnin' around the house. I told 'im, "Where'd you get that javelina? You're not supposed to have those things; pickin' 'em up like that." Well, he told me the story – he says, "His mother and one other was killed by lightning under an oak tree. This little fella was runnin' around there so I brought 'im in."

So I named 'im Snort. He was a real nice pig. He grew up, real friendly, and Christ, he liked to drink, too. He didn't care if you put him out a bowl of whiskey or wine or beer, he'd drink it! This uncle a-mine, my drinkin' uncle, we come out to the ranch there one afternoon and about a mile and a half from the house a little ol' spike buck run across the trail. I had my rifle and he grabbed my rifle and he killed this deer. And it was out of season! Anyway, we loaded this deer in the back of the pickup and got up to the ranch and course the hog was there and he was glad to see us. We skinned this deer out and gutted 'im and the damn pig, he's eatin' on these guts! We'd already give 'im some wine; my uncle liked to drink this Mogan David wine and we'd give 'im a drink or two of that. Then we went in and fixed supper and eat and this damn hog could get pretty drunk. He got to staggerin' around in there and it's gettin' on toward bedtime and this goddamn hog, he just urpped right out in the middle of the livin' room on the cement floor. I told Uncle Gene, "I'm goin' to bed. You and that damn hog can stay up and drink and get drunk, but I'm goin' to bed!"

I went to bed. I woke up the next mornin' and I look over there – we had twin beds in the bedroom – there's my uncle there, head on the pillow. Goddamn hog, he's in bed with 'im, under the covers! 'Bout that time, this hog, he kinda woke and then he reachs down as far as he could on this yellow bedspread and hang a tusk in it and rip a tear 'bout 18 inches long in it! By that time I'm startin' to get up and the ol' hog, he reaches down and makes another rip in it. I got up and I get the coffee pot on and ol' Snort, he gets outta bed and he goes over there where he'd urpped the night before and he licked it and cleaned it all up. Goddamn, just as clean as you could be! I said, "Snort, you're a better man than I am!" Because there's no way I could do that! Finally, I got my uncle up.

I was buildin' a barn there at the time and I had these two Mexicans and we started haulin' sand. We had to go down about a quarter of a mile below the house where the turnin' around place of the horse race we had was. There's good sand there and we'd get a pickup load of sand. The hog, he'd ride down in the pickup. Then we'd load up the sand and help the hog up and he'd ride back up on top of the load of sand. He'd watch the Mexican unload it. This one trip we come back and ol' Snort, he'd wandered off somewhere. So he wasn't there to ride back. We come back and one of the Mexicans was unloadin' this sand and Uncle's sittin' out there on a five-gallon can a-watchin' these Mexicans work. And here comes Snort and he's upset! He's slingin' his head and evertime he'd sling his head, he'd go, "Woof! Woof!" He got up there, oh, about 100 yards of my uncle and he saw 'im and he charged 'im! By god, he put him up on the goddamn bed of the pickup! With the sand! Finally, we calmed this here pig down and got back to work.

Another time with this pig, I had one of my trim carpenters come out, deer huntin'. There was kind of a shower the night before the season and I went out with another guy or two and looked around. But this trim carpenter, he drank Colt .45 beer. And him and the hog got drunk. He had his bed made out there with a big waterproof tarp on it. When I went to bed, Snort and this carpenter, they're still drinkin'. Along about 10:00 o'clock that night this carpenter's up; he's stumblin' around in the house and I said, "What's goin' on?" He says, "I'm goin' home! That damn hog, he gets in the bed with me; he wants to sleep with me!" I said, "Hell, you spent all damn afternoon and evening gettin' drunk! He thinks you're buddies!" He couldn't tolerate that hog anymore; by god, he's goin' home! And his son was with 'im. I got up and rounded up his son and told him, "You talk to your dad and help 'im move his bed up here in the bunkhouse. Hell, drunk as he is, if he starts back to town, he's liable to have an accident!" And we locked the damn hog outside so he couldn't get in bed with 'im.

I had a big ol' tiger cat and this tiger cat, he'd got to where he'd go to the gate at the section line that was just a half a mile from the house but the way the road wound around, it was a little more. On Friday night, this damn cat'd be there by the gate, waitin' for me. I'd open the gate and open the door and the cat would get up in the cab with me and come back. Wasn't long before the damn hog, he got to doin' the same thing! The hog and the cat, they'd both be there waitin'! Well, if I didn't have anybody with me, the ol' cat'd get up in the damn cab and ol' hog'd get up there and he'd sit up in the damn seat there, lookin' around. If I had someone with me, I'd have to let the tailgate down and let 'im ride in the back. I come out there one Saturday morning, I didn't make it on a Friday, and the hog's there at the house, but the cat's not. And the neighbor, he lives seven miles down the road from me and I met 'im that day across the fence. He's out ridin', too. He says, "Your cat was over at my place this mornin'." "Well," I says, "I missed 'im then." I come back and along about midnight Saturday night I heard the damn cat. He come in, jumped up on the bed – he'd come home. So I had to get up and open 'im a can of Pard dog food. He liked that Pard dog food. It wasn't too expensive and he'd get a can a-that a day and whatever he could catch and he was doin' real well.

The neighbor over to the north of me heard about these wetbacks. I had two of 'em there buildin' fence. And they'd found this here Pard dog food. They was tellin' me that this can of food was real good if it was warmed up, but it wasn't any good cold! "Well," I says, "you're not so damned busy that you can't build a little fire and warm it up for lunch." And I told this Guy Cates about it. God, he just couldn't rest on that! He had to go over there one evening and catch those wetbacks home. He started talkin' about this here meat, this can of food they was eatin'. He tells 'em that it's dog meat! He gets the can and shows 'em the picture of the dog on there. Then the Mexicans quit eatin' it! He had a big, ol' fat cow that was runnin' there in my pasture. I asked them Mexicans if they'd saw this cow up there and, oh yeah, they knew 'er. I says, "Well, I want you to butcher her and make jerky out of her!" I thought the next week when I come back I'd have all kinds a-damn jerky and I knew I was gonna hafta buy a cow, but that was all right – I'd have all this good jerky. God, I come out and there's no jerky! I asked the Mexicans, "How come you didn't butcher that cow?" "Oh," they said (in Spanish), "the cow didn't have your brand on it." So I lost on that deal!

The last thing I can tell about my hog is that I come out to the ranch one time and no hog! By the time I went back to town, still no hog! But I stopped in and talked to my neighbor and I told him about losin' my hog. He said, "There was a couple of deputies went up to your ranch and they said they was eatin' their lunch there and this javelina come a-trottin' down off the hill. He was real friendly and hell, he helped 'em eat their lunch." And they went on back to town. This neighbor had got the name of one of these deputies and I called 'im up. I asked 'im about this hog. He said, "Well, he did come in." I said, "You didn't haul 'im off, did you?" He says, "Oh, no." I knew the University had a little pen, really a pretty good size pen of javelinas there. So I thought, by god, they might a-give that pig to the University. One day, I went down there and here's about a dozen javelinas out there. And ol' Snort, I'd earmarked 'im, I'd put my earmark on 'im, a little swallowfork in both ears. I'm there a-lookin' at these hogs and one of the hogs just quit the bunch and he come trottin' right up to the gate in front of me like he was glad to see me! And this pig is got both ears with a swallowfork in 'em!. So I knew I'd found ol' Snort but there wasn't much I could do about gettin' 'im back! But it looked like he had a good home so that was what happened to Snort.

Round-up Stories

This one year when we shipped, I was workin' in Tucson as a construction superintendent, buildin' houses. I'd always take Christmas and New Year's holidays off; that's when I'd round-up and it was generally pretty cold. Sherry was on school holiday then, too. How that come to happen was that the first year Sherry was in high school, we rounded-up in November, same as always. Well, the school wanted to know where she was! Beryl made all kinds of excuses, but they weren't buyin' 'em. They finally said they might have to send the sheriff out to find her! So Beryl went in to talk to the counselor and explained that the ranch was a small family operation and Sherry just had to be there to help. So they agreed that if we'd round-up on the two-week Christmas break, the counselor would cover for Sherry when we went huntin' on long weekends.

One time when we come out, the hippies had come in there and they'd took ever bit of food there was in the house. They'd even went out to the woodpile and got a pickup load of wood! I always kept a good supply there for the fireplace; it was the only heat we had in the house. We got up the next mornin' with nothin' to eat. We went out and in the yard layin' there was a good pair of Levi's. Beryl, she didn't like me to wear patched Levi's on the job, so I took 'em out to the ranch. And all the patched Levi's I had out there – they stole them, too! But this one pair didn't have any patches, they threw them away!

Anyway, we went out and we rounded-up that day and come back and that evening we went into Benson and the first stop we made was the restaurant to get a bite to eat! We bought us some groceries and went back on the ranch and we got our cattle rounded-up. I got a neighbor to help us. We had to drive these cattle down to the San Pedro to ship 'em. God, this mornin' we were gonna ship, it was snowin'! But we went anyway; we went on down to the San Pedro where the shippin' pens were. No trucks! It started gettin' late and no trucks! So I went on up there to a guy I knew, an old bachelor, he had a dog or two that lived in the house there with him. I borrowed his truck to go up to Benson to call and find out about the truck. Before I got up there, I knew what the problem was – those trucks couldn't get down there! The roads was slippery. But I talked to 'em and they said they'd be back down next weekend. This neighbor and Sherry, they went on back that night. By the time they got in, it was real late and *cold*. Sherry was wet, too. The neighbor said, "Boy, she's a tough little gal; she never whimpered once and I was about to freeze to death!"

I got back from Benson and I eat supper with this old man Remmick. He'd write an article ever once in awhile for this farm magazine. One yarn I remember he wrote about was he was havin' problems sellin' all the cotton he was raisin' with nylon and all this stuff comin' on. He wrote this article and said that one of the ways we could use a lotta this cotton is to revert back to these bustles! We could pack these bustles with cotton and get all the women a-wearin' 'em, that would use up this surplus cotton! After we eat that night, hell, he was just a-settin' these plates down on the ground and let the dogs lick 'em out! Then he took 'em over to the sink and rinsed 'em off and let 'em dry! I wasn't too keen on eatin' with the ol' man Remmick after that.

Another time we were goin' down to ship and I had a neighbor there, he was a-helpin'; he was workin' for the ranch, he didn't own it. Earlier that year, I was ridin' and I had a tank up there about a mile from his house and I had a real sick cow – prolapsed uterus, I think they call it. She'd been in this shape and she was hot and feverish and her eyes was glazed over and there was no chance of savin' her, so I shot 'er. I went on about my business and here come this rancher. He said, "I heard a shot up here; I come to see what it was about." "Well," I says, "I shot a cow." He asks, "Well, what are you gonna do with it?" I said, "I'm not gonna do anything with it!" So he says, "Can I have it?" By god, he butchered that damn cow out and he had half-a-dozen kids and they eat that cow! And this one mornin' we was shippin', we come by there and he come outta the outhouse with his pants down. He was gettin' them up and scared these cows and we couldn't get 'em through the gate there. So Malcolm, he went up and let the fence down on a little ridge top and we went through. We didn't fix the fence up 'cause we figured we'd do that when we come back. God, he overtook us and he give us all kinda damn tongue-lashin' for lettin' his fence down. I told 'im, "We're too busy to argue, but when we come back this afternoon, we'll fix the fence." We come back; we fixed the fence up and he never showed up, which I was glad.

One thing about it, when you own a ranch, and you don't have it paid for, money's short.

I'm a-workin' there in Tucson and my brother, Dick, he's goin' to the University. I'm a-helpin' 'im through the University, hell, it took 'im six years to get through it, and I'm payin' 'im $50 a month back when I wasn't makin' much, wasn't makin' $400. And so I hired 'im this first summer I had the ranch. The first thing I had to do is develop the water; get some water troughs built and god, I worked 'im all summer. We put in three water troughs and fixed up three waters and all the time he's a-workin' for me, he's tellin' me how to run the ranch and what I should be a-doin'! After a couple a-months of that, I asked 'im, "Dick, this is all good advice but where did you learn it?" He said, "Aw, I learned it in the University." I says, "If they got a course there in the University to run one of these ranchs on bailin' wire and nerve...". "Oh no," he says, "They don't have anything like that!" I said, "Well, that's the way I'm operatin'. That's what I gotta study up on." After that, I run the ranch with wetbacks.

Ranchin' in Bad Weather

This story's about one of my ranchin' experiences. This was before I had Sherry to help me. I shipped these cattle – I was workin' in Tucson and I took off between Christmas and New Years and I shipped at Miramonte, out the Washburn. I had 57 cows to bring back and I left MacKenzie's place there in the morning, early, and he helped me partway with one of his boys for, oh, I imagine a couple a-hours. We got the cattle all strung out good and they was wantin' to go home and they're good stock cows. Goddamn, it turned *cold* and started spittin' snow and Mac says, "Hell, these cattle are goin' good; you just hafta follow 'em along and you can spend the night there at the Heart. There's plenty a-beddin' there and food and you can go on over to the ranch the next mornin'." Well, this spittin' snow turned into a damn pretty good snowstorm! Christ, it got so damn cold I'd hafta walk and lead my horses in the snow and I was gettin' wet and cold. Ever once in awhile there'd be a cow get in the outfit with mine and I'd follow along and watch 'er and if she got out on the side, I'd cut 'er out. Once in awhile at a gate, you might have a neighbor's cow to cut out but it never was a problem. But when I got to the Heart I still had about three or four hours of daylight left and these cows was a-goin' so good, I just let 'em go! Time I got 'em over to the ranch and opened the gate – there was this Deer Creek come down through there and I had a corral up there and a gate to go onto the Forest. I just went over and opened the gate into the

Forest and then I had some cows on the State land and I didn't open that gate. Next mornin' they were all there in the corral there where I'd opened the gate for 'em; they went back to where they're supposed to be.

But when I got in that night I was *tired and cold and wet!* I didn't think it was worthwhile to try to get a fire goin' in the damned ol' wood stove. Wet and shiverin'! I just went to bed! One thing I learned in my life when I was a kid, shippin' cattle in the wintertime – these old heavy quilts my dad had didn't make the best beddin' in the world. When I got outta the Army that was one a-the first things I did, I bought me the best sleepin' bag I could find, a down sleepin' bag, good down to about 18, 20 below zero! I already had a good bed tarp that I'd bought before I went into the Army and I got me a foam rubber pad 'bout two foot wide and six foot long, 'bout three inches deep. So when I crawled in bed that night, I had a good bed! I warmed up! I got up next mornin', put on dry clothes, got a little fire goin' in that cookstove and heated coffee water up. I had a half a pound of sausage so I cooked that up pretty good and broke three eggs in it and scrambled that all together; drank coffee and eat. That mornin' all I had to do was come back to Tucson but I had to go over to my rock pile and put about 500 or 600 pounds of rock in the bed a-that pickup on account a-that six inches of snow! Over on the other end where I dumped my rocks out – I never had a four-wheel drive and in the summer time there was a sand wash there I had to have rocks in the pickup to make traction and then in the wintertime if I got snow or rain, I had to have rocks for traction. If I'd had a four-wheel drive I wouldn't a-had to go to all that extra work. I'd haul those rocks one way when it snowed and the other way when it got dry!

That was one a-my worst days, I think, as far as workin' cattle in bad weather is concerned.

Smokey the Bear

I used to go to some of these Arizona Cattle Growers meetings and they'd have the Forest Service people there and ranchers. We always had a problem with the predators and lions. They'd always have a discussion on that, and this one particular discussion there was several ranchers that was losin' calves and it was a problem! Back in those days I was a little feistier'n I am now so I got the floor. I told 'em, "I had problems, too, but my problems was Forest Rangers!" They'd cut me ten head of cows and I said, "Then ever year I'd lose eight and nine calves off them cows! That's the predator problem I have! Lion problem is no problem for me 'cause I just killed the lion and that problem's over with! Up to now I haven't had the guts to kill a Forest Ranger!" I had several of 'em I think should a-been killed!

While I'm talkin' about Forest Rangers, I wanna tell about my Forest Ranger – I forget his name – but he was dressed up with one of these here Smokey the Bear hats and he was built a lot like Smokey the Bear. We all referred to 'im as Smokey the Bear! I had about two miles of fence there along, well; it was a mile and three quarters of fence, right along the Forest Service boundary. It was gettin' in bad shape and Smokey the Bear was out there and he told me, "You gotta get that fence fixed up!" I says, "Jim, the thing has been patched and re-patched and there's just not much I can do about it!" "Well," he says, "you're gonna hafta fix it!" I said, "Well, I was over in the Whetstone Mountains lion huntin' here a-while back and I run onto a Forest Service fence. You know, it's really in worse shape than mine. You got about two and a half miles of it and I only got a mile and three quarters!" "Well,", he says, "you know, money-wise, we just don't have the money to fix it!" I says, "Now you're just talkin' about my problems! I don't have the money either!" He told me then, "You know, we got some extra barbwire and I can allot you enough to just build a new fence." I said, "Now you're talkin' a language that I understand! You know, in order to get the labor out here and everything, you're gonna hafta allow me about six months to get it fixed." "Oh," he says, "that's no problem at all. Come in and pick up the wire."

So I went in and picked up a mile and three quarters of barbed wire and the posts and the wire stays for it and hauled it out to the ranch. I put out a few feelers to get some wetbacks to build a fence and here in less than a month – in fact, it was only about ten days – I get a letter from the Forest Service that I got 30 days to build this fence! I went back in there to ol' Smokey Bear's office and he's got his foot up on the desk there, smokin' a big cigar. He says, "Well, what can I do for you, Ollie?" I says, "Well, I just wanna know where you want this wire dumped off." He says, "Drop off wire?" I says, "Yeah. You know you promised me six months to fix this fence and that was our agreement." I handed 'im a letter and I says, "Here's a letter that says I got 30 days to do it! That's not the agreement and I brought this damn wire back and where do you want it dumped off?" He says, "Oh, Ollie, don't get excited!" And he called his secretary. She wrote me out a new letter, for six months to build the fence! I said, "I'm glad to get this, 'cause I can get it built in six months. I was kinda kiddin' you; I don't have the wire out there, either! I was figurin' on loadin' it up and dumpin' it out if you didn't, you know, question this error." Christ, it went along there, it wasn't 30 days, there's three of these little ol' wetbacks come by and I knew 'em and they're good fence builders. I put 'em on the job and Christ, they built a nice fence.

They got it all fixed and I went in and saw Smokey the Bear and I said, "Come out and check that fence, 'cause it's all built and a neat job and everthing's right!" That was one of the last deals that I had with Smokey the Bear because they gotta change 'em every two or three years. They don't want 'em gettin' too well acquainted with the ranchers.

I've always had problems with government people. It seems like they hire these penis-brains and then they give 'em dictatorial powers and the first thing you know, they're abusin' it! I always accused 'em, you know, if brains was dynamite, they wouldn't have enough to blow their nose. I come to this conclusion when I hired out with the Park Service. Hell, in a little while, I had a permanent rating of whatever kind they give you. I'm a-workin' for this Park Service and Christ, it seemed like ever idea I come up with, they'd have a better idea. And down in the Rincons there, up at Manning Camp, they had a nice spring down below the cabin, but it was about a 100-yard walk. You'd walk down there and get you two buckets of water and bring back up. Down at the pack base, we had a canyon that run down there and there was several big pools of water up there. We had a little gasoline engine and a pump and we'd go down there and start this little Briggs and Stratton gasoline and pump up some water. I got the bright idea that if we could just take that little pump up to Manning Camp and 100 yards of pipe and some kind of little tank, we could just pump this water up. Down there at pack base, we had electricity. We could get a little electric pump and pump that water down there with electricity. All we'd have to do is just throw a switch and when the tanks run over, turn it off.

They sent this into headquarters and back comes a letter. They thought the idea was fine but we already had the gasoline and pump all set up there at pack base, so just take the electric pump up to Manning Camp. We don't have any electricity up there and they're bound to know that, but that's when I decided Christ, this stupidity is more'n I can take. After another little deal or two like that, I turned in my resignation and had to go to work for myself. I'll tell you, Park Service Rangers, I don't know where in the hell they get 'em, but I never did see one that was overloaded with brains!

We got these two tanks that was government surplus and we set them up. They were 10 foot across, 10 foot tall. This little Park Ranger, he wasn't completely dumb 'cause he flew B-17's in World War II and he got outta that alive, but he said he damn near wrecked one one morning when he was takin' off there and he rolled his wheels over a freight train! He went on and made their bombin' run and come back and landed – it hadn't hurt the plane any! But anyway, we was puttin' these tanks up and he was worryin': how much water they would hold. I said, "Christ, just get your paper and pencil and figure it out!" He said, "Well, I don't know how to do it!" I said, "Get you a piece of paper and pencil and I'll figure it out for you!" I forget the formula now, but you gotta measure the height and then you gotta measure the width and this pie r squared and a few things. Then you get the number of cubic feet in the tank and you multiply that by 7.5, 'cause there's 7.5 gallons in a cubic foot. That amazed him, a goddamn country kid, barely educated, could figure a little bit!

They sent me down to Tumacocori and I worked for a superintendent they had down there. He was kind of a – oh, I don't know how you'd describe 'im – I referred to 'im all the time as "Mother Jackson." He had displays up there behind glass but the doors opened, you know, to change bulbs and stuff, and he'd put in different displays. But there was a crack all around the doors and he asked me if I could fix that. I said, "Well, Christ, there's no problem to fix that!" Down in the shop they had a lot of this quarter inch lathe, about an inch and a half wide, so I went in there and on the inside, put this lathe in there so when you shut the door, you couldn't see the light. Hell, that took me a half a day or so and ol' Mother Jackson come up and says, "Well, where's the lights?" "Hell," I says, "Isn't that what you wanted fixed?" "Yeah," he says, "but how did you do it?" I said, "Just open one of the doors and you'll see." He opened the door and then says, "You know, I've had half a dozen guys work around here and none of 'em could ever fix that thing!" I said, "Hell, they didn't think how the hell they could stop that light!" He says, "I've got another job for you. That adobe building down there's got a tin roof on it. It's a new roof and it leaks! Fix that." I went down there and I looked at it and they had this corrugated roof and they had all the nails down in the valley, instead of on top. When he come down there, I had about half of the roof all taken off. He said, "I thought I told you to fix it, not take the roof off!" "Well," I says, "I gotta take the roof off to fix it!" He says, "Why?" I said, "Well, whoever put it on – you can look, it's got all the nails down in the valley and it's leakin'! I gotta take it off and turn 'em over where I can get the holes on top and re-nail it!" Oh Christ, he got to thinkin' then that I was about half-smart! But I was about half-full of that job around there and that's where I turned in my resignation.

And that was the end of my career with the Park Service.

Trail Riding Stories

I remember several trips I made checkin' the ranch. I'm goin' up Turkey Creek one morning and here's a car passed me and parked up the road a little bit. When I caught up with 'em, it was a couple of University students. I visited with them a little while and they were gonna go up the sand wash a ways and have a little picnic lunch and go through their studies. They had an armload of books apiece and I noticed that they had a blue sheet. I thought that maybe they were gonna spread their picnic lunch on that sheet and their books. So I went on and made my ride and I was comin' back, ah, it was along about noon and I could see somethin' goin' on down in this sand wash. And from a distance, it looked like this guy was up astraddle of the gal and was a-chokin' her! Her legs was agoin' like she was peddlin' a bicycle! I couldn't really see what was goin' on so I dropped down outa sight and come in where I was about 50 yards from 'em and, Christ, they're havin' intercourse! And this ol' boy, he was up there on top and her ol' legs is a-goin' like she's on a bicycle. Then he would stop and he'd kinda lay off to the side and her legs would slow down and then finally he'd get back up in the saddle and the bicycle business would go on. Then I realized what was goin' on was no concern of mine so I went on home. Later, I told my wife about this. I said, "This here bicyclin' business – I think you oughta try that!" Well, she wouldn't have nothin' to do with that! We had an old caretaker there named Homer Smith and I was tellin' him about – he was an old bachelor. "Hell," he said, "let's saddle up and go back! I'd like to see it!" "Aw," I says, "hell, they're probably through by now! You're too late!"

Then one morning I was goin' over to what we called the "Red Rock Pasture." When I was goin' in the summertime, I'd leave early – about 4:00 o'clock, just startin' to get daylight. I'd get down the road about, oh, I'd guess it was a mile, and I see this pickup with a camper on it parked off to the side of the road. Everybody in it's asleep and I noticed that it's got a Utah license plate. I went over and made my ride and I came back about 11:30 or so and this couple's out in this pool of water there, skinny-dippin'! And there's another lady, she's sittin' on the bank there with a couple of little kids. She's a red-headed gal and I could see they're skinny-dippin' and so I just rode on up there. Then they discovered me! She jumped up and covered her breasts with her hands and bent over and out of the water she went! But this ol' boy wasn't concerned, he just stood there buck-naked, a lot better blessed than I am. The other ol' gal was just sittin' there with the kids, watchin' the whole thing. I got to wonderin' if maybe he was a Mormon and had two wives! They weren't very talkative so I went on.

Another time we had a real cold spell and we had a bunch of these hippies had moved into the upper part of Paige Canyon. They were camped there and had a hospital tent and had their beds all rolled out on the ground, probably ten beds on each side. There's an ol' boy out there cuttin' wood with a bucksaw. He wanted to know what we were doin'. I didn't think we needed them there on the ranch – they were prowlin' all over, eatin' lots of oranges – every where I'd go there's orange peelings on the trail. I had a couple of guys with me and I told 'im, "These guys are the Fish and Wildlife Service. There's a trapper here and he's caught a couple of foxes that are rabid!" I thought if I could get a little scare into 'em about rabid foxes around, maybe they'd move. But he wasn't too concerned. "Well'" he said, "we haven't saw any foxes. There's a skunk foolin' around here at night but he don't bother us." So I rode on down the trail aways and here sat two ol' gals up on a big ol' rock. And this one gal is wrapped up in a blanket. I could see her legs clear on up past her hips and she didn't have any panties on. But she had a little baby in her arms and she was nursin'. She told me that the baby was born right there in their camp. She seemed to be real proud of the fact that she'd had this baby out in the woods. Christ, there was a lot of ice on the ground; I don't know why she wasn't cold because she wasn't very well covered up with that blanket! There was a little boy and a little girl and they're runnin' around naked; they don't have a stitch of clothes on 'em! I visited with her a little while and I left.

Chapter Five   The Army Years

Drafted and Into Basic training

I was drafted and went into the Army in January 1941. Since I've been out for close to 60 years, I think maybe I should've stayed in. But I disliked it too bad to even think about it at the time. When I got out, I definitely wanted out! I must've been the kind of man they wanted in the Army 'cause I went in a poor ranch kid, dumber than hell, didn't know a whole lot. I got drafted in the Army and the first thing they did, they loaded us up on a train and took us to Fort Sill, Oklahoma. Of course, we played a little poker on the train and drank a little whiskey and I got off the train with a pretty good hangover.

The next thing they did, they undressed us and put us in a overcoat and I had a short one that didn't come quite to my knees. There was a cold breeze a-blowin' and they set us out in a open shed to take our IQ test. Christ, I was a-shiverin' in this overcoat and I took my IQ test – never did finish the thing – but I was gettin' up towards the last end of it. We had an hour to do it in, as I remember. Then they issued us some uniforms, everything is either too big or too little, and they put us in these pyramid tents with a Sibley's stove that burned this soft coal that was full of sulfur. The whole area had this sulfur smoke in it and I was kinda allergic to that. I didn't do too well; I felt about half-bad.

The first week, they started us on our drillin' and short-order drill and I had a little four-eyed Arab that was actin' corporal that was a-runnin' the squad I was in. He always took pride in showin' up my damn weaknesses. The first problem I had with 'im was I wouldn't get off on my right foot, or my left foot; as I remember, you had to take off on your left foot. He didn't like the way I was respondin' to orders so he put me on the Awkward Squad. They had some Mexicans in there and a few Indians that didn't talk English. Anyway, they put me in this Awkward Squad and we're out there drillin' and I thought we was doin' pretty good and a major come up. He told the sergeant-in-charge to halt his squad. He did. And he walked up to me and he says, "Soldier, what are you doin' on this Awkward Squad?" I says, "Hell, my corporal, he thought I needed some special trainin'. I didn't argue with 'im." So he says, "Soldier, you think you could drill this squad?" Hell, I'd been around there for a couple of weeks by then so I said, "I'm sure I can!" "Well," he said, "let me see you drill 'em."

By god, I called 'em to attention and I told 'em to port arms and present arms and then I told 'em, "Forward march!" And I give 'em a Column Left and a Column Right and To-The-Rear, March and halted 'em and told 'em At Ease. This ol' major come over and says, "I'm takin' you back to your squad. Sergeant, take over your squad." So I got back and the major told my little four-eyed actin' corporal, Nackerd, he said, "Corporal, I don't think I need to see this soldier on the Awkward Squad again!" He responded real well.

One thing I learned early was to not do too much volunteerin'! One time I remember they had us all in the mess hall, the weather was bad, and the sergeant was teachin' us the nomenclature of the Model 1911 .45 caliber automatic – he took it all apart, named the parts and put it all back together again. He turned to me and said, "Recruit Barney, you don't seem to be a-payin' much attention!" I said, "Oh yes, Sir, I'm a-payin' attention." But I didn't tell him I owned a .45 automatic and I knew how to take the thing apart, and listenin' to him, I'd learned a lot of the part names. He said, "Well, if you're payin' all the attention you claim, let's see you take it apart and reassemble it." Well, I shook it apart quicker than he did, named the basic parts of it, and put it back together quicker than he had. For that I got four days KP!

The next thing they wanted us to learn was the General Orders. They promised the first few guys that could recite them would get a pass. Well, I went right straight from the mess hall where we was gettin' our instructions and went in to the sergeant and recited the General Orders from one end to the other. Another four days KP! I decided then not to be too knowledgeable! It just got me a lotta washin' dishes and peelin' potatoes.

Then we got into how to shoot a rifle. Nackerd had us in there tellin' us how to sight a rifle and then he got around to askin' me, "Did you ever shoot a rifle?" I said, "Corporal, my dad bought us boys a BB gun one time and about the third or fourth day we shot a songbird and he took the BB gun away from us and that's the only experience I've had with a gun." "Well," he said, "we'll teach you how to shoot a gun." They worked on us for several days and finally it come around to where we had to shoot. They had these Model 52 Winchester target rifles; they were as good a rifle at that time that you could get. So I walked up and down the line 'til I found one that looked like it was sighted in right and I got in that line. The corporal, he's there, and I get down and fire two or three rounds I'm a-callin' 'em bullseyes and he's a-questionin' me whether they're bullseyes or not. "No," I said, "Corporal, I've done everything just like you say to do. I get the line sight picture just like you say it's supposed to be and I'm squeezin' the trigger and I guess they gotta be bullseyes." "Well," he says, "we'll find out." After about 10 shots – they give us a 50-round box to shoot – I could see down there at 5:00 o'clock, well in the black, I could see a hole openin' up. And then I tell 'im, "Corporal, you got to help me. I know I'm pullin' this gun off and it just seems like they're droppin' down to 5:00 o'clock. And it's just where the sight picture is when it goes off." "Aw," he said, "I don't think so." I shot the whole box there and he gotta go over and check my target. Well, they're all right down there just over 5:00 o'clock and you could cover all 50 of 'em with a quarter! And he got real excited then! Boy, he grabbed me and my target and we run to see the captain. He says, "Captain, I want to show you the way Recruit Barney shot!" The captain, he's a-lookin' at 'im and "Boy," he says, "that's a good target!" And then the corporal told 'im, "The only gun he's ever shot was a BB gun his dad give 'im and he only had it for two, three days before his dad took it away. That's all the experience he's had!" The ol' captain looked at him and said, "Corporal, how gullible can you be? This soldier learned how to shoot a gun before he ever got here!"

So we went on and finally got our basic training in. Four months was up so they gave out a few First Class promotions. I made First Class right with the first of the draftees brought into this National Guard outfit. They were all, most of 'em all, from the Flagstaff College up there and our captain was a professor at the college. So I made First Class with the first bunch.

We went along there for awhile and they give out some Corporal ratings. And I got a Corporal rating on the machine gun squad. I was one of the first ones to make corporal out of the drafted bunch. Anyway, this first job on the machine gun squad was pretty easy duty. I'd been through the rifle course and I made expert on the Springfield rifle; I'd made expert on the Gerand M1 and I'd made expert with bayonet. They had me pissantin' a BAR around for several years, over most of Texas. And I made expert with it. And when I got this machine gun squad, I got to shoot it and made expert with it, too. As far as the weapons the Army had to fight with, I was doin' pretty good!

And it went on and they give out some sergeant ratings. I got a sergeant rating first. Hell, I'm one of the dumbest ones there but I'd learned a little bit about the Army. If I took any kind of a test, I didn't use my judgment on it, I just answered the way I'd read in the manuals. So I'm a sergeant and I got a squad of men and they were all Arizona boys. They filled up this I Company of the National Guard outta Flagstaff – the first draft they had, they drafted us in Arizona to fill up the Guard outfit. So I had all Arizona boys and several of 'em had two or three years of college, which I never had. Anyway, they was real good guys and real easy to work with. I went through Panama with 'em and I went over to the South Pacific with 'em, but I never got to fight with 'em in combat – it was all trainin'.

After finishin' basic training at Fort Sill, Oklahoma, we were sent to Camp Barkley, Texas. There was a sergeant there who had been given some kind of a compass program to take and we went off on a night trainin' exercise. He got us lost and finally just stopped and said, "You know, I could shit better directions that I'm gettin' outta this here compass!"

But there was a goat or sheep shed nearby so we went over there and laid down until daylight in about two feet of goat shit. And that goat shit's warm! Hell, we done pretty good. After it got daylight he found his way back to our Command Post without the compass.

After Camp Barkley we went to the Panama Canal Zone.

Figure 6. Ollie in Basic Training Camp in Lousiana

Panama Canal Zone

Eventually, we got down in Panama and I don't know, we'd been down there six, seven months, and I don't know what had happened (but this was before I got my sergeant rating). They put me on KP. Prior to gettin' on KP they give a aptitude test for all the people in the Canal Zone. Then I got on this KP and I'm in there a-peelin' potatoes in the afternoon. I had a big pot I had peeled already and I'm a-workin' on another one and my platoon sergeant come in. Eventually, he got to be the First Sergeant. He sit down on a sack on potatoes and, "Barney," he says, "what do you really think about the Army?" I said, "I think you already know I don't like it. I'm just waitin' 'til I get out of this damned outfit. I think there's a lotta bullshit goin' on. I'm not overly impressed! Hell, we're down here in this damned jungle and we're trompin' around out in the damn jungle with mosquitoes and leeches and chiggers gettin' on us. We're supposed to be a-guardin' the Canal, but, hell, we got a big Navy out on both ends of the thing and we got a Air Corps here and it seems to me they're actually the ones that's a-guardin' the damn Canal. We oughtta be over there somewhere killin' Japs or Germans or somethin' instead of pissin' around in these damn jungles!"

"Well." He says, "these results come back from this appitude test and you made the highest score in the whole Panama Canal Zone! I think maybe you're right – making a score like that and they gotcha in here peelin' potatoes!" There was probably a lotta guys who made good scores, but he said I made the highest one. I'm sure it was because I didn't answer the questions the way I thought they should be answered; I answered them the Army way! I'd learned my lessons earlier when I got all those days on KP.

But I found out later that what they were doin' was givin' us jungle training. So we got sent to Australia in a Regimental Combat Team – 3,500 of us. And then they took me out of the machine gun squad and made me a squad leader. That way I rated staff sergeant rank and I'm one of the first ones to get a staff sergeant rating out of the recruits, draftees.

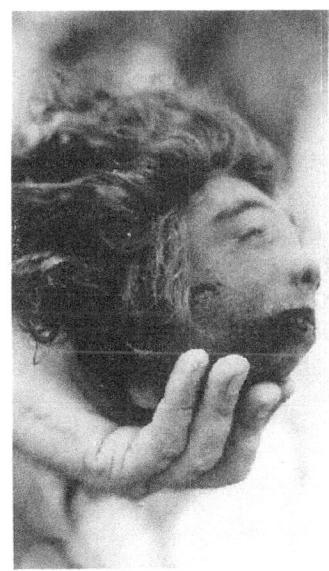

Figure 7. Panama Native Headhunters

One night in the canteen there, right along the canal, we had this Colorado boy on guard duty – to keep peace and quiet with all these guys drinkin' beer. There's quite a lot of regular Army guys there and they wasn't above startin' a fight with a National Guard guy if they thought they could whop 'im! They got on this Colorado boy and took his pistol and belt away from 'im and threw it in the canal. And, of course, he was in real bad trouble for that! He had to pay for that pistol and belt! The next night, they put me on there. I knew I'd have to watch what was goin' on. Pretty soon this same bunch, I think there was five of 'em, got 'em a table there and ordered their beer and they started pounding their glasses on the table, sayin', "I got Beer Number One! Who's got Beer Number Two?" They'd go all the way through that. I went over and I asked these guys, I said, "You know, you guys are gonna hafta quiet down!" Well, the spokesman of 'em, he jumped up right in my face and said, "What you gonna do about it?" I said, "Well, I'd just like to get you to quiet down, 'cause I don't wanna hafta run you into the guardhouse!" Now, he was real belligerent. I thought to myself, I'll fool this bastard! I had my nightstick in my right hand and I knew he was gonna grab it so I put it over in my left hand. And, sure enough, he grabbed it! I come right from the floor with my right and clipped him on the jaw and, I tell you, it knocked him cold – right out! And I turned to those other guys and said "Now, if you guys just pick 'im up and take 'im back to your barracks, I won't have to call the Sergeant of the Guard – put you all in jail!" So they gathered 'im up and took 'im out and in about 30 minutes or so, they come back and apologized to me. They said that they was wrong and they really appreciated me lettin' 'em take 'im home and not puttin' 'em all in the guardhouse!

Figure 8. Panama Native Transportation

After guard duty in Panama, we were put on the USS Hermitage. At that time it was the fourth largest transport ship in the world. It was an Italian liner that was captured in the Canal Zone and converted into a troop ship. There was 10,000 troops on it and about 3,500 Navy guys. It took 21 days to get from the Canal Zone to Australia. We went by one island – it was the first land we'd seen in a long time so everbody went to the side to see it and the boat started leaning over! They had to get us off the one side and scattered around to get the boat back on an even keel!

Ever damn boat I got on, I got seasick! Until the time they shipped us up to the Philippines, when they gave us seasick pills. But by then, I had already made 13 or 14 boat trips.

Anyway, we went on and that's the way I fought my war, as a squad leader.

Port Moresby

From Australia we was shipped to Port Moresby, New Guinea. We was diggin' in because the Japs was expected to land there, but they never did. We was livin' on C-rations and decided that we'd go out and kill a kangaroo for some fresh meat.

We killed one way off down at the bottom of a damn steep hill. We nearly had 'im back to the top when we got tired of packin' him and stopped to rest. While we was restin', we saw a big worm, looked like an angleworm about 18 inches long, crawl out of the bullet hole! So we just give 'im a kick off down that hillside 'cause we'd lost all interest in eatin' 'im.

From there we went down to Milne Bay. They had us sleepin' in hammocks and to get water, we'd take the liners out of our helmets and set the helmets out at night to catch rainwater. In the mornings, they'd be runnin' over and we'd fill our canteens. There's where I almost drowned. There was a small freighter of some kind that the Air Force or Navy had crippled and it had beached, oh Christ, it must have been five miles over there, but we could see the thing with binoculars. The captain sent me and my squad over there in a rubber boat to check it out and find out if anything was going on and what it was. When the tide was out there was almost an island out there between us and the boat. We got over there and the tide went out and I left three guys with the rubber boat and the rest of us walked over to the beached freighter. When we started out the water was up, well, about to our belts, I imagine. We walked over there and checked it all out – Hell, it was abandoned but it was loaded with .50 caliber ammunition. When we headed back, the tide started comin' in and, Christ, covered up our island. The water was gettin' up to our belts and a little higher and we'd lost our rubber boat. So I fired three shots and the guys answered me – they'd gone about 200, 300 yards away from us. They came back and got us before the water got much higher – probably saved us from drownin' since none of us could swim a mile and a half. Especially a ranch kid from Arizona.

First Action

The first action we saw was up in Rebal. They sent us over there and one of the battalions had had a firefight or two, but we never got involved in one. There was a big river that ran through there – I forget the name of it – and the Japs had crossed it. They'd dropped a lot of their guns and ammunition off in the water when they did. So we went up there and rescued one of their machine guns and several rifles and we picked up a big box of ammunition – probably had 1,000 or 1,500 rounds in it. We shot that machine gun out in the river; all of us shot it. The Army sent it back to the States and it's supposed to be in Fort Tuttle in Flagstaff in the museum there. I've never been to the museum to see if it really is there.

When we first got to Hollandia, New Guinea, the Wakde Army Area, we were bivouacked along the edge of a swamp. It was round and there was a drainage that went out there and a bridge. L Company and another company was over on the far left flank and we was on the right flank. We had the medics in back of us about 100 yards. During the night the Japs attacked out of that swamp and hit L Company – it was a hell of a firefight! We'd put down booby traps along the edge just under the bank. We were dug in there where we could lie down in the hole and we had ponchos stretched over the top to keep the water off us when it rained. Then, goddamn, these booby traps started goin' off and the bullets started flyin' through our ponchos and the medics got excited and started shootin'! Hell, all we could do is stay down with our bayonets fixed and wait for the Japs to come at us and try to shoot or bayonet them before they could kill us. The next morning, we found that the booby traps hadn't gone off! Some guys had gotten excited and thrown a bunch of hand grenades over there and it just sounded like the booby traps.

Sergeant Johnson, from Colonia Juarez, Chihuahua, was a good friend of mine. He was a white Morman. He'd got drafted into the Army 'cause when he turned 21 he had to declare himself either a Mexican citizen or an American citizen. He declared himself an American citizen and went up to Bisbee and got a job in the mines. Consequently, he got drafted, the same time I did. That morning he went down to the edge of the swamp and was washin' his face. He looked up and about 20 feet from him there was a Jap wadin' through there, so he shot 'im! Everbody asked, "What the hell are you shootin' at?" He said, "I killed a Jap!" They all yelled, "Aw, bullshit, you didn't kill no goddamn Jap!" So Johnson waded out there and dragged 'im out on dry land.

There was a Tor River that flowed through our area and we had an outpost along it. The Japs attacked it and they sent us out to rescue the guys in the outpost. There was a good firefight goin' on and when we got closer, I saw a Jap a-layin' there on his side with his back to me and he had a sound power telephone wire and he was twistin' it in two! I shot 'im in the back and he didn't die real good so I just emptied the clip in his head. Goddamn, it made me sick to my stomach! I actually threw up. Hell, I'd murdered the poor son-of-a-bitch! But, by god, I got over that! I learned the only damn way to win a war is to kill people! And lots of 'em!

But the first real combat we got into was there in Hollandia. When they shipped us over there our G2 told us there was about 3,500 or 3,600 Japs comin' up from Hollandia and we wouldn't have any tough combat 'cause they was sick and starvin'. But when we got there we found they'd shipped three transport loads of Japs right out of China with all new equipment and Christ, we fought 'em there for three weeks. I know the first push we made there, our Third Battalion made the push, we lost 30% of our men there that day

That scrap we had that day was a damn tough fight. We got pinned down and the Japs was chargin' in from our left flank. We had three tanks out there and several squads of men. We went in that night – there was a small stream runnin' through there – and we come across some water-cooled machine guns, four or five of them. There was a damndest pile of spent ammunition beside one of 'em – I'd never seen so many .30-.06 shells in my life – and a couple a-burned-out barrels and that ol' gun was just a-boilin' and a-smokin'. I asked this gunner, "How many rounds did you run through that thing?" He said, "We run 60,000 rounds through it!" But I know there was tracers comin' back and forth over the lines, both ways, lots of 'em.

I don't know how many Japs we killed. They had had a camp up there and a supply dump. I guess it was the second day when we went through the area where the Japs was a-chargin' in, and there for about 100 yards across and I don't know how long a distance it was, you could walk on dead Japs. They was just piled up there; you couldn't hardly walk through there without steppin' on 'em. I know we got credit for killin' 18,000 in that three weeks. We never did find any of those 3,600 sick ones.

There was a sergeant in the outfit from Panguitch, Utah. He was one of the first to get killed; it happened on the first day. Sergeant Johnson, from Mexico, knew where he was, so they sent three of us with a litter to bring 'im back. I know we

74

walked in about a quarter mile and there wasn't any place on the ground where there wasn't a damn bullet hole or where shrapnel had hit. All the trees were scarred higher than you could reach from bullets and shrapnel. It was a wonder anybody lived through that!

One of the guys in the squad, a little guy, was from Brooklyn. That little bastard went through that whole thing, come back when we did and he never was wounded! I know several times he got bullet holes in his damn clothes but hell, he wouldn't weigh 135 pounds then, soakin' wet. All of his clothes is too big for 'im, his shoes is too big for 'im, everthin' is too big for 'im. But he did get bullet holes through his damn clothes; I know that. One day he was leanin' against a tree not too far away. A damn sniper shot at 'im; the bullet hit about two feet away. He looked over at that but didn't move. The next shot hit about one foot from him! Goddamn, he moved then! About the time he moved, the third shot hit the tree. All he said was, "Huh, piss poor shot!" That damn little bastard was a good soldier, but he wasn't a garrison soldier. He never did get a promotion. I don't know how many times he got bullet holes through his clothes and never did ever get touched! He went through the whole damn campaign and never got hit once.

When I first got 'im he said, "You goddamn sergeants think you're smart!" I said, "You dumb bastard, you're just as smart as any of us! You could be a sergeant if you'd just behave yourself!" "Aw," he said, "I don't want to be a damn sergeant." He stayed in touch for years after the war – always sent me a Christmas card. He'd gone back to New York and went to work for the Post Office.

For 10 or 15 years, ever Christmas, I'd get a letter from 'im, wantin' to know how ol' sarge is doin'. Then he kept track of some a-them buddies he'd made. Most of 'em was down south there somewhere. They didn't get out when we did; they was replacements. He kept track of 'em; he'd tell me how they was a-doin' and then one Christmas, I never heard of him again. I don't know what happened to 'im, whether someone killed 'im or he died or what happened to him. The first time we went to Africa, we stopped there and had a couple of hours layover and I went out and was gonna get the New York phone book and see if I could find 'im. And Christ, they only had about three or four phone books and all of 'em about six inches thick! I finally got to the Bermans and Christ, there was half-a-dozen Bennie Bermans – hell, I just give up on it. Course, I hadn't heard from him in several years before that. I'd always liked to know what happened to him. He had to die or got killed; he wouldn't just stop writin'. Hell, some irate husband might a-killed 'im!

I did a lot of damn scoutin' over there. I'd have to pick out the guys to go with me and I'd try to rotate 'em; generally I'd just take three. At least half to two-thirds of the time, he'd volunteer! I'd ask him, "Berman, aren't you afraid?" He said, "Hell yes, I'm afraid! But I'll go with you. I'm not afraid of these other sons-of-bitches!" He was a rough-talkin' little bastard!

They relieved us with a Division after three weeks. Those guys had been into those sick ones – the Japs we was supposed to have found – and they sent their noncommissioned officers over to spend the night with us. They was braggin' to us, "We'll go through 'em like a dose of salts!" I don't think they knew what they was gettin' into.

Burial Detail

After we was relieved from that first combat mission, we got assigned to the burial detail. That was the worst damn detail I was ever on! They was bringin' in guys by the truckload! Stacked up there like cordwood! They was all shot to hell and bloated and full of maggots. We was camped right there by the graveyard, too. We'd dig holes in the sand about three and a half or four foot deep and we'd wrap the bodies in mattress covers – stuff 'em in and tie it down at the feet. We'd take one of their dogtags and pry their mouths open and put it in there. The other one we'd nail to a stake and put on the grave.

Christ, it was awful! We was camped there and ate there and the maggots was crawlin' all over the goddamn ground. Damn flies was everwhere and blowin' the blankets in our beds. That was one damn place I was glad to get the hell away from!

When we was on that detail, they put up a big screen and was goin' to show us a movie. We're all out there sittin' on our helmets or layin' on the sand – I read this story, someone sent it in to *The Reader's Digest*, but I was there when it happened – we'd been waitin' for about an hour since they was havin' problems with the projector and it had gotten really quiet. Pretty soon three or four shots rang out on the perimeter and some clown just jumped up and yelled, "Now count your men, you Tojo son-of-a-bitch!"

The Silver Star

I told you about the time we were sent to Hollandia, in the Wakde Army Area, in our first real combat to fight those "sick" Japs that was supposed to have been left behind. Turned out to be six divisions right out of China with all new equipment.

We made our landin' there and everything was fine. Bright and early one morning we pushed off toward the airstrip up the coast we wanted to take. Our Third Battalion was in the advance and right away we got into some real tough opposition. We got held down. They give me a note to take back to the Battalion CP, a good half-mile back down the way. I'm a-joggin' off down there and snipers are shootin' at me most of the way. That kept me movin' pretty well. When I got up to the CP, there was a general out there, a one-star general, and of all things, he's out there with his star shinin', directin' a little traffic! And there's sniper fire around! I knew that from my way up. So I went into our CP and delivered my message, my note I was carryin', and when I come out, this general was layin' there dead! The snipers got 'im! General Gavins was his name. I think he was one of the few generals killed during World War II.

77

I still had to go back to where my unit's pinned down – course, the snipers worked on me all the way back. Fortunately they didn't shoot too well! When I got back the Japs were counterattackin' on our left flank. There was an open draw that was probably 150 yards long with very little vegetation in it. We got three tanks up there and a couple platoons of men and they broke this counterattack, but we're still pinned down with artillery. I got back there with my squad and, God, we're gettin' sniper fire! Finally, one of the men said, "It's in that ol' tall tree out there! That's where the sniper's firin'." I looked it all over and I couldn't see anything but there's a real thick clump of leaves and stuff in there and you couldn't tell what's in there. I emptied my rifle in there – eight rounds – and nothin' fell out, but those snipers would tie themselves in there. But we never got anymore sniper fire outta there!

Twice that day, right there where we was pinned down, I damn near got myself killed. One time I got back there with the rest of the squad to see how they're doin' and here come a artillery shell. It hit a big stump there, about three feet in diameter, and I had bark and splinters and wood all over me! I look up there about three foot from my head and there's a three-inch hole through that thing where the shell went through it and didn't go off! If it had I wouldn't be here today!

I'm pinned down and there's this damn tracin' fire comin' through, Christ, it was like a swarm of bees, both ways! Pretty soon – I'd been layin' there for awhile with all this tracer fire goin' over and it was hittin' the ground and the trees around there really good – I thought, by God, maybe I've been here too long! And I just got moved when a damn tracer shell come down and hit what would've been right between my shoulder blades! It bounced around and burned out. But that's twice there in about a hour that I should a-got killed. And, I guess, I could a-got killed goin' up to the CP and back.

Along in the afternoon we finally got orders to pull back. I had a little Italian boy and goddamnit, before we got to movin' good, a damn shell hit in there and wounded 'im real bad. When I'd been up to the CP, I saw there was about three or four Jap litters layin' up there about 100 yards. I had it in my mind that I'd get one of those litters and get someone to help me come back. We're gettin' a lotta damn fire and I told my corporal, "Just grab a-hold of the other end of this damn thing and let's go back and get that guy." I forget his name now. We went back and he's a-moanin' and a-groanin' and he thought that we'd gone off and left him – which we had! When we went to put him on the litter, I saw that one of his testicles was lying there in the dirt but it was still attached by its cord. So I picked it up and put it on the litter with him. I think the guy survived; I never did hear where he died. I don't know whether they cut that testicle off or cleaned it up and put it back in his scrotum. Then we got back outta there! We delivered 'im to the aid station and found a big shell hole near there.

We spent the night in that. We got a lot of shellin' from our ships that night and the Japs was still throwin' in a few shells. Next mornin' everthin' is quieted down. There was a stack of Jap bombs all crated up in boxes. They was 50 Kilo bombs. I don't know how many of 'em there was but they was stacked up about five foot high and probably 10 foot across and about 50 yards long. If one of those shells had ever hit in that damn thing we'd have been just one big crater there!

The next day three of us went in to pick up the sergeant who'd been killed, a Mormon boy outta Panguich, Utah. He was goin' to the university in Flagstaff. We went in and picked up his body and there was a couple of sailors in there who come in lookin' for souvenirs. This sergeant friend of mine, this Sergeant Johnson from Mexico, got the dead sergeant's billfold out. He'd been in a poker game a few days before and Johnson knew he had several hundred dollars. He didn't want the damn grave people to get off with that! One of these sailors asked 'im, "You findin' anything worthwhile?" And I thought that goddamn Johnson was gonna kill the bastard! He got mad! He said, "This is as good a friend as I ever had and I'm gettin' his belongings so I can turn 'em in! And I want to see you get the hell outta here before I hafta kill ya!" I tell you, they left!

Both of us, the corporal and me, got Silver Stars for going back under fire and rescuin' the Italian boy. I was put in for the Distinguished Service Cross but they didn't think we'd seen enough combat for anyone to be worthy of that. So they gave me the Silver Star, same as my corporal. This was the summer of 1944.

Our outfit was really chintzy about giving out unit medals. I also picked up a Bronze Star – haven't got it yet – still waitin'. Sherry's workin' on gettin' the medals I never received; besides the Silver Star, there were two Bronze Stars, a Purple Heart with three Oak Leaf Clusters for being wounded four times and a whole batch of campaign medals – even got a Good Conduct Medal!

More about my corporal: he was a Mexican outta New Mexico. He wasn't a big Mexican, but he was a bright Mexican. When we got in the Philippines and they shot us clear down to practically nothin' and I was wounded and gone, and there for a week or so, this corporal was the company commander! That's how high he went, the little son-of-a-bitch. He'd got a battlefield commission and was a second lieutenant, but he was actin' as company commander!

I still have the original write-up from the Army that went with the Silver Star. It reads:

"(GO 32, Hq XI Corps, 5 Nov 44)

Staff Sergeant Ollie O. Barney, Jr, 38000563, Infantry, United States Army. For gallantry in action near Wakde-Sarmi area, Dutch New Guinea, on 24 May, 1944. During a strong enemy counter attack in which his company moved to more advantageous positions, Sergeant Barney voluntarily returned under intense enemy rifle and mortar fire in order to rescue a wounded comrade who had fallen. In order to accomplish this mission, he and one other volunteer traversed a distance of approximately two hundred yards over rough open terrain that was fully exposed to enemy observation and fire, and succeeded in bringing back the wounded man to safety of the battalion aid station. Sergeant Barney's courage and gallant conduct so inspired the other men of the company, that they renewed their efforts and repelled the attack with severe losses to the enemy."

(Editor's note: The medals were finally received June 2005)

Noemfoor Beach

From that first combat mission we were sent to Noemfoor Island. They give us a bunch of lumber to build rafts so we could float our machine guns and extra ammo to the beach. The timber was from eucalyptus trees in Australia and was really heavy. We drilled holes in it and nailed it together with spikes and when we got ready to make our landing, we threw that thing out in the water and it sank like a rock! We had to pissant that damn ammunition in! When I went off our converted destroyer, it shifted a little bit and I dropped off in a hole and Christ, I thought I never would quit goin' down. But I had two floatation bladders under my jacket and I finally came back up. Somewhere on the beach I got hit with a piece of shrapnel across my knee – ruined a good legging, tore up my britches and cut a pretty good gash on my knee.

There was six Army planes with us during the landing to protect us from any bombers or fighters. I never learned 'til just a few years ago that Lindberg was over there showin' these Army pilots how to fly those planes and how to get more out of the aircraft. He was the head of the group that was with us! I've read his autobiography and Lindberg shot down one Jap Zero and had another one smokin' really good before it disappeared into the clouds! When the big shots found out that he was takin' an active part, they got him the hell outta there!

Anyway, after we took the beach, they dropped some paratroopers there. One planeload they dropped too low and killed or crippled most of 'em. We went up on some limestone bluffs above the beach and dug in. It would rain durin' the night and several times the Japs would come around and we drew a little fire and did a little firin' and just as it was getting daylight, the captain come around and told me to take three men and go out a mile ahead and check out what was goin' on. Christ, we went out and there was a lotta ferns growin' there with dew on 'em and we could see where the Japs had been walkin' through 'em. I got a real funny feelin' out there about six hundred yards or so and I stopped. Ol' Berman came up and said to me, "Sergeant, we're gonna get killed if we keep goin'!" I said, "How the hell do you know? " "Well," he said, "I got a feelin'. By god, we'll get killed if we keep goin'." I said, "I got the same damn feelin'. I don't feel good about it either. So we'll just stall around here 'til about the right time and we'll come back in."

About that time they sent a patrol out to get us – they was hollerin' for us to stop. We got back and had just gotten back when the Navy put a barrage out there, Christ, for a mile out there they shot down ever damn tree! Three ships just smaller than battleships and some destroyers was firin' and they had a bunch of rockets they were firin' in there. I tell you – nothin' could a-lived through that! And we would have been right out there in the middle of it!

Later we went on out because there was an airstrip they was buildin' up there we had to take and we ran onto a Jap. He had a clean, dry uniform on and he had a stick, a green stick, about eight feet long and he had a bayonet tied on the end of it. He was just walkin' along, just rum-dum. I was gonna take 'im prisoner but someone off to the side shot 'im and killed 'im. Where that bastard was, I don't know. He had to be down in a cave or some damn thing. But he was sure rum-dum. He didn't know what he was doin'. Hell, that old stick was green; he couldn't a-stuck it into anybody, it was too limber.

Then we went up there to the airstrip and the Japs had a bunch of Javanese prisoners, slave labor. They all had Japanese uniforms on and the guys up front shot two or three of them figurin' they was Japs until we found out they weren't. We rescued 25 or 30 of 'em and they was the happiest damn guys I ever saw in my life. There were several of 'em lyin' in racks they had built up in the trees to sleep on. There were half a dozen of 'em up there that had been asleep and the Japs bayoneted 'em just before they left. And all 'em had just masses of sores on the backs of their legs because if they slowed down at all, the Jap guards would prick 'em in the calves of the legs with a goddamn bayonet.

It was the last week we were in the Wakde Army Area; we hadn't finished with that scrap yet. They sent me on a patrol up the Tor River and we found a permanent Jap camp but there was nobody in it when we got there. They'd been livin' there and I don't know where they went to, but I went on up the river and came back the same way. The next day they sent another platoon from another company and they loaned me out as a scout. We went up there and this Jap camp was occupied! I was with the lieutenant, we were up in front and saw a Jap there out on his little porch − he was repackin' his pack. The lieutenant didn't know what to do, so I told him, "Before they find out we're here, get your men to back off and call in artillery on these bastards! I'll kill that guy fixin' his pack and that'll get their attention." When they backed off, I shot the guy on the porch and he fell on his pack and another guy came runnin' out of a little house and started around the corner and I shot him. By that time, there was automatic weapon fire comin' in, so I backed off. The lieutenant said that he had the artillery zeroed in on the camp, but here come brush and trash floatin' down the river. I told 'im then, "Hell, I think your damned artillery is off! "Oh no," he said, "It's right!" There was a couple of guys in his outfit that let four Japs walk right by them. Apparently those four walked right into that artillery fire. When I went back the next morning with our platoon − we found two fresh graves in the camp − which the artillery fire had missed, but the Japs had moved out anyway. Further on up the river we found a wounded Jap layin' behind a log. Six guys went up there lookin' at him. I didn't go up to look at the bastard; I stayed back. They said that he jerked a hand grenade out, rapped it on the log and held it up to his stomach and killed hisself when he could have thrown it over the log. He would've wounded or killed all six guys. That tells you somethin' about that damn Jap mentality. He didn't want to be taken prisoner, so he just blew hisself up.

So we went on up the river and never did find out where the rest of the Japs went. After that day, I never went back to the camp, so I don't know if they ever occupied that camp again.

At one point we were told that the Japs was eatin' one another! I didn't believe it. But in some of these camps we found, they'd have lean meat cooking. And because of their religion, they wouldn't kill a pig and eat it. Then one afternoon on patrol, we killed a Jap and left 'im layin' there. When we went by that same place the next day, his britches had been pulled down and all the meat was cut off of his butt and thighs! When we trailed 'em up and found the meat cookin', I had to believe it! Some of our paratroopers who had been killed were found with meat cut off of them, too. You know, I felt pretty sick about the first Jap I shot, but by now I was startin' to feel good about killin' 'em.

After the main fightin' was over, they sent our whole company out on a patrol. We went through a lot of jungle and camped on a beach. A Super Cub would find us and drop our supplies. They come in early one day and dropped a note with our groceries that said there was 12 armed Japs walkin' up the beach right along the edge of the water. The beach was pretty narrow there between the jungle and the water. They sent me out to set up an ambush. I didn't know exactly how far but I went down to where I was feelin' right about comin' out on the beach to set up our ambush. What we did was walk right into all 12 of 'em! They had stopped for a break – their rifles was leanin' up agin bushes, some of 'em were layin' on the ground. Me and my two scouts was in front and we walked right out among 'em! Another guy was close behind and I tell you, there was a firefight took place right then! I like to got my damn head chopped off by the Sergeant

Major with his little Samurai sword. I had run in there and he was jerkin' out his sword but he was in the wrong position! He had to turn around to swing and I was right there next to him. As he turned to swing I jammed my rifle against his head and pulled the trigger! The muzzle blast was huge and the top of his head blew off, blood and brains flyin' everwhere! When it was over, we found only 11 bodies; we was missin' one. We got to lookin' around and this one Jap had crawled headfirst down in some Mango roots with one leg stickin' out. We pulled 'im out and there was no blood on him, but he wouldn't respond; he was playin' dumb. We stripped him naked and there wasn't a scratch on him. He was just a kid, looked like he was 16 or 17 years old, but he was probably older than that. We couldn't get 'im up, we couldn't get 'im to do nothin'; he was just playin' possum. He wasn't shell-shocked but I was sure he was scared to death. I told the guys, "We're supposed to bring in some prisoners, but we're gonna hafta pack this bastard and I tell you one thing, I'm not a-gonna help pack him! You can either pack him in as a prisoner or you can shoot the bastard. I don't care!" So one of the guys put his rifle down close to his head and pulled the trigger and that was the end of him.

I suppose the way they fight wars now, I'd be tried for a war criminal! We wouldn't have had to pack 'im more than a half-mile or so, but not a man in the squad was gonna do it. I got one guy killed in that damn deal. I was positive that he was shot by one of the other men in the squad. I hate to talk about that because that happens in war all the damn time; havin' people killed by "friendly fire." I think I know the guy that shot 'im. I had this one misfit that grabbed the Samurai sword; you know those Sergeant Majors carried one that was only about three foot long and officers carried one that was almost four feet long. They could sure whack your head off with one! I never could talk that guy out of the sword. Eventually he went psycho. I had him out on a wharf, guardin' it with another guy, when all of a sudden, along about midnight, he just screamed and run down that wharf into the ocean. We lost the submachine gun he was packin' but we got 'im out alive. They sent 'im home and I never did hear anymore about 'im. But he'd already sent my sword home.

Another morning I was sent out to scout and found a trail that run down on this peninsula. I was to go several miles and then make a right angle turn toward some hills, little hills, and check 'em out to see if there was any Japs in 'em. Ever once in awhile on the trail, there would be a little clearing and when we came back, we walked over one clearing and came onto an ocean where there wasn't supposed to be one! I thought back and realized that we had walked over the trail and missed it. As we started back we run into a Jap officer and his aide and we had a little firefight there. I shot the Lieutenant and someone else shot his aide. They had a little utensil all full of clams they'd gotten from the beach and the Jap had a regular Army Samurai sword. I got that sword and his pistol and the rest of the guys got the other souvenirs. Later I sold the pistol for 100 Guilders ($103 US) to some guy in the Air Force that come up lookin' for souvenirs. We had a sergeant goin' home on furlough and I knew I couldn't hang onto that sword – it stuck six inches out of the barracks bag and someone would a-stole it – so I sold 'im the sword for another 100 Guilders.

It was a guy up in Globe that bought it from the sergeant, he's dead now, and I'd like to find the owner and maybe buy the sword back. I'm not gonna work on it, but it would be quite a souvenir. I guess I could a-sent it home but, hell, it would a-meant a lot of damn paperwork and they kept me pretty busy around then; I didn't have a lot of time. I was runnin' patrols and makin' scoutin' trips.

After these main campaigns was over with, these Japs, the survivors, would just go off out into the damn jungle and live around, off a-these native gardens. For some damn reason, I got a-way more than my share of the patrols. I kinda think the reason I did was because practically ever one of 'em out, we'd have a pretty good body count. Back in those days there, you know, they liked to keep a pretty good body count. And this one I remember, we went out on it and most of 'em I'd take my full platoon. On some of the more dangerous ones, I'd take a smaller patrol where we could get around and not be seen so easy.

These Japs was real bad about runnin' around with fixed bayonets. Wounded guys, you know, they'd just stick a bayonet in their belly and not finish 'em off. There was a couple other sergeants and I, we'd made up our minds, by god, we were gonna bayonet one a-them bastards. Just let 'em know that it could be done. This one bunch of Japs, we trailed up and found their camp. I had a system of takin' care of these camps. I'd have my two scouts out and they were mostly watchin', keepin' their damn eyes open. I was a better tracker, you know, and I'd kinda keep track of their tracks. When they'd smell smoke or hear somethin' then we'd just ease up and get up where we'd see the camp. Generally, they're in under this lean-to they got there and they'd have a little fire a-goin', cookin' up their vegetables they'd stole outta these native gardens. The first scout, he'd stop right there and the second scout would come up on the side of 'im, you know, about five or six foot. Then I'd come in on the other side and then the guy behind me'd come around and we'd form a firin' line there. We just keep gettin' in position 'til they spotted us. And then all of us on the firin' line, we'd just empty our guns in their camp.

On this particular one, I saw this Jap run out on the side there and so I took after 'im. I fixed my goddamn bayonet and I was gonna bayonet the bastard. He didn't have a gun and I was gonna bayonet the bastard. I got up about 15 foot of 'im and he saw I was after 'im and he saw I had a fixed bayonet and he went down in his damn pocket clear to his elbow! He come out with a hand grenade and those Japanese hand grenades, you pulled a pin on 'em and they had like a firin' pin there, just like in a rifle, but you had to rap 'em on the butt of your rifle or a tree or somethin' to ignite 'em, burn 'em. Christ, when he come out and he headed for this tree to rap that thing on a tree, I shot 'im! But before I'd shot 'im, he started hollerin' ahead – there was someone ahead of 'im. I shot him and then I run up and overtook the other one and shot him. But I, after that damn grenade business, I'd lost all interest in bayonettin' one of 'em!

Generally, all of us had our hand grenades and they still had a few rifles. We'd come in on these here native gardens and walk around 'til we'd find fresh tracks where Japs had been pilferin' some of these native vegetables. We'd take the tracks and trail 'em up and we'd find and form our firin' line and Christ, damn near ever patrol we'd get four to six Japs to turn in for a damn body count. I done a lotta that. I don't know how many damn Japs – we probably killed as many as a hundred on what they called Combat Reconnaissance Patrols. If you saw a Jap, it was a Combat Patrol! If you didn't find one, you'd keep your eyes open and see what you could see and report.

This Sergeant Johnson, from Colonia Juarez, he was another one, he got a-lotta these Combat Reconnaissance Patrols. He was real successful with comin' back and reportin' killin' four to six Japs. Like I said, we got more'n our share of 'em.

One time, we're out patrollin' around and we hit this trail. We trailed it in and it come to a water hole. There was three Japs there fillin' up their water deals and we killed all three of 'em and threw 'em in the water. We come back through there a day or two later and someone had pulled 'em out. By that time they're bloated up and full a-maggots. We threw 'em back in. It turned out that these natives, some of 'em was usin' that water and they'd complained and it come down to me. First Sergeant knew who in the hell had done it. He called me in and he says, "Ollie, these natives is complainin' about findin' these dead bodies in the water! Don't throw any more of 'em back in the water!" I assured 'im I wouldn't.

Ever patrol we made we killed four to six Japs and we made a lot of patrols. We'd check 'em over for any papers they had or for souvenirs. We was supposed to turn in their dogtags and any papers they had, but I saved a couple of dogtags for my dad. He wanted a scalp but I didn't get that – didn't know how I would get that back! He kept those tags 'til he died and I have 'em now in a showcase in my trophy room.

In all that damn fightin' I never had but two men killed, but I had a bunch wounded. I've thought back and it seems that our company was responsible for somewhere between 300 and 400 Japs killed, probably closer to 400.

Noemfoor Island Natives

One of the first things we did when we got on the island was dig slit trenches to get in when the Jap bombers came in. The natives would come up and look in the trenches and just couldn't figure out what they were for until 10 or 15 bombers came over one night and bombed the island pretty good, includin' their village – killed quite a few of 'em. The next morning, the survivors was all diggin' trenches; they realized what they were for!

We had a cowboy in the unit from Williams, Arizona. We called him "Pappy" O'Hara since he was a few years older than most of us. He chewed Copenhagen snuff that his folks sent to him in a roll and when he'd get kinda low on it, he wouldn't chew it, he would sniff a little up each nostril and then he's sneeze and fart and take on! And that's the way he used it until he got a new supply! He had a world almanac that he studied all the time and the man was practically a walkin' encyclopedia. If you wanted to know somethin', you just asked 'im and he'd almost always know the answer! We was camped one time in a coconut grove and we had to walk about a half a mile down to where there was water, where the natives got their water. They didn't have containers, just coconut shells that they had cleaned all the meat out of. They'd have 10 or 15 of them tied on a stick and they'd go down there to the coral and get water. It was terrible water – salty, briny water – and after all the natives waded around in it getting their shells filled, it wasn't the most potable water in the world! Of course, we had Halazone to purify it. But ol' Pappy said, "I'm gonna dig a well!" And, by God, he got a couple helpers and started diggin' and down about 10 feet they got good water. So we got busy and dug a couple more wells near our camp. We had good water then and didn't have to walk a half-mile for it. Several times some of the natives would come by and look down in those wells and shake their heads and taste the water but not one of 'em ever went back to their camp or village and dug one for theirselves. They kept goin' back to the old water hole with their shells. Any kind of can we threw away, they grabbed up and used for water containers.

Figure 9. New Guinea Headunters

The missionaries had been in there years before and I guess they stayed until the Japs killed or imprisoned them. But they'd taught those natives to read and write. They could read the labels on the cans! They didn't know what it meant, but they could read those labels. That's one thing I fault the missionaries for – they taught the natives to read and write just so they could read the Bible but they never gave 'em any kind of a tool. The only tool the natives had was a machete – the missionaries never gave 'em any seeds to plant in their gardens, never brought in any fruit or nut trees for better food. Just taught 'em the Bible.

The native women done all the work; the men didn't do anything. When folks got old, they were given little lean-tos near the gardens where they could get somethin' to eat until

90

they died. Then they'd burn the bodies and put the bones in caves and crevices on the rocky beaches.

Figure 10. Some Neomfoor Inlanders

I remember one time we were out on one of these patrols and we saw a whole passel of these natives – a few men and mostly women and kids. And those women and kids hell, they'd have a big sack or a basket of stuff; they packed this stuff on their heads. This one ol' boy we had, he was from Alabama. There was a little ol' native woman there and Christ, it looked like she had 50 or 60 pounds of damn vegetables in there. This old man, a fuzzy-wuzzy, he was walkin' along there with nothin'. The ol' kid from Alabama, he stopped 'em and made this guy pack the vegetables on in. Boy, that hurt his pride, doin' woman's work!

We called 'em fuzzy-wuzzies – they had these big ol' hairdos, you know – and it was greased with coconut grease and it'd stand up and hell, it was probably a foot across. Ones that had a real good one, most of 'em stood up six, eight inches above the head. I always wanted, sometime when I could a-got away with it, I wanted to shoot a tracer bullet through that hair and see what would happen!

Whether it'd set it on fire or what! But I never did get the chance to do it where I could get away with it. That was one of my ambitions that I didn't never fulfill.

These natives, they'd go out when the tide was out. They'd go out and scrounge around when the tide was out and they'd get fish and shells and different things. They'd put 'em in their baskets and take 'em home and cook 'em. We used to have to stand guard out on these damn beaches, too. I'm out there on guard one time with two, three guys and here come a whole herd of these native women in their grass skirts. They wore grass skirts but nothin' above. They was goin' in there to take a bath. I've got my binoculars and I thought this would be interestin' to watch. Goddamnit, it turned out they got about three or four a-these grass skirts on and they take 'em all off except one and then go in the water. So I never got to see one completely naked!

That's the way we had to shower, too, is go out in that damn salt water. Hell, you couldn't lather soap in it. It'd knock all the dust off you, but it didn't take a lot of dirt off. At least you'd get in water. I guess it was better than nothin'.

Figure 11. A Family Gathering on Neomfoor Island

South Pacific Incidents

We were on a perimeter and it was just gettin' daylight. The partner I had in the foxhole, he says, "I gotta crap! I don't have any toilet paper!" I scrounged around in my pack and I found a little packet of toilet paper but I said, "By god, you better take your damn rifle with you, too! It's about as important, when you're gettin' outta this damn hole this early in the morning to go take a crap, to have your rifle as it is toilet paper." And he left out there and it wasn't long I heard a shot! And pretty soon he come back. I said, "What happened?" He said, "I'm sure glad you reminded me to bring my rifle. I had it a-layin' right down there beside me and I was about half through with my crap and I see a Jap come a-sneakin' up through the bushes! So I got my rifle and I just shot 'im; he's layin' out there dead! Christ, if I hadn't a-had that rifle and he saw me, he'd a-shot *me* for sure!"

Another time, we were campaignin' along the beach and with a lotta this sand and salt water and it would rain. The BAR (Browning Automatic Rifle) man never could get but about three or four shots in a burst and the thing'd be jammed up. I told 'im, "You're gonna hafta get rid of that damn gun." He says, "Hell, where am I gonna get another rifle?" We was walkin' up along through another camp there one time; they were medics. There was an M1 rifle a-leanin' agin a tree. I saw it from a distance; I went up and tapped 'im on the shoulder. I said, "When you go by that rifle, you just set yours down there and pick it up." And that's what he did. He packed that rifle along 'til he got wounded. That was the last BAR I ever packed or had anybody pack in the damn service. I guess in the European Theater, they might a-worked, but I'll tell ya, they damn well didn't work long in them jungles, along the ocean and that salt water.

The M1 rifle – we never had any problem with them a-workin'. There was only one problem and it wasn't a problem with the rifle, it was a problem with the ammunition. They had these corrosive primers and you'd shoot it a few shots and that night, if you didn't take your cleaning tool and put a patch on it and oil that chamber, the damn chamber would rust! Then when you fired it, the cartridge would stick in there and it would jerk a section of the rim out. You had a damn rifle that you couldn't operate! You gotta get a ramrod and beat the damn empty shell out. Somebody always packed a cleanin' rod and it didn't take the guys long to learn that whenever they fired that rifle, that night to get their Army tool and oil the chamber and clean it out. The tool had a screwdriver on it and a few other little things to take your rifle down and apart.

South Pacific Wasps

This is a story that happened when we were campaignin' in the South Pacific. We always had a water problem over there and we got to where we'd have a little time and we had some tree climbers that fasten to your boots. We'd climb up in these coconut trees with a machete and chop off these coconuts and drink the milk out of 'em and a lot of 'em, we'd open up and eat the meat. That coconut milk outta these fresh coconuts is a lot better than the ones you buy in a grocery store. This one day I climbed up in this tree and I started whackin' off these coconuts and there was a bunch of wasps up there! They got after me and hell, I'm up there 30 feet and it's too far to jump! I gotta come down that tree on those climbers and I'm pretty sure I made better time a-comin' down with them wasps after me that I did goin' up!

I had one other run-in with these wasps. We were campaignin' and a machine gun opened up on me. I dove in behind a log that was probably 30 inches in diameter and this machine gun kept on a-shootin' on this log and that stirred up some more wasps! Christ, I had two choices: I could stay there with the wasps and the machine gun a-workin' on that damn log or I could jump and get killed! The decision was made right quick to stay with the wasps! I was layin' down as close to the ground as I could get and was real still and I don't think I ever got stung, only once or twice. Those bullets couldn't get through that log so I was safe and

I don't know what happened to the machine gun. After a bit he quit shootin' so someone might a-shot him off his gun.

The swarms weren't as big as the killer bees, probably wasn't over 35 or 40 wasps, but they had a potent damn stinger!

Invasion of Luzon

We started out on one a-the islands off the coast of New Guinea. They put us on, our Regimental Combat Team, they put us on these converted destroyers that were haulin' troops. It was the first time this ever happened – they give us seasick pills. We had a young Navy crew on there that had very little experience and had no experience in the South Pacific. They'd made a trip or two across the Atlantic and when they saw us takin' these seasick pills in the South Pacific, they just laughed theirselves silly. They said, "Aw, you guys, they don't have any rough weather in the South Pacific! If you wanna see rough weather, you gotta get into the North Atlantic!" Course, there was several of us told 'em, " Well, hell, we've gotten seasick in the South Pacific and if they work, we're glad to take 'em!"

Out about the second day, we got into a typhoon! A real Typhoon!! Hell, I thought it was gonna sink that damn converted destroyer – it would go clear, the front, clear outta the water and then it'd drop down and then it'd go back under six, eight, 10, 15 foot of water. Waves'd come back over the decks about four foot deep. 'Bout a half a day of that, these sailors was startin' to get seasick and they were turnin' different colors of green and layin' around in there, sick and throwin' up and just havin' a terrible time! And a-course, none of us was seasick. So we told those sailors, "Hell, this is nothin'! You should a-been here last year!" And I'll tell you, it was a goddamn mess! I didn't get seasick, but I was spooked a little bit!

After we got through the typhoon, and there was about probably 800 or so ships in this here convoy, a Jap sub got in the convoy. They start throwin' those damn ashcans out there and they threw some of 'em close enough to our damn converted destroyer that it damned near knocked it outta the water! And just scared the livin' hell out of those guys. So we told 'em, "This isn't anything, hell, there's just one or two of 'em out there. You should a-been here last year when we got several of these here subs in there and they sunk about half the convoy! God, that was scary!"

But we got through and everything was runnin' along fine. We got up to Luzon and anchored there and we got off and got out on shore and back off the shore quite a little ways. We kinda bivouacked there and that's one of the times I saw General MacAuther. He was paradin' around there and watchin' his troops and seemed real businesslike. He was a kinda gutsy ol' bastard and a damn good general! The Australians referred to him as a "Bloody good general but a bloody cunt of a man!"

Next morning it come along just about daylight and we heard these Jap bombers come in. Now, we knew what the hell a Jap bomber sounded like and pretty soon we could see 'em – there was four of 'em come in and they was comin' in right over all these ships parked out there and they told us there was over 800 ships. The reaction of these boats, warships and everthing that was out there – ever one of 'em just turned ever gun they had just shootin' straight up! We could see these tracers goin' up; hell, it looked like a huge pile of coals that someone was throwin' up with a shovel. We watched these four planes, they just flew right into it and Christ, it shot 'em all down! As soon as they hit that volley of fire, hell, they just exploded and burned and fell! Knocked ever one of 'em down right now! Why they flew into it, I don't know. I guess Japs, they was just used to doin' what they were told. But after a minute or so that shrapnel started fallin' – hell, it sounded like a hive of bees, that shrapnel comin' down! There was several pretty good chunks fallin' around on us but no one got hit with it. And then that afternoon we had to go on up to where the fightin' was, where the Japs was dug in.

We went along the seacoast there for about a mile up there and the Japs was shellin' us with the 155 mm cannons. Ever once in awhile they'd hit in a column of men and, Christ, they'd just wipe it out. When we got up there to where we were gonna get into that artillery, the Captain got a-hold a-me and he says, "I want you to fix your bayonet and get behind our company. Anybody falls out, just prod 'em out with your bayonet and get 'em back in the damn column. If they refuse to come in, just shoot 'em!" I says, "I might prod 'em with the bayonet and leave 'em bleeding a little bit, but I'm not a-gonna shoot 'em! If you gotta get 'em shot, you get somebody else." "Aw," he says, "you can handle the situation." And we had one guy there in the company from one of the Southern states, I think he was from Alabama, and he was a guy that was, oh, ten years or so older than me. He was a new replacement we'd gotten down in the islands before we left and he fell out. I walked up to 'im and told 'im to get back in the column. He says, "I'm not a-gettin' in." "Well," I says, "you're gettin' in unless you wanna be bayoneted! 'Cause my instructions is to put you guys back in or, by god, bayonet 'em! Kill 'em! And I don't want to do that, but I will." On the strength on that, he got real damn reluctant, but he got back in the column. We all got through and it was just a few days later than that we were makin' a push there and he fell out. Everbody went off and left 'im and he was just sittin' there and there was a Japanese had an anti-tank gun saw 'im and shot 'im – made a direct hit on 'im and cut him in two pieces. By god, if he'd stayed with the column, stayed in there, he mighta gotten killed but he would a-had a chance to live. He was just terribly afraid; I could see he didn't have any battle experience at all and it was pretty damn rough.

So we made the push into Luzon - we got up and had to fight ever damn inch of the way. I remember when we got stopped up there, where we was gonna bivouac and start our push, there was a division of men that was workin' across this mountain in front of us and they were gettin' shelled. There was six guys there that, when they got into the thick of this damn artillery, instead of keep goin' they stopped! All in a bunch! They was bunched up in a little depression that a shell had made earlier. I was watchin' through my binoculars. I thought, "This is a terrible damn thing, a stupid thing to do, you know, to bunch up when artillery is comin' in like that!" Goddamn, I saw the shell come right on in – it hit right in the middle of 'em. Hell, it scattered them out over 15, 20 feet there. And there was one guy, he raised up and kinda got on his hands and knees and then he shrunk down; he was dead! It killed every one of 'em! It was a good example of why not to bunch up – it was a real problem for the sergeants, especially with the new men. The ones with combat experience, hell, they knew enough not to bunch up.

We were losin' a lotta men and water was a hell of a problem. They issued us two canteens a day - at night - and then we get wounded guys and, Christ, they'd already drank up their water and we'd end up givin' most of our water away. But at night we'd send a detail down to get water. Each guy would pack two five gallon cans of water. Well, by that time, you know, I'm burnin' up for water. Ever evening I'd volunteer to go down and bring up a couple five gallon cans and then when I got down there, I'd get my canteens full and then I'd take on all the water I could drink. It was so hot and humid. Water was a terrible damn problem! As I was sayin', we was gettin' these wounded guys and they'd walked far as they could and when you get guys all shot to hell and dyin' for water, you give them your water! And then we'd take their ammunition. That was how we re-supplied our ammo. We'd take the bolts outta their rifles and throw 'em away so those damn Japs couldn't get to 'em. We was hung up on this damn hill there for two or three days and finally, to break out of that damn place, they told us the next mornin' we was gonna take this damn mountain with hand grenades and bayonets! So we fixed our bayonets and got 'bout a half dozen hand grenades apiece and we headed up the mountain – and found out that durin' the night all the damn Japs had pulled out!

We got over the hill and formed a skirmish line down in the rice paddies where we could hold the damn mountain. We was gettin' a lotta damn fire there. I put my squad out on the right flank and I put two guys on the far right side and told 'em: "There's a draw right out there and you watch that some damn Japs don't sneak in here with some hand grenades!" I was probably 50 feet from 'em and somethin', I don't know if it was a knee mortar or a hand grenade, dropped right on those guys and knocked 'em both out. Finally, one of 'em came to and hollered for help. I told 'im to hang on and we'd get to 'em as soon as we could. He kept on yellin' so I crawled over to get closer to 'im and quiet 'im down. I got about half way to him when I saw this damn hand grenade comin' up behind the rice paddy. I knew it was gonna hit right on me but if I'd get on my feet and get eight or ten feet away from it and then get back on the ground, the shrapnel would go over me. But the Jap had held the hand grenade and as soon as I got on my feet the damn thing went off! Everthing went black and I went numb and all of a sudden, I could see and hear again and there was this Jap right in front of me, maybe 30 feet away, aimin' at me! He was all covered up with a fish net with grass tied in it. I let off three or four rounds from my rifle and he fell over. Then I started blackin' out again. I didn't know how bad I was hurt or if I was mortally wounded so I fought it as hard as I could, but I passed out again. When I came to, the medics had dragged me around to kind of a protected area and they had my boots off and my pants cut off. They were wrappin' me up and shootin' morphine into me to kill the pain and then they packed me out on a litter. They got me to a makeshift hospital where they operated on me and cut a lot of the shrapnel out. There was a lot in my knee joints and my lower right leg was broken. Then they transferred me to a hospital ship.

The day after I got wounded, we were down then, we had just enough men in the company to make up one platoon. I think we had about 27 men left. Of course, I'd been wounded the day before but this is what the guys told me. They'd sent this Johnson out on a patrol and he come back and reported in. He said, "The damn place is alive with Japs out in there!" It was kind of a low country and a lotta kinda brush and stuff. He told the captain, he says, "By god, we can't go in there! Hell, we'll be killed!" The captain says,

"That's our orders, to advance out through there." So Johnson told 'im, "We're gonna get shot up!" After he knew he had to go, and he was in charge of this squad that was to lead out, he just told the boys, "Come on, let's go get killed!"

And the first thing, they got down there, the opposition was a machine gun. And it opened fire on 'em and wounded several guys, maybe killed one or two. And Johnson stopped and he shot the machine gunner, shot the gunner off it. Another Jap jumped on the gun; he shot him. And accordin' to this guy that told me the story, he killed three Japs off that machine gun and his gun was empty and the guy on it killed him, when his gun was empty. By that time they had just a few over 20 men left in the company and of course, the whole regiment was all shot down. Hell, they only had 20 or 30 men left in the company outta, you know, close to 200. And they relieved us, relieved the guys. And then they filled 'em up again with replacements. And the next campaign, they went into this Batangas Area and made a landing down there. They lost a lotta men there.

The Machine Gunners

This happened in the Philippines. We'd been pinned down up on this hill there for two or three days and we were losin' a lotta men. Back across on the hillside, just right along the top, there was six holes in there, dug in there, looked like they're about four foot in diameter. The First Sergeant had gotten a-hold of me to take a patrol up there and see if we could find out what those holes was, what was goin' on there. Down below us about a quarter mile, there was two grass shacks there and we hadn't never saw anybody around 'em. Or ever got any fire outta them. Hell, I never paid any attention to 'em. I got down in front of a rice paddy and was explainin' to my scouts how we oughta approach those holes; take as much cover as we could a-gettin' up there. While I was explainin' to 'em, outta one a-these grass shacks there was a machine gun opened up on me!

Those Jap machine guns, they loaded 'em in strips, 31 rounds in a strip. They could hook those strips together when they was firin' the gun and they fired off a full 31-round clip at me! And, goddamn, it kicked dirt up all over me and my Number One scout, he was a-lookin' over the top a-this rice paddy and a bullet caught him right along the inside of his eye and took the back of his head off! That sure killed him! And that stopped the goin' out on patrol but all these line companies, they had two machine guns. So I called the two machine guns down and the gunners and I told them, "Now, you guys put a full belt in each one a-those shacks. You take one and the other guy take the other one." And they fired at them and the tracers set 'em on fire and in one of 'em, there was all kinds of ammunition burn up in it! But no one ever come out of it!

And while I had the machine guns there I thought it'd be a good idea – we had what they call a T-32 rifle that shot a 37 millimeter anti-tank cartridge – and I got it up there. It was a pretty big gun, mounted on a tripod and had about an eight-foot barrel on it and a scope sight. I told him, I said, "I want you to take the right-hand hole and lob a high-explosive shell in it!" And about the third one he had the range and everthing right and he put this high-explosive shell in there and there was eight or 10 Japs come a-boilin' outta that hole. These machine gunners had already test-fired and they were right on the right aim so they opened up on 'em and Christ, they killed all of 'em, oh, 15 or 20 feet was as far as any of 'em got! Hell, no one got away! So we went to the next hole. We went through all six of 'em and hell, there was always five to six or eight in every hole. We tried to count' em and the lowest count we had, you know, lookin' up there in our binoculars, was 45 and the highest count we had was 50! So that between 45 and 50 Japs I killed there one afternoon and never pulled a trigger! And that's not a-countin' the machine gunner down in the shack; there was two or three in there. And them shells goin' in the holes might a-killed one or two in there!

Recovery and Rehabilitation

While I was on the hospital ship, a chaplain came by one afternoon. He was wantin' to check on me, check on my mental condition and give me a little spiritual guidance. I told him, "I don't need any spiritual guidance; what I need is a good leg and a catheter to drain my bladder, 'cause I'm in misery since I can't pass my water!" So he went off and pretty soon here come a corpsman and he drained out nearly a liter. I felt considerable better then.

I was on that boat for about a week gettin' this antibiotic and they give all of us a bottle of beer. That was the drunkest I ever was in my life! The old bed was a-turnin' and a-turnin' and when it'd start to turn over, I'd grab the side and then it'd start back the other way. Hell, there wasn't anything happenin', I was just drunk!

They put me on another hospital ship and took us down to Hollandia. There was a lieutenant on the ship I met when we was trainin' for the invasion of Japan. Then, he was just out of West Point. He was a First Lieutenant and he'd been through Fort Benning, Georgia and had all the latest training. He got me to explain how to take a pillbox. I'm up in front of the whole company and I says, "The first thing, you're gonna find out where that pillbox is when you've probably got some machine gun fire and maybe killed or wounded a man or two. 'Cause I never saw a damn Jap ever shoot a machine gun where he didn't kill or wound somebody. The way you take 'em, you get it spotted, you get the coordinates on it and you call artillery. You get the 105s and get about a five-round burst on the bastard and that takes care of your pillbox!" "Aw," he says, "Sergeant, that's not the way you do it! You deploy your men and you work up and someone throws a hand grenade in it!", "Well," I said, "that don't work here. They got snipers all 'round these goddamn pillboxes! Hell, you'll get men killed tryin' to do it that way! Artillery's the best way. If you can't get artillery, put your mortar fire on it. That works pretty good." He says, "Well, that's not the way you do it." I said, "That's the way we do it. That's the way we've found that works." He said, "What would you do if I gave you a direct order to take one with a hand grenade?" I said, "I'm not a-gonna do it! I'll tell you right now, I don't get good men killed doin' foolish, stupid damn things! Goddamn it, if you think you can do that, you go throw it in there yourself! I don't take goddamn fool orders. I've smelled dead lieutenants and I've smelled dead privates and they both smell the same to me!" By that time, he's pretty pissed! So he turns to another sergeant and told 'im to explain to the company how to take a pillbox. He said, "I don't need to. Sergeant Barney's already explained how to take a pillbox!" And that stopped everything!

We broke for lunch and when we come back the other sergeant and myself got called up in front of the captain with the lieutenant. This captain asked what happened and when the lieutenant explained it, the captain said, "Lieutenant, I hate to tell you this, but those sergeants is right! They know somethin' about how to take a pillbox. That's the way we do it!" But he told us he didn't want another discussion like this comin' up in front of all the company. And dismissed us!

So while I'm on this hospital ship, the same lieutenant come by and sat on the foot of my bed and said, "You know, I owe you an apology. That little discussion we had? I only lasted ten days but I found out that a lot of things they teach at Fort Benning don't work!" He had been shot in the leg. He did apologize and asked if there was anything I needed, anything from the PX, did I have money, was I doin' OK? I don't know if he was doin' that because I was a wounded sergeant or if he thought I was a lieutenant. I had gotten a battlefield commission, or thought I had until I got paid and found out it had been rescinded. The Regimental Colonel had turned it down because he didn't think I'd ever be back.

Anyway, I ended up in a hospital in Hollandia and it was over a month before they could get me out of bed with crutches. I was there for about four months before they discharged me from the hospital and put me in a casual group to get back to our outfits. They was sendin' us out on details and I'm a sergeant, so they put me in charge of 'em. One day we had one of these "stateside" corporals with us when we was loadin' cross arms for telephone poles. A little private was up on top handin' 'em down to the guys and this corporal got on him somethin' terrible! I told the private, "Just drop one of those goddamn cross arms on his damn head! We don't have to put up with this bullshit!"

I finally got back to the outfit and somewhere along the way I got issued a new rifle. An M1 rifle made by Winchester and the workmanship was just like one of their regular guns. It had a nice finish and a good piece of wood for the stock and it had never been fired. I always regretted that I didn't bring it home with me. (Sherry struggled with US Government bureaucracy for three years and finally got me a surplus rifle.)

I was on guard duty one night with Bennie Berman, the little guy I told you about that was always gettin' bullet holes in his clothes. This was before I got wounded. He told me, "Sergeant, you know, a man could get killed around here! You know, I can put up with dyin' and gettin' killed 'cause it's liable enough to happen, but I'd like to kill just one a-them goddamn, squint-eyed sons-a-bitches before they kill me!" After I got back from the hospital – he was one of these misfits that I had – they'd transferred him down into another company. But when he found out I was back he come back; he had to see his sergeant. Goddamnit, he's packin' a real nice, clean, practically new M1 rifle! And the old one he had, it was a beat-up bastard, 'cause I think he'd drug it through that jungle more'n he'd packed it! A nice rifle! "Bernie," I said, "Where in the hell did you get that nice-lookin' rifle?" "Oh," he says, "one a-these recruits had it. I tried to trade 'im but he wouldn't trade with me. I told 'im he'd get killed and I'll get it anyway! We got out and we got into artillery barrage and goddamn, he got killed! But I stopped long enough to pick up his good rifle!"

**Figure 12. Ollie with His Replacement M-1 Rifle
(About 1985)**

Then he says, "They can kill me now. I'm ahead of 'em. I killed three of 'em!" In this Batangas deal, it was right at the closest beach there, they had their perimeter set up, you know, facin' away from the beach. He said, "I'm out there a-guardn'; I'm watchin' and it's startin' to get towards daylight and I thought I could see somethin' out there in front of me. I kept watchin' it and it got light enough to see and it's a goddamn machine gun out there with Jap sittin' behind it! I waited 'til that light got a little better and I just shot 'im. I shot three of 'em off it! I started a damn war!" He says, "These Japs come around and landed the boats behind 'em and by god, it delayed our breakfast! When the war was over with and this mess sergeant was tryin' to get us somethin' cooked up, the bread's all got bullet holes in it and most a-the canned goods is shot up! I started a goddamn war!"

One funny thing happened not long after I got back to the outfit. Not long after the First Sergeant gave me the Third Platoon a runner come from Battalion Headquarters sayin' the Colonel wanted to see me. I pretty much knew what he wanted, so I told this recruit runner, "Hell, just go tell that goddamned Colonel that if he wants to see me, he can come and see me!" Well, he come! Here come Mr. Colonel! When he got up to about 30 foot a-me, I come to attention. And I give him as good a salute as he ever got in his damn life! I said, "Colonel, I kinda got outta line, didn't I?" "Well," he said, "it depends. What's your problem?" I said, "I know what you want. I took this thing one time and ol' Bulldog, when I got wounded, he cancelled it! And now, if I take it, we got to go to the invasion of Japan. And, Christ! We're on the point system here now and we all got a-way more points than it takes to go home. We're just patrollin' around here thinkin', hell, I got a good chance to get home alive! And that's what I wanna do!" He said, "Sergeant, I don't blame you one iota. I'll tell you one thing. Until you do go home, you'll be to all officer's meetings and you take that platoon over as an acting lieutenant. And there'll be no promotions!" I told him, "Colonel, you couldn't be any more fairer than that!"

So I went to all my officer's meetings, with my little notes; I'd take down my notes and come back and sit down with my patrols. These recruits, they was all around there – there was a few old guys there, two or three, who knew I was just a sergeant – but the recruits was all callin' me lieutenant.

Higgins Boats

The last thing I did in the war was to take my platoon and the two Navy Higgins Boats with crews they'd assigned to me and go around the southern tip of Luzon Island in the Philippines. Our orders were to check all the villages for Japs or Jap activity or what the Japs had been in. The Navy crew kept the boats about a quarter mile off the coast and when we'd see one of these native villages or see a little smoke comin' up, we'd try to turn in and land up a quarter of a mile or so from these villages. The boats would run up on the beach, drop the ramps and then we'd come around in back of the villages. If we missed and had to come in too close, we'd go on down past a half a mile and come on in. All I had was mostly recruits - some had a little combat experience – and after the second day they wanted to know why we had to go down and fight this jungle and come in the back way. Why couldn't we just go up and drop the ramps in front of the village and just walk ashore? I told 'em, "The main damn reason is that I want to go home alive!! If we ever dropped those ramps in front of one of these villages and there's a Jap in there with a machine gun, there won't be any of us ever get off. We'll all be dead!" I told them *I* wasn't taking any chances!

We'd go in and talk to these Philippinos and they was tellin' us about these Japs had come in and interrogate them wantin' to find out everthing. If they was a little hesitant about talkin', Japs would grab up a little child and throw it as high in the air as they could. A Jap would set his rifle down under it and catch the little baby on his bayonet. So the villagers talked, but told 'em as little as they thought could get by with.

One of these nights, we stayed all night in the village – it was getting late when we come in. They brought us some eggs – boy, I'll tell you, we hadn't been used to gettin' fresh eggs! God, we cracked those eggs and there's these "blutes", I think they called 'em! Those Philippinos like to let them sit under a hen 'til a little chicken starts to form and I'll tell ya, we weren't hungry enough for fresh eggs to eat blutes, so we had to turn 'em down on that!

Anyway, we made it right down to the southern tip of Luzon. It was about a ten mile hike across there – we was supposed to walk across the southern tip on this trail that went all the way across it. It wasn't a road or anything, not even an ox-cart path. These Philippinos along there had these dried fish, little minnow-lookin' outfits, dried out. We eat some of 'em and they weren't all that bad, but I didn't relish them. When we got across on the other side, they were there with the trucks to meet us since there was a road that went back. And our orders there was to come home, and by god, they took us back. All I had a chance to do was go in the camp and grab one of my barracks bags and get down to the docks where we were going to disembark. (That's a Navy term and I probably got it wrong, but we was sure about leavin'!) Anyhow, I picked up the wrong barracks bag! I had Army Bausch and Lomb binoculars that was practically new; I had just been issued 'em and then I had some of my souvenirs in there – one of my souvenirs was some Japanese chop sticks made out of ivory and they was in a little carved wooden box with a lid on it that slid out. And I had a few gold teeth in there. Anyway, I lost all that. But, I got out of the Philippines and out of the Army with the one damn thing I was interested in saving – my live ass!!

Going Home

They put us on a troop ship and we started home. We'd been a Regimental Combat Team of 3,500 men and now there were 69 of us goin' home. There were probably another 15 or 20 off on furloughs, but there weren't 100 of us left.

The first damn night I got stuck with a detail of takin' about five men and myself and go down and do the laundry on this troop ship, and it was all just Navy stuff. At the time we was gettin' two meals a day, a breakfast and an evening meal. Our detail started about 4:00 o'clock and we worked 'til midnight or so. We got off at midnight and we'd go in the kitchen and fry us a steak. We had a lot to eat! And then we could run our clothes in the laundry and get 'em washed. Them ol' troop ships down around the equator, it's hot and it'd be sweaty and Christ, we'd take a shower and I told these guys, "This looks to me like a real good detail! If it's agreeable with you guys, I'm gonna volunteer for the whole trip." Well, they was all for it! And, damn, we eat good and we run around in clean uniforms all the time.

One night, at the bottom of one of the washing machines – they're big, huge things – there's a little silver coin in there. I got it out and checked it and it was an Indian coin made in 1690 somethin' – the last letter was wore out where I couldn't read it. This ship had been to India just before it came to get us so some Navy guy had gotten this coin and lost it in the laundry. I kept it – still have it. It oughtta have a little value to it, bein' so old, but I never have priced it out.

I was in the chow line one morning and there were these "sea-going bellhops" (Marines). One of 'em threw out his arm in front of me and pushed me back and gave me a damn lecture about crowdin'. There was a fire axe on the wall near me, so I grabbed it and told him, "You son-of-a bitch, treat me with a little respect or I'll chop you down to my damn size!" And he apologized!

We went down, we went through the Panama Canal; we'd spent a year there when we first went to Panama. We went through the Canal and landed at Newport News, Virginia. This is clear over on the Atlantic Coast! We got reassigned then on a troop train to come home. We had a few days there before they put us on a train to Fort MacArthur in California. We had a little guy from Bisbee, Arizona – Sidney P. Quales was his name. One of the quartermasters started givin' Sid a bad time and a sergeant told the man, "Goddamn it, you leave him alone or I'll shoot your damn legs out from under you!" He let his tommy gun go off and shot a heel off the quartermaster's boot. The guy got right back in his car and left Sidney P. alone!

While we're there on the train, we're visitin' around with some of these European Theater of Operations (ETO) boys that was gettin' out. One of our guys was a Staff Sergeant from Alabama. One ETO boy, I heard 'im ask 'im, "Did you ever kill any Japs?" He said, "Well, I done pretty good if I count my three blacks."

That story there happened in Batangas, in the Philippines, after we took it. There was a lot of colored quartermasters there and they give us all furloughs to go to town. Some of the quartermasters started givin' us a hard time – tellin' us to get out of town, that this was their town. That didn't sit well with the guys. So they all come back to camp and got their guns and came back to town. I'll tell ya, there was a few little shootin' scrapes started around there and accordin' to the report, there was eleven of 'em killed and 22 or 23 wounded. The ol' general there, I don't know what they called 'im, but anyway, he was in charge there. He went to our Regimental Colonel and told him our men had created a problem in town and to keep his men out of town. The Colonel told 'im, "Goddamn it! My men are fightin' men and they need their time in town and their recreation. If they was half as rough on them niggers as you say they were it's gonna be a lot easier for you to keep your niggers outta town than my men! My men are goin' to town!"

This sergeant from Alabama, he come in early, he was one of the guys in town, and told us, "I just killed three niggers and I thought I oughta get outta town." We asked, "What happened?" "Well," he said "I'd gone to this bar. There were these three blacks who crowded up to me and told me to get the hell outta town. I told 'em I was a fighting man and I want to drink a beer or two. Then I moved down to the other end of the bar. They come down and started hassellin' me again so I just got up and shot all three of 'em off their goddamn barstools with my tommy gun." He went to bed so we got his tommy gun and looked at it and Christ, it was half a clip short and it's been fired! So we cleaned the gun up real good and loaded up the clip. The next morning, we asked him about it again, and he claimed, while he *had* been in the bar when it happened, he didn't do it! This is the same sergeant who kept Sidney P. Quales from bein' hasseled.

We were 7 or 8 days goin' across the United States. It seemed like we had to stop for every other damn train and let them go through. We come through Tucson and some of the guys jumped off the train to get a bottle of whiskey and Sidney P. Quales was one of 'em. He got his bottle of whiskey but the train started pullin' out before he got back on. He was runnin', tryin' to get up to our car. Several guys had their hands out to get the bottle and he handed it to one but he couldn't get back on. He missed the damn train! We got out to about Red Rock and the train stopped and pretty soon here come a handcar up with Sidney P. They put him back on so he went through the train lookin' for his jug – never did get it back!

We went to Fort MacArthur; we went from one ocean to the other. We were all issued new uniforms right out of the bales - they were all wrinkled from being packed so tight. Sergeant Gordio from Benson, Arizona went on furlough, course we all went on furlough then. He went into a bar and there were three "stateside commandos" there who started calling him a recruit 'cause he was dressed like one. He explained to 'em, "Hell, we're just back from the South Pacific and we're fightin' men and I don't wanna listen to your BS!" Then he got up and moved clear down to the other end of the bar.

And here they come, so he ordered another beer and now he's got two bottles of beer. They started hassellin' 'im again and he said, "I told you guys I'm gonna put up with just so much of your damn BS. Leave me alone! I'm a fightin' man!" They started on and he just took those two bottles in his hands and broke 'em and he laid into 'em with these broken beer bottles! With the necks of 'em! And Christ, he cut them up and got 'em in pretty damn bad shape but he got 'em off of him. And here come the MPs. They ordered an ambulance and put these three guys in and sent 'em to the hospital. The MPs told Gordio, "We oughtta throw your ass in jail for what you done, but we're not a-gonna do it – we're gonna take you home but we don't wanna see you around town anymore tonight!" And they did.

While we were at Fort MacArthur gettin' discharged there was this ol' gray-headed Border Patrolman – how he got my Army history, I'll never know. But he said to an officer, "There's a Sergeant Barney being discharged and I wanna interview 'im." So I went to 'im and this ol' Border Patrol introduced himself and asked if I'd be interested in goin' to work for the Border Patrol. I said, "Well, I'm gettin' outta the Army and I'm gonna hafta get a job somewhere." "Well", he says, "you're the person we're lookin' for. We wanna hire you and I'll tell you what we want done: over in Texas we've got two smugglers over there bringin' in dope." Apparently they'd killed a Border Patrolman and maybe a customs man. He says, "We could arrest 'em but we don't want to – we want 'em killed! And we know you're the guy to do it because I know your military history. Plus you was raised on a ranch and you know how to ride horses and you definitely know how to take care of yourself in a gun fight!"

He went on: "I'll tell you again, we don't want 'em arrested; we want 'em killed! That's what I'm hirin' you for: killin'. You'll not go through the Border Patrol trainin' and you've got a fair knowledge of Spanish. We'll put you with an older Patrolman and he'll get you to these guys. We're gonna hafta lie a little bit because after you've found them and the first little thing goes wrong, well then, you just revert back to your Army experience and we'll have two dead Mexicans." Then he said, "You won't get in trouble for it; we'll cover for you, but you may get fired. But I definitely want to know that you'll kill these Mexicans." I said, "Well, I'll kill 'em for you."

So we wrote out all my damn papers for me and said, "You're hired!" Then he said that since I had been gone for close to four years, he wanted me to go home for 20, 30 days and then send the papers in and I'd be officially hired. So I went home for 20 days and sent my papers in to get hired by the Border Patrol. In the meantime the war was over and they informed me that they'd stopped all hirin'! The Border Patrol still had their Mexicans and how they took care of 'em, I've no idea how it ever happened. I never did get involved in it. Now, I'm glad I didn't, but at the time, hell, I wouldn't thought no more about killin' a couple a-Mexicans that needed killin' than I would shootin' a jack rabbit!

Anyway, the next day we all got discharged and I headed home. I don't think any of us has ever been back there. I went to the ranch and spent a year with my dad.

Figure 13. Ollie's Army Medals

Top Left: **Silver Star** The Silver Star is awarded to a person who, while serving in any capacity with the U.S. Army, is cited for gallantry in action against an emeny of the United States while engaged in military operations involving conflict with an opposing armed force. The required gallantry must have been performed with marked distinction.

Top Center: **Purple Heart** One of four earned during his Army service. The Purple Heart is awarded to a member of the U.S. Armed Forces who has been wounded or killed in action against an enemy of the United States.

Top Right: **Bronze Star** The Bronze Star was awarded to a member of the U.S. Armed Forces who has distinguished himself by heroic or meritorious achievement or service while engaged in an action against an enemy of the United States.

Second Row Left: **Good Conduct Medal** The Good Conduct Medal is awarded for exemplary behavior, efficiency, and fidelity in active Federal military service.

Second Row Right: **American Defense Medal** The American Defense Service Medal was awarded for service in the Armed Forces between September 8, 1939 and December 7, 1941. Army members had to serve 12 months to be eligible.

Third Row Left: **World War II Victory Medal** The World War II Victory Medal was awarded to all members of the U.S. Armed Forces who served on active duty in World War II at any time between December 7, 1939 and December 31, 1946.

Center Photograph: Ollie at the conclusion of Advanced Infantry Training, carrying a Browning Automatic Rifle (BAR). Note that the standard WWII helmets had not yet been issued.

Third Row Right: **American Campaign Medal** The American Campaign Medal was awarded for 30 days continuous service outside the Continental United States if that service included active combat against the enemy and that also resulted in a combat decoration for that service.

Bottom Row Left: **Asiatic Pacific Campaign Medal (with three Bronze Stars)** The Asiatic Pacific Campaign Medal was awarded to a soldier in active combat in the Asiatic-Pacific Theater of Operations against the enemy and who was awarded a combat decoration. Bronze service stars were awarded for participation in designated campaigns.

<u>Bottom Row Center:</u> **The Combat Infantryman Badge** (top), **The Presidential Unit Citation** (bottom left), **The Honorable Discharge ("Ruptured Duck") Lapel Pin** (bottom center), and **The Philippine Liberation Ribbon** (bottom right).

There are three requirements to earn a **Combat Infantryman Badge**: the soldier must be an infantryman satisfactorily performing infantry duties, must be assigned to an infantry unit at such time as the unit is engaged in active ground combat, and must actively participate in such ground combat. Campaign or battle credit alone is not sufficient for award of the CIB.

The **Presidential Unit Citation** is awarded to units of the Armed Forces for extraordinary heroism in action against an armed enemy occurring on or after December 7, 1941. The degree of heroism required is the same as that which would warrant the award of a Distinguished Service Cross to an individual.

The **Honorable Discharge Lapel Pin** is awarded to personnel honorably discharged since September 9, 1939. The reason for the "Ruptured Duck" nickname and the originator of the phrase are unknown, although many have claimed to have originated the phrase.

The **Philippine Liberation Medal** was awarded for service in the liberation of the Philippines from October 17, 1944 to September 2, 1945. In order to qualify, a service member had to participate in the initial landing operation of Leyte and adjoining islands or participate in any engagement against the enemy during the Philippine Liberation Campaign.

<u>Bottom Row Right:</u> **The Army of Occupation Medal (Japan)** The Army of Occupation Medal was awarded for 30 or more consecutive days of duty in one of the occupied territories after World War II.

Chapter Six   Family and Other Interesting People

Homer Barney

My brother Homer was killed in World War II bombin' Berlin. He went through basic training here in the States; he trained with a B-24 crew. After they was out of trainin', they pulled him out; they wanted to keep 'im here in the States as an instructor durin' the war. He was a bright young man and he could talk good. When he was in high school, he taught a class in leatherwork. They wanted 'im for an instructor but he told 'em he didn't want to be an instructor. Then they offered to train 'im to be a fighter pilot. He said he was already trained as a gunner on the B-24 and that's what he wanted to do; he wanted to get in the war.

So they shipped him over to Germany in the Eighth Air Force. They put him in a new crew there and he was a waist gunner and a crew chief. At that time, they were losin' 20% or more of the bombers when they went out – that's not right, it has to be 5% because if they made 20 missions, they sent 'em home. He got killed on his 17th mission. They shot one of the motors out of the plane and that motor fell down through the formation and knocked out another plane. Half the crew got off Homer's B-24, parachuted off the plane and they was saved, but the other five was killed on the plane. Apparently this plane crashed and never burned because they sent our mother his watch and billfold and they weren't burned. The watch was wrapped up in a piece of parachute cord and the face of the watch was just ground off. So he rode the plane down. They buried 'im over there in a German churchyard. After the war was over with, they sent the body back and he's buried there in Benson with my mother. The VFW Post there in Benson is named after my brother and a Mexican boy; the first two men killed out of Benson in World War II. They call it the Barney-Figueroa Post.

A funny thing about his bein' killed: I was in New Guinea at the time, on burial detail. One night I woke up and this Homer – he was my favorite brother, we were real close – he was tryin' to tell me somethin', tryin' to get to me. And it was so damn real that I lit my flashlight and wrote down the time and the date in my notebook. Afterwards when I found out approximately the time he was killed and allowin' the date changed and the hours and everythin', hell, it was within minutes; it was the same time. I've never been able to figure that one out. And I haven't told a lot of people about it because it seems screwy, but there was somethin' that happened there that I don't understand.

Alvin Barney

My brother Alvin worked for me when I was a construction superintendent. I had a retired railroad engineer by the name of Bruce workin' for me at the same time. He wanted a farm in Arkansas. He did a little correspondin' down there and he'd got ahold of a real estate man and he took a couple of weeks off. He went and bought a farm down there just outta Beebe. He come back and told about another little farm there with close to 1,000 fruit trees on it. Young trees, all barren. The guy wanted $5,600 for this orchard, 186 acres. He talked to Brother Alvin about it and hell, he didn't want any farm in Arkansas. Ol' Bruce asked me, "Would you be interested?" I said, "Well, the price is definitely right! Are you goin' down and live with your wife?" He said, "Yes, there's a nice house on my property. And this other little farm has two houses. They're not much, but they're livable." I asked him, "If I buy it, could you use that property? Work it in with yours?" He said that he could. Then I said, "I'll buy it if you can use it and all I ask of you is just pay the taxes on it. There'll be a day come along when I can sell and make some damn real money on that place 'cause you're gettin' it for practically nothing."

On the strength of that, my brother went down there and talked to the guy and jewed him down a couple a-hundred dollars and bought it! And he stayed there. He'd joined the

Mormon Church and he's real hot on the Mormon religion. God, he went around tryin' to convert them Arkies into joinin' the Mormon Church and he just let his farm go to Hell. He couldn't make any money off the fruit; then he got cattle and he didn't make any money on the cattle. He just lived there for 42 years – went to seed, his health went bad and Christ, I finally went down there with Dick to see if we could get him to sell the place and move to Arizona. Buy 'im a little place or build 'im somethin', but he wouldn't have nothin' to do with that. He had a good investment there and he's gonna stay there and take care of it. So I propositioned him, I said, "Alvin, if right here where you live you just deed me five acres of land I'll build you a duplex on it. You can move in on one side of it and have a decent place to live and get some ol' Mormon family that needs a little help to live on the other side, an old couple, and they can kinda take care of you. You'll have a place to live." He wouldn't do that. There just wasn't any way to help 'im so we finally left.

About a year later his mind just completely deserted 'im and we had to take 'im down and put 'im in a home. That was one of the hardest things I ever done – take 'im and leave 'im down in that damn home! I went down there once after that and visited with 'im and Christ, poor guy didn't know where he was or what was goin' on. I had a problem gettin' away from 'im; he wanted to come with me. I couldn't take 'im so this Arkansas lady I got down there wants me to move down there and live with her! I said, "No, I'm afraid of Arkansas. I know what it done to my brother! I'm not a-gonna do that!" You get out in the woods and Christ, you get covered up with ticks and chiggers! The deer down there have little horns and there's just nothing down there for me! Her roots are in Arkansas and that's where she's gonna stay. Mine's in Arizona and that's where I'm gonna stay.

Beryl Barney

I never married until I was 35 years old and I married a real nice lady. We were married for 42 ½ years and I have to admit they were the happiest years of my life. Another thing I'd like to admit, you know, I don't think there's anything better than a good woman or a good lion dog.

Actually, I was engaged a couple of times before I got married. And my wife, I never had really proposed to her! We'd been goin' together for a year and a half or so and we got along real well. We'd been off down to Benson to the rodeo and come back – she was staying with her folks at the time. I dropped her off at the door and kissed her goodbye and I said, "Beryl, you know this cold weather's comin' on and I think maybe we ought to just throw our two blankets together!" I went on home and, Christ, the first thing I knew I was engaged! She took that as a proposal! And, hell, in less than three months I was married!

But one of these engagements I had was with an ol' gal I'd been seein' in Tucson for several years. It got to the point where we were goin' up to Globe to get married at her grandmother's. So we left this one afternoon and we were up about half way to Globe and we got in a discussion of some kind. By that time it's dark. It was kind of a little argument and things didn't look good to me. So I turned around right in the middle of the road and started back towards Tucson. She said, "Well, where're we goin'?" I said, "We're goin' back to Tucson." She said, "I thought we were goin' up to Globe to get married!" I said, "I did, too! We're not there yet and we've already got into this big discussion or argument and if we can't get along single there's no damn way we're gonna get along married! This wedding's off as far as I'm concerned!" Later on, she married an ol' boy over in Wilcox, I found out later, and they had seven kids. She died about the same time Beryl did; both of 'em died of cancer.

I remember one time at a party my wife got kinda upset with me because all the women were over on one side of the room visitin' and us men were on the other side and we got to discussin' things, you know, things we'd like to do before we die. Or should've done. Or some of the things we had done. I just causally mentioned one thing that I'd like to experience before I die. There's this blackberry wine, not wine but some kinda drink, and I like it! I said, "Before I die, I'd like to get a fifth of it, put a nipple on it and go to bed with a flat-chested woman!" Well, I just barely got this outta my mouth and my wife, Beryl, she jumped up and took exception to this! "Maybe I'm too big for you!" she said. I just ignored her, but I didn't say anything more about goin' to bed with this blackberry brandy.

Out of a clear blue sky one day, Beryl asked me if I washed the bottom of my feet! And I told her, "No, hell, I never thought anything about washing the bottom of my feet. When I get out of the shower, hell, I dry, but really, I've never washed the bottom of my feet."

Figure 14. Beryl and Ollie Barney at the Safari Club International Convention (About 1980)

Another time – this happened after we'd been married a year or so – you know, this woman, she believed everythin' I told her. She didn't think I was capable of lyin' or misrepresentin' the truth at that time. I was helpin' my neighbor, MacKenzie, round-up. It was durin' deer season

120

and I had a license and back then, you didn't have to have a tag or anything. This one morning this Mac says to me, "Ollie, strap that .30-.30 on your saddle and if you see one of these nice, fat mule deer bucks, shoot it! It's a little early to butcher and hell, deer meat will come in real handy." Hell, we hadn't got a mile from the ranch and up above us there's two nice mule deer bucks, they were probably four years old or so and I killed one of 'em. And I'm a-walkin' up this steep, rocky hillside, packin' my rifle, this .30-.30, in my right hand and I fell! With this gun in my hand, my middle finger got caught between the rifle and a rock and just mangled the fingernail and battered up the finger pretty bad. I had it all wrapped up and when I come home on the weekend I was havin' to wrap this finger up; I was changin' the bandage and Beryl asked me what happened. "Well," I said, "you know I'm a-stayin' down there in that guest house below the main house and there's no lights in it. We're gettin' up early in the morning. So I got up this one morning and got one sock on and got my boot on. I couldn't find the other sock so I'm up there walkin' around bent over feelin' for this sock and I stepped on that finger and mangled it all up." And Beryl, she believed every word of it! She went to the office and she was tellin' 'em how I stepped on my finger and mashed it all up and they liked to a-laughed her out of the office!

We were married 42 ½ years and there's about 40 years where I don't think she ever believed another word I told her!

At my age, hell, I'm 85 years old and I've been single for nearly nine years – it will be nine years the 12th of June (1994) – and I realize that I'm at a kinda awkward age to remarry. These women that're somewhere near my age are either happily married, or they're senile, or they're on walkers or they got other mental or physical problems. And the younger ones…I can't afford! This one ol' gal that I've hunted with – she's a great person – I've had her out lion huntin' a couple of times and I was kiddin' her. I said, "Rena, if you ever feel like you're up to buryin' another husband, I'll volunteer!" And she kinda laughed and said, "No, I'm not up to it right now. Not to bury another husband!"

Sherry's Story

When I started courtin' her mother, some 50 years ago, Sherry was just a little girl. Her granddad was pretty well taken with me and they kept workin' on Beryl about whenever she was gonna marry me. Her dad told her I was a nice young man and as good a man as she'd ever meet. And then Sherry, she was so taken with the ranch and the little calves and occasionally a colt and she was after her mother, askin', "Honey, when are we gonna marry Ollie?" (All the kids called their mother "Honey".) Well, Honey didn't have that answer! Eventually, we married and from then on, until Sherry went to college, I had two shadows. Everwhere I was at, Sherry was there if she could possibly arrange it. She got to be where she was quite a lot of help on the ranch. We'd get out to the ranch and her and my two dogs, they'd wrangle the horses and eventually the damn dogs got to where they didn't need Sherry's help. As soon as I unloaded them, they'd head out to the horse pasture and pretty soon, here'd come the dogs and the horses. I actually worked Sherry; I didn't just have her around to look at. I had chores for her. I realize now that with the laws we have, if we'd had the same laws then, they would a-probably got me up for child abuse for overworkin' this little girl.

But she loved it and eventually I'd give her a calf every spring, a heifer calf. I had my dad's old brand and she was usin' that brand on her little herd. And she had ever one of 'em named; she always named 'em with a name a-startin' with a "J". And then she got a scholarship to the college in Flagstaff, so I kinda lost some of my good help then durin' the wintertime.

When she got this scholarship to Flagstaff we were out at the ranch ridin' and I stopped my horse up on a ridge where we could see any cattle around and I said, "Sherry, there's something I want to talk to you about. Are you listenin'?" She said, "Ollie, I listen to you! What do you want to talk to me about?" So I said, " Well, you know, you're goin' off up there to this college and you're gonna be dealin' with college boys. You're not gonna have your mother checkin' up on you; you're pretty much on your own. I can tell you right off that these college boys is gonna be a little harder to fight off than those high school boys. My advice to you is that keepin' your fingers crossed is not good enough – you're gonna have to keep your legs crossed!" Bein' raised up on a ranch and knowin' where calves come from and all this, she was pretty well up on this. A few days later, her mother approached her on the same subject. Sherry says, "Honey, Ollie and I have already discussed this." That ended that conversation! But that night, Beryl asked me what I'd told Sherry. I says, "I told her that she'd be up there on her own, wouldn't have you lookin' after her and these college boys was gonna be a lot harder to fight off than the high school boys and by god, keepin' her fingers crossed wasn't good enough – she's gonna have to keep her legs crossed, too!" And Beryl says to me, "That's a terrible way to be a-talkin' to a young lady!" "Well, damnit," I said, "it's the solution to the problem!"

But earlier, she got into huntin' – god, she really liked that huntin'. I bought her a rifle but she had killed her first deer with my rifle and she always liked it, so before long I had to trade rifles with her. And she's still got this here Winchester Model 88 lever action, .308 caliber. I can't wean her away from it! She's hunted all the way around the world with the thing – she's had it to Africa and Australia – and accordin' to her count, the gun's killed over 100 head of big game. I had a good Mouser rifle and I decided I'd re-barrel it as a .308 Remington and give it to her. I got that job done but she still liked her .308; I can't wean her off of it!

She's hunted Africa twice with me but she's never killed a buffalo. She's killed three water buffalo and an American bison, but she still wants to shoot this cape buffalo in Africa. She's got a boyfriend now who thinks it's too dangerous to go back and hunt in Africa. And here awhile back, my good friend, John Bessett, he talked to him and he says, "John, I wish you'd try to talk Ollie out of the notion of going back to Africa." John says, "Why?" Well, he says, "It's too dangerous!" John told him, "I'm not gonna try to talk him out of goin' to Africa. If he goes, I'm goin' with him!" Right now, I don't know what I'm going to do, but I'm seriously thinkin' of threatenin' him a little bit! But I don't think I oughta do that because I might get in bad with Sherry and I definitely don't want to do that. He's not a bad guy. I get along with him fine, but if he's gonna start interferin' with Sherry goin' hunting with me, we're liable to have a clash of personalities.

Another story I want to tell on Sherry: when she was up around 16, she might a-been 15 goin' on 16, I heard her mother talkin' to her about smokin'. I just didn't enter in on it and when it come round-up time and we was all through roundin' up and I had my replacement heifers cut out; I think there was 11 of 'em out there. I told Sherry, "Why don't you get on your horse and we'll go out and look around, see what you think of these here replacement heifers." And there was one in there that we'd missed sellin' the year before and instead of comin' yearlin', she was comin' two-year old and she was with calf. We went out, Sherry and I, and rode around through these heifers. I asked her what she thought of 'em and she said they were fine heifers; they'd make good cows. Then she jogged my memory; she says, "You wanted to talk to me; you said you wanted to make a deal with me. What kind of a deal do you want to make?" So I says, "You know, I've heard your mother talkin' about this smokin'. I don't want to advise you one way or the other and I don't want to get crosswise with your mother, either, lecturin' you on smokin'. But the deal I'll make you is: if you'll tell me that you won't smoke cigarettes until you're 21 years old, you can just ride out and look these 11 heifers over and if you promise not to smoke, we'll just re-brand one heifer for you." She said, "I've already looked at 'em – I'll take that springin' heifer. She'll have a calf in the spring!"

I always impressed on the kids, Beryl had four when I married her, that they oughta have a savings account. So I opened up a savings account with $5.00. Sherry, she added to hers and she never has been broke! There's been times when she had quite a little of money in that savings account.

You know, now my hearing has gotten bad and my brain has deteriorated quite a lot, so I refer to Sherry among strangers as "my ears and my brain". It's worked out pretty good because she does have good hearin' and she's got a good brain.

Interesting People in My Life

I'll start off with my dad. He was sure enough a real good dad and he give us boys good advice. Some of it – I never realized how good advice it was until I was grown. One of the things he droned to us quite often was, "To have good friends, you've gotta be a good friend. To have good neighbors, you have to be a good neighbor." And he believed that; that's the way he led his life. He also said that there'll be times when you'll meet people that you absolutely couldn't get along with. So just stay away from 'em, have no association whatever with 'em, 'cause it's agin the law to kill 'em!

Another thing he told us boys several times is, "You know, durin' life, there'll be times, there'll come a time when your back's agin the wall and you have to 'fess up to somethin'. You can try to lie out of it, but that'll just get you in more trouble. Just tell the truth and take chances with that! You got better arguments when you're tellin' the truth than when you're lyin'."

I worked with several good cowboys before I went into the service and they really were good hands. There's one of 'em by the name of Klute. At that time he was as good a cowboy as I ever saw. He could ride a jackass, I believe, and still make a hand! Goddamn, he's just one of those guys that, anything happened, he'd always be in the right place. If he had to rope somethin', he'd rope it right now! No foolin' around!

I remember this one guy in my outfit; the I Company of the Arizona National Guard unit that was activated for duty in September 1940. It became the 158th Regimental Combat Team; named the Bushmasters. He just died here a year and a half or two years ago. His name was Chuck Lawson. He was a real good, great guy. After we got out of the Army,

125

we kept in contact. When we was in the Army, we'd talk about marryin'. I said I wanted to marry a big woman. "No," he says, "I wanna marry a little woman." Well, he married before I did and, hell, he married a big woman – weighed 170, 180 pounds! She was pretty well built, but she was big! And when I got married – Beryl at that time weighed 110 pounds! We were wrong on those assumptions!

There was another boy there from Wilcox: Bloodworth, Forest Bloodworth. He was a hell of a good guy and he was in my squad. He finally got out of the Army and he went to work for the state highway, runnin' a road grader and other equipment. He's gone now. The First Sergeant we had when we went in was a big Cherokee Indian. He'd weigh about 250 pounds. He was a *big* Indian. And he was a good First Sergeant. I know one night there in Panama, we'd had a beer party and we had this Navajo Indian there. He was, I guess, he was on a fightin' drunk. Someone tried to reason with him, and he'd done a little boxing, and he whacked the guy on the jaw and just knocked 'im cold! Then this little guy from Bisbee, Sydney P. Quales, (we called 'im Dr. Gloom because he could always see the bad part of anything) tried to talk to this Indian. Goddamn, the Indian just whacked him and out he went! I saw these two guys knocked out, and I used to be able to hit a pretty good lick myself, so I started trying to reason with 'im. And I'm watchin' 'im real close. When I see he's gettin' ready to hit, I whacked him on the jaw – knocked him out! About that time, this big Indian come up. He says, "What's the ruckus up there?" He didn't wait for any explanation; he says, "I'll give you five minutes to get back to bed and I'm turnin' the lights off. And if I hear another damn word, I'm gonna come up here and knock your heads together!" That got us in bed! End of ruckus!

And this Zanzuki, Paul Zanzuki, him and I are the only two left outta the original bunch that was put together when the Guard was mobilized. Course, we come a couple, three months later to fill 'em up to full strength. And this Paul Zanzuki, he must a-saw potential in me, because he give me a lotta breaks that I didn't think I really deserved. He give me promotions along, too. I got 'em, hell, bein' a newcomer and

126

all these guys from Flagstaff was all college boys. And the captain we had, he was a professor in charge of the National Guard company. Hell, he had all of his boys there and I can tell you, promotions for a year there didn't come to us draft boys. I was jerked up in front of the captain a time or two. (One of the times I got jerked up was when we threw these four Japs in the waterhole on Noemfoor Island.) Anyway, I went out on some special training; out of each battalion they had a squad or two. We had this little lieutenant and he wasn't overly bright. The first time we got into some tough fightin', he went psycho. He give my captain a bad report on me and he jerked me up after lunch. The First Sergeant had told me, "Captain is gonna eat your ass out and he's probably gonna break you. But stand up to the bastard!" That's just the words he used! He said, "Don't take any fuckin' shit off 'im! Just stand up to 'im! 'Cause the worst he can do is break you down to a private and hell, you've been there before! If he breaks you, ever damn one of us noncoms is gonna turn our stripes in! And we'll put him in a goddamn hot spot!" Well, I went up there before him and he started in and I just took over myself. I says, "Captain, you're chewin' on my ass, which is fine. And if you wanna bust me down to a goddamn private, let's do it. Let's not just bullshit around about it!" And he's gettin' kinda goddamn big-eyed, you know? I said, "Hell, you'll get transferred outta the company and I'll get my stripes back!" And then he tells me, "I can carry an extra sergeant on my roster (or record-book or some damn thing or other) but I'm gonna take your squad away from you."

That's when I lost my good squad. He took 'em away from me and for about three days around there, I'm just an extra sergeant. And then he got all the damn misfits in the company and give 'em to me! They were good soldiers but they was mighty poor damn garrison soldiers. They was always in trouble on their damn inspections and whatnot. I got these guys and that backfired on 'im. 'Cause it wasn't too long after that that they had an inspector general come through. He run ever squad in that regiment through on takin a pillbox. At that time I had a bazooka man and when I got ready to run through this thing, I told all these misfits, I said, "Now listen. We've done a little fightin' and we've got a pretty good idea how to take a damn pillbox. But we're gonna do it by the book! We're gonna do everything by the damn book!" So we run through the course – we done it by the book. We got up within range of that pillbox and this little Bennie Berman, the sorriest one I had, he's got the bazooka and he made a direct hit on that bastard! And there was a 55 gallon drum in the middle and that drum went up in the coconut palms, I bet it went 20 foot in the air! When it was all over, he checked every damn squad in the regiment. He told my captain, he says, "You've got a Sergeant Barney. I want him up here, 'cause I wanna tell you somethin'." So I got up there and he told that captain, "Sergeant Barney here, I give him the highest score in the regiment and he's officer material!" Most of the guys I had in that squad ended up as squad leaders!

Then when I got out of the Army, there was a few guys I met, like Malcolm MacKenzie. He had a ranch right next to me and we used to help one another. I'd got a little ol' collie dog that was half Australian Collie and half Border Collie and a hell of a good cowdog. There was one hound I had, an ol' pet hound, he was a hell of a good lion dog, and he was a good cowdog. Malcolm and I learned that a couple a-good cowdogs was more help than a couple of cowboys! And a hell of a lot cheaper! We worked together and we worked with our dogs. Christ, we took care of all the cattle on my place and all the cattle on his place and that's all the help we ever used was those two dogs 'til we got ready to ship or move a bunch of cattle somewhere. I tell ya, a good cowdog, they're more loyal than most cowboys are. I've learned that ever man is entitled to one good dog, a good horse and a good wife. And I've been real fortunate; I've had all of 'em. The best thing a man can have is a good, loyal wife. They're even a hell of a lot more help than a good dog!

I should run in my good friend, Layne Brandt. We've hunted together for the last 20 or so years and caught a few lions together. We've been good friends and he gives me a lot higher marks than I really deserve. We do click together!

Chapter Seven   Construction Companies

First Years Home

I come home on a Greyhound Bus and stopped off in Phoenix and spent a week with my mother before I went to the ranch to see my dad. My dad, he wanted to hear these damn war stories but I never would talk about the war – I'd just tell 'im I didn't want to talk about it. Christ, ever so often I'd have a goddamn nightmare, wake up and the sheets would be soaked with sweat. Christ, if I talked about it, it would bring these damn things back and then I'd liable to have a nightmare and I wouldn't go right off to sleep. It took years – the kids grew up and never heard any of these war stories. I never even talked to my wife, Beryl, about those times. I remember hearin' one of our neighbors tellin' my dad, "I don't know about Ollie – he's not quite right! He's been affected or something!"

After I was wounded, the first time I got on a scale I weighed 153 pounds. That was down from 186. When I was discharged I weighed 159 pounds, so I was pretty lean. And maybe about half mean; I don't know.

When I was with my dad he asked me one day if I was registered to vote. I said I was. He asked, "How're you registered to vote?" I said, "Well, when I was in the Army, they had us all sign up and I registered as a Democrat. When Roosevelt run for the last time, I voted for 'im. But after I got outta the Army, read the paper and listened to a little talk, I realized, Jesus Christ, I'm not a very good Democrat! So I went down and re-registered as a Republican!" Dad said, "Hell, you may make a man someday! In my whole lifetime, I voted for one Democrat. He was a horsethief and I voted to hang 'im!" He claims it was one of those early Udall people.

So I spent a year with my dad, a-helpin' on the ranch, and then went to work for the Park Service. I was hired by the Forest Service and had worked for the Park Service in the Rincon Mountains; they reimbursed the Forest Service for our wages. The head Park Ranger found out that I was back and talked me into goin' to work for him again. I spent about four years working with 'im. Hell, I had a permanent Civil Service rating but I just couldn't cope with the damn Park Service stupidity. So I bought the ranch from my dad and quit the Park Service. I had the ranch for 28 years. I know I never made any money at it. (But after the 28 years, I figured I'd made $100 a month.) So I had to have another job.

I had an uncle there in Tucson that was a carpenter and he got me a job, got me on as a helper. There was a big kid there from Arkansas whose dad was a sharecropper back home. He'd been there about three months and just took me under his wing and showed me how to do things and was a-helpin' me along. We was pretty good buddies. He'd come to Tucson on a Greyhound Bus and the only thing he had a-goin' for him was that his brother-in-law was the carpenter foreman.

The first thing I did when I went to work there was to help the sawman – the Arkansas kid. He did all the cuttin' for the rafters and studs and upper and lower plates – all we had to do was go in there and put it together. Ever night after work I'd quiz my uncle on this stuff. And he taught me how to lay out a house, how to cut rafters and the other stuff. After about three months, this sawman wanted to go fishin'. The foreman argued with him sayin', "You can't go fishin'! We got to have you here to cut out these houses!" I volunteered; I told him, "Hell, let him go fishin', I can cut out the damn houses." He looked at me and said, "You think you can?" I said, "Hell, I know I can!" "Well," he said' "I'm gonna let you do it! If you get into a problem, you can ask me or your Uncle Gene."

I cut out three houses while the regular sawman was off fishin'. One a day. That's when this kid got back and the foreman told him, "Damn you, you can just stay fishin' if you want to; Ollie can cut out these damn things just about as fast as you! And he hasn't made any mistakes and he's a hell of a lot cheaper than you are!"

I sawed out one house, a hip house, and on one a-these hips, I sawed two pieces for the hip, goin' up the same side. Christ, when my uncle come to assemble the house behind me, he come a- ravin' down on me askin', "What the hell were you thinkin' about?" I thought maybe I had sawed all the rafters a foot short or somethin'! It just turned out these two jack rafters wasn't a pair; there were two alike. My uncle could a-sawed one out and went on, but he felt better about chewin' on me for a while and makin' me saw it out. He took it back and it worked.

But that damn Arky was ambitious and he learned fast. It wasn't long before he was biddin' on framin' some a-the houses. His brother-in-law had a carpentry and remodeling license and he was biddin' the jobs under that license.

Don Carr

Don Carr is the young man from Arkansas that I met when I first started workin' with my uncle. I told how he was workin' under his brother-in-law's license. When I started the Enrico projects, Jimmy Noonan and I told him that he should get his own license and bid on our job. He says, "Hell, I don't know whether I can." I told him, "I got a book and if you read that book and learn it, you can pass the license test." He did just that and started biddin' the jobs on his own.

Don had a pet finish carpenter and he done something that I didn't like so I kinda chewed on him a bit. Don came up to the office after that and he was mad; he was upset! I'd eat one of his men's ass out and by god, he was quittin'! And he wanted his money right now! He went on for about five minutes and I listened to him and he got all wound down. Then I says, "Don, now I've listened to you, heard your problems, so will you listen to my problems?" He said,

"Yeah, I will." I told him, "Don, you've had these pushy jobs like I've got here, and you know to get anything done you gotta push everbody to their damn limits. And I've found out your limit and if you just want to forget everything and keep on workin', I'll guarantee that I'll never get to your limit again." He quieted down and told me, "Well, Ollie, if that's the way you feel about it, that's good enough for me!"

And he went back to work and hell, we were good friends. He got some dogs and we started huntin' together. There come a kind of a lull in Tucson; work was short, but by that time he'd gotten 'im a concrete license. He was pourin' concrete and hell, makin' money. Then one day he come to me and said, "You know, Ollie, I'm gonna quit. I'm goin' back to Arkansas. I've already went back there and bought a three-bedroom brick house on about 30 acres of land. I've put together a quarter of a million dollars and I'm not a-gonna let these goddamn subcontractors go broke on my money!" And he did; he's still back there. He built several churches around there and then he got to building houses – he said, "I taught them Arkies how to build a house!" The last time I saw him was four, five years ago – he was livin' in a four-bedroom home he'd built there on about five acres of lawn. He'd bought and sold land; Christ, he had a brand-new GMC pickup and his wife had a brand-new Dodge. They were livin' the good life!

Enrico Building Company

I worked at the carpenter trade for 16 years and I eventually got to be the sawman – sawed out a lotta houses. I finally got my license for carpentry and remodelin' and I had a partner – together we formed a construction company and worked at it for several years. Then he got to drinkin' pretty heavy and run up a bill or two that I had to pay for 'im so we dissolved our partnership.

Then I got a job with Enrico Building Company as the Construction Superintendent. I built well over 300 houses for them. When I went to work for them, I told the owners,

"Now, if I'm workin' for you and runnin' the job, I'm gonna do all the hirin' and all the firin'. And I'll run the job. And anytime you're dissatisfied, let me know and I'll leave. But I can't work with the two of you comin' in and interferin'." They agreed to that. There were a few subcontractors on the job, but after that I hired all the subs and ordered all the materials.

That company had bought a cotton field. We had to plow the cotton under and put in the streets and sidewalks. They had started three model homes when I come on the job. There were two two-bedroom models and one four-bedroom model. I finished 'em up and started on the main project. I sent the three plans to the lumber company and when I was ready to start a house, I would call and give 'em the house plan number and the lot it was goin' on and they'd drop off the lumber and supplies the next day. The saleslady was selling those places like hotcakes. In 11 months we moved 102 families into their own homes!

But the first thing that happened was one of the subcontractors the owner-partners had already taken on started draggin' his feet and gettin' behind. I went down to the field and told him, "Goddamn it, you got to get caught up! You're three houses behind!" I went back on up to the office and I'm shufflin' through my papers and he come in and talked to the partner who was mainly the boss. He told 'im, "Ollie come down and eat my ass out – said I was gettin' behind and I had to catch up!" Then I interrupted. I said, "Listen, goddamn it, if we can't keep our problems in the field and you gotta drag 'em up here in the office and start thrashin' 'em out with my boss, then you finish the three Formica jobs you got goin' and your ass is fired!" He turned to Jimmy Noonan and says, "Can he do that?" Jimmy says, "Sounds to me like he's already done it!"

So I got another Formica man and he was $15 a house cheaper and done over 350 houses for me – done a better job and never got behind. The only subs that was paid by the hour was the carpenters and the laborers. I had a little pot-bellied Mexican that run the labor crew; he did all the hirin' and firin'. I didn't work on Saturdays and Sundays – that was when I worked the ranch. And this Jimmy Noonan, he didn't like my little pot-bellied Mexican and he fired him on a Saturday when I wasn't there. So he come to work the next Monday and told me that Noonan had fired him. I says, "Noonan doesn't do the hirin' and firin' on this job – I do! So you just get back and do your work." Noonan come in later that day and said, "I see your little pot-bellied Mexican is back on the job." I told him, "Yup, you fired him and I rehired him." He asked, "Can't you get along without 'im?" I said, "Yes, I can. But I'm not goin' to." That was the last time Jimmy Noonan ever fired one of my men.

We went along and I hired a guy and his brother. This guy was kind of a rabble-rouser and he got to creating problems with my carpenter crew. They had to have this. They had to have that. One of the things they wanted was ice water on the job. Up to then we'd been letting someone pick up a block of ice and the guys would ice their water jugs down. So I called all the guys together and I told 'em, "You guys is got ever damn thing you want now, I brought your ice water to you, but there's one thing you don't have…I'm firin' ever damn one of you! And there's three guys here I'm keepin' – they're workin' on the trim crew and they're not involved in this framin' crew. By god, I'm firin' the lot a-you." I fired eleven carpenters that morning.

Jimmy Noonan come by later and said he didn't see any carpenters workin' and asked what happened. I said that I had fired all of 'em! And he said, "Well, what are we gonna do?" I said, "I got names of a few guys lookin' for a job and I'll call 'em up tonight, or today, probably won't get a-hold of 'em 'til night, and I'll hire some. And all these guys I let go will be back in three days askin' for their jobs and I'll hire 'em back – but then they'll know who in the hell they're workin' for!" And it happened just that way. Except I never hired back the instigator and his brother.

The next thing I found out was that the instigator wrote a letter to the Labor Department in Washington, D.C. He complained about bein' fired and ol' Jimmy showed me the letter he got from the Labor Department and he asked me, "What am I gonna do about it?" I told him, "Hell, you don't have to do anything, just give me that damn letter and I'll answer it for you!" So I took the letter and I wrote on the back of it that I had hired this guy and he wasn't qualified to do the job he claimed he could do and besides that he was an instigator and I fired his ass! It's that simple. We put it in an envelope and mailed it back and that was the last we ever heard about it.

There were two houses that I hadn't even started because the lots were covered four or five feet deep with dirt from the water line, sewer line and street construction. I was trying to get rid of that dirt; I was even trying to give it away! Ol' Noonan come around and says, "Ollie, what in hell are we gonna do with that dirt? I've been tryin' to give it away and I can't!" I told 'im, "Hell, I tried to give it away around here for a month! I couldn't give it away – so I sold it! The guy said that he'd start haulin' it off here in a day or two." He said, "You sold it? Then you can have the money! What'd you get for it?" I said I got $1,500. He changed his mind then and told me, "Well, hell, that's a lot of money! Let's just divide it up!" So I had to give 'im $750, but I didn't feel bad about that.

So we got rid of the dirt, finished that project and started another one

I built more than 300 houses for that company in two separate projects. Then sales slowed down about the time I heard about the Maxim Brothers down in Green Valley. One of 'em come to Tucson to talk to me about runnin' the job for 'em. They were financially over-extended, but I went down there with 'im and looked the job over. Christ, they had a pickup with a phone in it for me and I went over the job and I could see all kinds of problems – the subs was a-draggin' their feet and gettin' behind. I knew the only way I could run the job is to fire all the help. And some of 'em was pet help, and bring in my own people from Tucson. By that time I'd been workin' pretty steady and I was kinda burnt out on this here carpenter work so I didn't take the job. The brothers went belly-up not too long after that and sold out to Fairfield. If I'd went to work for 'em, I might a-pulled it out for 'em, but I would a-ruffled a lotta damn feathers!

Wilbur Bessett

I went down to talk to Wilbur Bessett, the plumbin' subcontractor, about the schedule because he was gettin' a little bit behind. He was havin' some stomach problems and I was, too, at that time. I told 'im, "Wilbur, you're gonna have to get caught up and stay that way! I got to get these houses built!" Now Wilbur was pretty short-fused and he threw a tantrum, tellin' me, "Goddamn it, I'm doin' half your work, I'm a-orderin' all this material for these houses and that takes up a lot of my time!" I says, "Wilbur, I'll come back this afternoon when you've cooled down and we'll talk. And here, take some of my stomach pills, they make you feel a little better."

I come back that afternoon and he had cooled down. I said, "Wilbur, I realize you are doin' a lotta my work, but all you gotta do is give me the materials list on these three models we're buildin' and I'll see that the material is here when you need it. But you just hafta get caught up!" The next day he give me the lists. I already had a crew up there building a yard and I ordered 20 houses worth of material for 'im. Christ, after that all he had to do was go up to the yard and take out his material – he even started workin' at night! He started puttin' the underground plumbing all together and then come back in the mornin', set it in the ditches, caulk the joints and hook it all together! That old man plumbed over 300 houses for me and never got behind again. And never got upset with me again!

His son, John Bessett, he was about 13 years old then. I took a real likin' to him and he started huntin' with me. He didn't even have a driver's license. He's 66 now and we've been huntin' together all this time. We've hunted Australia twice and once in Africa we got together even though he was huntin' with a different outfitter. John and I has never had one cross word in all these years. We can hunt together now and don't even have to talk! We know what the other is going to do. He was a great huntin' buddy! And Wilbur just passed away this year – 2006 – he was 95 years old!

The Carpenter and the Whorehouse

This story happened back years and years ago, probably between 55 and 60 years ago. It was when I was a carpenter and single. This crew we were on hired this new carpenter outta Kansas. I've forgotten his name now but he was single and I was the only other single one on the crew. He was wantin' to go down to Mexico and drink some a-their tequila and fraternize with some a-their Mexican whores. So bein' the only single one, I was elected to go with 'im.

This is durin' the middle of the week and it's his birthday – that's what he's wantin' to celebrate, his birthday. That evening after work we started off down to Nogales and hell, we hadn't even got outta town, Tucson, 'til he was a-wantin' to stop and have a beer! I says, "Hell, if we stop and have a beer, we'll never get to Nogales!" So we went on and when we got down to Tumacacori they had a sign there: "Beer." I think that's all they sold in that little liquor store. So we stopped there and we're sittin' in there drinkin' our beer and I can see the door there and what should come through the door but an ol' gal that when I was workin' down there, hell, I used to date 'er on a regular basis! I nudged 'im and I says, "You know, this lady that just walked through the door – I'm gonna hit on 'er!" She got about halfway into the room and I said, "Lady, you look like you could stand a drink!" By god, she come over and we ordered her a beer and was just carryin' on a conversation, not sayin' anything. She's drinkin' her beer and finally she says, "What are you guys doin' down here?" "Well," I said, "this friend a-mine, it's his birthday and he wants to go down to Nogales to one a-those fancy clubs and see these Mexicans goin' through some a-these exotic dances they put on. Hell, why don't you just come along?" She says, "I think I will!"

And I can see him startin' to squirm now; we got this lady I picked up! Anyway, we went down there and on Canal Street, we drove up there to one a-the places that had lots of lights and stuff on it and I dropped 'im off. I said, "We're gonna go get somethin' to eat. We'll be back about 11:00 o'clock and pick you up." So we went and we eat and come to pick 'im up and I says, "Hell, you might as well come on in with us." And she did! Really, she didn't know where she was a-gettin' into! And when I got in there, I can see he's partin' stuff with this Mexican whore and I got to visitin' with the whore, askin' 'bout what kind of a lay he was. How long his pecker was and how many times he'd went and I see her really startin' to squirm then 'cause hell, she could talk better Spanish than I could! We gathered him up and went to drop her off at Tumacacori to get her car and meantime she decided she'd just take me to Tucson and turn him loose on his own!

We did and went back and spent the night at my place and got up next morning, had bacon and eggs. I says, "Your landlady, where you gonna tell her you been? You're not a-gonna tell her you spent time in a Mexican whorehouse, are you?" She says, "No, I don't think I will!" God, I come back that evenin', she's gone, but she'd tidied up my trailer a little bit before she left.

That nexy day, you know, my carpenter friend was kinda draggin' around with his hangover and the boss fired 'im! I don't know whether he fired 'im for not getting' his work done or for leadin' me astray!

Chapter Eight

Hunting in Arizona and Mexico

First Lion; First Dogs

The first lion huntin' I did was when I was a kid; my dad had bought me a couple of hound pups and I worked with 'em for several years. My dad poisoned both of 'em: accidentally, of course. This one, he saved him once, but he finally got a dose that killed 'im. I never did catch a lion with 'em but I tried and I trailed several times with 'em. One time I went up on the Rincons and camped up there and I found a deer kill. This ol' hound, he started that and I lost 'im. 'Bout midnight he come back into camp.

Figure 15. Ollie with His Two Hounds

Then, after I'd got back from the war and worked in construction 'til I was gettin' burned out on that, I told my wife one morning, "I'm gonna turn the key off; I'm gonna quit this damn construction. I've learned my capabilities. I'm not smart enough to make a million dollars and I'm too smart to make it for somebody else!" She says, "Well, you're quittin'? I'm quittin'!" She went to Europe for three months.

But before that happened, you know, after I got back from the Army, I eventually bought the ranch from my dad. As I said, I'd had a couple of lion dogs when I was a kid, but nothing much. Now I had a little time and I was seein' a lion track out at the ranch once in awhile, so I started lookin' around for a hound pup. I already had a cowdog that I got from a daughter of a neighbor, Roddy MacKenzie. He was half collie and half Australian collie; a nice little dog. I didn't have a cowdog and I got to thinkin' hell, I needed a cowdog, so I started negotiatin' with the daughter – what would she sell 'im for? Well, she had to have a quarter and back in those days, I didn't have a lot of money, but I did have a quarter in my pocket! So I bought Ike. Then I bought Abe – I tell about all the Abe dogs in another story.

Anyway, I'm still not havin' any luck on lion. I saw in the paper that someone had a burro they wanted to give away, so I picked this burro up and took it up on a Forest Service trail, oh, about 50 yards off of it. I shot this burro and put a couple of traps there and, goddamn, that ol' lion would come by there and hell, he wouldn't go down and check that burro at all. He just went by 'im. But I caught a deer in the trap. And then I decided I'd better find out somethin' about how to catch a mountain lion!

So I went over to Saint David to see this old man by the name of Jim Wilson; he'd hunted lion for years. So I went over and talked to him. He was a barber by trade and when a government hunter over in Safford wanted to quit and retire and he come to Jim Wilson and told him he could get him this government job. It was huntin' bear and lion for, I think, it was Biological Survey back then. Wilson told 'im, "I don't know anything about huntin' bear and lion!" The hunter says, "You buy my dogs and you don't have to know anything. All you gotta do is just take them dogs out where they got a complaint about lion or a bear and just turn them dogs loose and follow 'em! They'll teach you all you need to know." He said that's the way it worked out.

I don't know, for 35 years or so he'd hunted for the government and he said – he never told me how many bear he'd been on – but he said he'd been on 535 lion kills. He said he had one old dog that he'd got from the prison. It was a bloodhound and he called it "Major". A big red dog. When that dog was 13 years old, it was the best dog he ever owned and it was durin' the Depression, he sold this dog to a guy that wanted to train some pups for $150. That's back in the Depression and a 13-year-old dog!

I told 'im, I says, "God, a dog I'd had that long and was that good a dog, it'd a-been hard for me to sell." He says, "Ollie, you was growin' up in the Depression but you didn't have a houseful of hungry kids to feed, either! That's the only reason I sold 'im. By god, I needed the money to feed those hungry kids!" It would a-been hard for him to sell that dog, but he had the incentive.

I asked 'im, "How in the hell do you train these damn dogs to quit runnin' deer?" "Aw hell," he says, "you can slow 'em down, but you can't train 'em. But they get to be three, four years old and they find out they can't catch a deer or a coyote. If they're any good, then they'll start catchin' lion for you." And it's pretty much that way.

Anyway, he says, "Trappin' lions is no different from trappin' skunks. All you need is the right bait. That's javelina. You kill a javelina and you find a place where there's lion sign and where they've scratched in some saddle and you get you a little tree there and hang this javelina up in the tree. And where this lion has to walk between a bush and the tree there smellin' this javelina, you put a couple a-traps in there and you'll catch the first lion that comes through." Javelina season was comin' on so I shot a javelina and I figured well, if a whole javelina would work, why wouldn't a half work? So I put out two sets, one on one end of the mountain and one on the other. First time I come to the one that's on the north end, I had a lion caught. I let my dogs trail it up in the trap and fight it. I had some binder's twine; I tied up my dogs and put binder's twine in the loops of my rope and got it on this lion's neck. I pulled the rope around a tree and stretched 'im out good and got my feet on the two springs of the trap and turned 'im loose. Then, with the binder's twine in the loop, I jerked the rope off of 'im and, a-course the lion took off! Then I cut my dogs loose and Christ, by then he's outta sight! But they got on 'im and treed 'im. I done that three times. I caught one lion on the north end and I caught two on the south end. By then, ol' lion dog, the hound, was workin' good and the cowdog was workin' pretty good.

There was one big tom there, I kept seein' his tracks; I never could catch 'im! After I'd caught these three lions without the traps, by releasin' 'em, I run onto this lion track one morning. Goddamn, my hound took it backwards! Little cow dog right with him! Goddamn, I rode better in those days and I'd ride good horses, so I overhauled that hound and got 'im turned around and got 'im on the other end of the track. And god, we trailed 'im for probably three or four miles and he went into Deer Creek. There was a Ponderosa Pine that grew up about 30, 40 feet and it'd been broke over the top for, oh, about six or eight foot and then it grew back up straight. And this lion had been layin' under a ledge right there by this tree and when these hounds come, hell, he just jumped up on that pine and climbed up there. I couldn't see the damn lion, he was layin' up there in this thick boughs coverin' the tree and I looked all around and finally, I could see about six inches of his tail stickin' out. And this friend a-mine with me, Stan Corey, we both just have pistols, he climbed up there where he could see this lion and he killed 'im with his pistol. And the lion never fell out!

Ol' Stan, he wanted to go back to the ranch to get an axe and chop the tree down. But this tree's about 20 inches, at least 20 inches in diameter, maybe two foot – that looks like a lotta work to me! There was sycamore trees a-growin' along there; there was some a-these saplin's that was about 18, 20 foot long that was dead. I broke one a-them off, climbed up in this pine and ol' Stan, he handed me up this saplin' that was dead and with that, I could reach this lion. I

142

poked 'im out and saved about a two hour ride back to the ranch and another two hours comin' back and however long it'd take to chop that tree down.

That was the startin' a-my lion dogs. I caught, I forget how many bear, but I think that dog – I lost 'im when he was four years old – and I'd caught 21 lion with 'im and maybe five bear.

This Mexican friend, I'd hunted with him a little bit, Alfredo Aredia, he had a blue tick-type hound, a good dog. And he said he'd sell 'im to me for $500. So I wrote 'im out a check for $500. It went along there for about three or four days and he called me up. He says, "Ollie, I can't sell that dog. You can use 'im, you can borrow 'im, but I can't sell 'im." I said, "OK." It went on about a month or six weeks and him and his wife drove up to the house. "Ollie," he says, "A partner a-mine has a lot of equipment, mining equipment and he wants $750 for his half of it. I wanna buy it. I'll sell that dog to you for $750." He apologized for raisin' the price and everthing and I said, "Well, that's fine. But I've gotta go over to New Mexico. There's a guy over there's got three young dogs he wants to sell and I promised 'im I'd come over and look at 'em. If I don't buy 'em, I'll buy your dog." "Ollie," he says, "I need the money!" I said, "Well, if you need the money, I'll loan it to you!" I got my checkbook and wrote 'im out a check for $750. This ol' Alfredo, I guess he's real honest, he says, "Draw up a contract where I owe you the money." I said, "I don't need a contract. Your wife's here, my wife's here and you know I loaned the money to you. The women know I loaned the money to you and I damn well know I loaned you money and that's just good enough!"

So I went on to Reserve, New Mexico, and went huntin' with this guy and they was three nice little dogs. But we got on a lion track and they'd trail along and then one of 'em would climb up on a rock and they'd look all around. And then they'd go back to trailin'. Then another one'd stop and start lookin' and listenin'. We didn't catch the lion and on the way back, this fellow at Reserve said, "Ollie, what do you think about these three dogs?" I said, "Well, I think you're showin' me the wrong dog. I'd like to see the dog that these young dogs is huntin' with. I think that's the one I wanna buy." "Well," he says, "last winter I went out huntin' and got in a big snowstorm and I lost this dog. I never have ever been able to get him back. I don't know whether he died or someone hauled 'im outta the country. If I had 'im these three young dogs wouldn't be for sale!" I told 'im, "I got a dog back in Arizona I can buy for just what you want for these three dogs – you want $750 and that's what this guy wants for his dog. I've hunted him and I've caught lion with 'im, so I'm gonna pass on your deal and go back and buy this one dog. He can do everthing these three can do."

The guy was nice about it. I went back and I called Alfredo up and I told him, I said, "You don't owe me $750 dollars now. But I own the dog." That was agreeable. From the time I had 'im, I caught around...I don't know, but I caught quite a few lion with 'im. A guy I had out huntin' stole the dog. I know he stole 'im but I never have been able to prove it. But I do know that he had a couple of friends up in the Kingman area that he'd hunted with. And he'd went down into Mexico and hunted with 'em. I found out through the record book that he'd went up with these guys and caught 'im a record-book lion on the Walapai Indian Reservation. I know that's where my dog went. I told it around that I knew this guy had stole the dog but I couldn't prove it.

I had pretty good evidence, 'cause it was up in the Catalinas near this Control Mine. This Spaghetti King I was huntin' with, we'd lost all of our dogs up there the day before and some of 'em come in that night. We met two of 'em goin' back up the trail the next morning – I did; I'd sent him around to the Control Mine to get our truck and trailer up there so we'd have somethin' to come back in. I told him where to meet me, up in Dan's Saddle above the Control Mine. He should a-been there when I got there but he wasn't. He was about 30 minutes late and I'd started back down the trail lookin' for 'im and I run onto 'im. His story he told me was that he got up to the Control Mine and the dog wasn't there, so he drove on up the mountain to the sawmill up there, thinkin' maybe he'd come in there. We come on

Figure 16. Ollie and Ol' Blue

back and I went back and I spent a couple a-days lookin' for that dog. I rode up and down the road and up to the sawmill and not a hound track nowhere. I had a picture a-that dog and the guys there at the Control Mine said that dog come in that afternoon. And there was a couple of Fish and Wildlife men up there that was trappin' some a-these wild pigeons and they'd told these guys at the mine that there was a hound, a couple of hounds barkin' treed down there in a deep canyon all afternoon. They said this dog come in that evening and I had a picture of several dogs and they picked out the one that was gone. I know this Spaghetti King picked that dog up and hauled 'im up to his cabin up there and went back and got 'im later and took 'im up to those guys in Kingman. He'd caught that good lion with him.

When I come back that evening, I barely had enough damn gas to get back to Oracle. So when I went back the next day or two, lookin' for this dog, I drove up to the Control Mine and back to Oracle. But I still had too much gas, about five gallons more, so he'd taken that dog on over the mountain to his cabin and left 'im there. I was in Myrmo's shop one day and he come in there and he started buttin' in on the conversation. I picked up a piece of hand steel there and told him, "Goddamnit, don't butt in my business anymore or I'll knock you in the damn head!" He said, "You think I stole your dog!" I said, "When I prove it, I'm gonna kill your damn ass!" He says, "Well, I didn't steal 'im!" I said, "Accordin' to circumstantial evidence, you did steal 'im. And someday I might be able to prove it. And when I do, I'm gonna damn well take care of you!"

And I know I can prove it. All I'd have to do is go up there with my good friend John Bessett...he's good for gettin' information outta people...go in there not knowin' who he is and get to talkin' lion hunters. Have a few lion-huntin' pictures to show 'em and maybe they'd drag out a picture of ol' Blue. I'd know where he'd come from but I'm kinda reluctant to do that because if I did find out he done it, I'd feel obligated to take care a-this bastard. He's still alive. Everbody's that hunted him dislikes him. He's a mouthy bastard. I guess I'm a little bit chicken because I haven't done anything. I don't want to hafta kill the bastard! But he needs killin'!

George Parker told me, "We oughtta kill the bastard! I'll help you!" I told him, "I'm not damn sure he's really guilty!" "Aw," he said, "He might not be, but he's guilty of somethin'. He needs to be killed!" Then I found out George had had a fallin' out with the guy, too. But we let it go.

146

George was like ol' Judge Bean in Texas. He was known as the "Hangin' Judge." This story was supposed to have happened down there in a little town where Judge Bean had his law office. And there was a fellow who lived there, kinda on the outskirts of the town, and he had a real good-lookin' wife. There was some peepin' Tom around there and when she'd take a shower, he'd be a-peekin' in the window. This guy, he didn't like that! So he borrowed one of these Number 6 bear traps and set it out there and caught the guy!

By god, he got ol' Judge Bean over there to prosecute 'im after they got 'im outta the trap and ol' Judge Bean turned the guy loose! And that pissed this husband off, you know, and he told the judge, "Goddamn, you oughtta prosecute 'im!" And ol' Judge Bean said, "Mister, with the bait you was usin', you could a-tempted the honorable court!"

Anyway, that's how I got started lion huntin'. I've owned a lotta good dogs since then; I've owned a few sorry ones. I know I used to hunt outta Tucson on weekends, not every weekend, but a lotta weekends, and sometimes between jobs I could hunt for four or five days. I had guys in Tucson that was always wantin' to go huntin' with me and I'd tell 'em, "Hell, I can't take you out 'cause I got clients that's payin' me and they're not a-gonna want you around in the way. But I can tell you in the fall of the year I take my dogs out and work 'em. I'm always workin' a new pup or two. Same thing in the spring, when the season's over with, I'll take my pups out and work 'em a little bit, where I catch a lion and turn it loose and let 'em tree it. I have the old dogs tied up. Let 'em get experience. If you wanna go then, you're welcome to come, but I wanna tell you right now that I'm gonna treat your dogs *exactly* the way I treat my dogs." "Oh," they'd say, "we don't mind if you whip our dogs for runnin' a deer." I says, "I don't whip dogs for runnin' a deer. But I'll tell you what I do do: when my old dogs catch a lion, I kill ever damn young dog that don't get to the tree! The reason I do that is I don't end up with a bunch a-damn worthless dogs!" And no one ever hunted with me under those conditions!

I'd excuse one once in awhile for runnin' a deer if he was doin' a good job of it. But by god, I wanted, when I caught somethin', I wanted these young dogs to get to the tree. Those were the ones I kept. They're the ones that'll make you good dogs.

I had hundreds of hunts for lion and I did catch 13 bear with dogs. Clients shot all them. I've only killed óne bear in my life and I didn't do that with hounds.

Taking The Arizona Big Ten

This started back 30, 40 years ago and it was real popular at the time. Everbody wanted to shoot the Arizona Big Ten. There are ten big game animals to shoot in Arizona and at that time, there wasn't anybody had done it. Hunters got to concentratin' on it and ever once in a while, one of 'em would get it. I was interested in gettin' it myself but I was hung up on a bull elk.

I was over 20 years time in shootin' a big bull elk and when I got it, I was the 26th guy to get the Big Ten. I've actually taken this Big Ten about five or six times with other people, most of 'em was hung up on a mountain lion and I'd catch 'em a lion and they'd have the Big Ten. I've helped get five or six big horn sheep and a number of elk and the lions was what was hangin' these guys up on. Then it kinda died down for several years and then the Safari Club, they took it up. So I've got two Big Tens now, one's issued by the Wildlife Federation – the first one – and I was about 3rd or 4th on the Safari Club. It's still goin' on now. I think there's maybe 30, 35 guys now that's taken all the Arizona Big Ten.

They mostly get hung up on mountain lions and big horn sheep; buffalo, too, 'cause it's so hard to get drawn. But I've been with six, seven guys when they shot their buffalo. I was with Sherry when she got her buffalo and that was a real interestin' deal. My brother, Dick, and my daughter, Sherry, both got drawn for buffalo bull the same year. We went up to House Rock Valley and Dick, a pretty fair politician, got down there the evening before. He'd brought a liter of whiskey and had everyone a drink and he tells this game warden who's in charge, he says, "You know, if you've got an ol' poor cow out in the pasture, I'd rather shoot one of them out in the pasture rather than one of these in the corral." This ol' boy says, "Why sure, I sure like to hear that! We're short of 'em; we don't have enough buffalo in here!"

So the next morning, we're supposed to meet 'em there early, 6:30 or so, and when we got there, there's an airplane parked there, there's four rangers mounted on horses and we start out lookin' for a couple of buffalo. After a while, up on the hill, there's a couple of bull buffalo and Dick, he gets the first shot. We made a stalk on 'em and Dick had first choice and he picks out the one with the biggest horns; what he thought was the biggest horns. And he shot it. At that time I had a .270 Weatherby and Sherry used that – she took the other one. And boy, she laid it down right now! When we get up there and look at it, it's one of their herd bulls that they just brought in from Kansas! And he's a big fella! And that's the reason his horns looked small – he's so big! Dick, he got the little buffalo, the little horns, and he had the first pick! Then this game warden looked at it and he realized then that we'd shot a herd bull. So he called up the boss back in camp on the radio and says, "By god, we've shot a herd bull!" This guy asked 'im, "Has it got the yellow paint across its hindquarters?" Our guy says. "Nope." "Well," the boss says, "They sent us out to shoot buffalo and we shot a buffalo, so forget all about it!" Then the damn thing's so heavy they like to never got it loaded on a truck, you know, with the winch!

In Arizona and Mexico I've been in on 13 Desert Big Horn Sheep kills. There's a doctor here in Phoenix that would contact these people to get to guide 'em on sheep hunts. Twice, he had me guide one of his hunters. One of 'em was an old fella from Louisiana; he was 78 years old. The first evening in camp, the doctor took 'im out and he found 'im a ram that had a couple of ewes with 'im. He got to talkin' to this hunter, he tells 'im, "Now be sure and shoot the ram; don't shoot one of those ewes; be sure and shoot a ram!"

And that got 'im all nervous and he missed the ram. Course, Doc, he's all upset 'cause he missed the ram and then he turned 'im over to me.

I took 'im out and about the second day I located a real good ram – the bastard made the record book! We watched 'im; he laid down and we put a stalk on 'im and got up to 150 yards of 'im and this ol' ram's a-layin' there asleep. But he's got his head up. My hunter got to thinkin' that, since he'd missed that other ram, maybe his rifle wasn't sighted in right. So he asked, "Can I use your rifle?" My rifle's always sighted in. God, he got a rest over a rock; I put my down jacket on it and I said, "Now, he's about quartered in there so you aim right there at his rib cage, back about a foot, and it'll break the shoulder on the other side." And he shot. And the ol' ram's head just fell down and then he couldn't see 'im! "Goddamn," he says, "I missed 'im! I missed 'im!" I said, "No, he's dead! He's layin' there deader'n hell." The ol' man couldn't believe it! Anyway we went up there and he got his ram and it's record book and he's real happy.

Another guy killed a ram with my rifle. We'd hunted there several days and this one morning we went around there behind this mountain because I'd seen a good ram in the evening, by himself, go over the mountain but it was too late to do anything about it. We went around the next morning and found a road up there. When we get out, we see a vehicle comin' up behind us. It's a local guy who got a sheep permit. He said, "I guess you saw that big ram; there's three rams with that big one in it." Of course I said that I did. Which I hadn't. He says, "You was here first and you saw 'im. You just let me know where you wanna hunt and I'll hunt the other side of the mountain." So we went up and hunted around on the other side of the mountain and we got back together. I saw these three rams – they was layin' down. I told both of 'em, "Now, we'll put a stalk on 'em and my hunter's got the first shot. And you can take the second ram. But don't make any noise! Don't say anything! Don't get up or nothin'!" The other hunter had my rifle because the day before, he'd backed up and run over his rifle! And he was kinda leery of it, so he wanted to use my rifle, which was fine 'cause, sheep huntin', I always pack another rifle. I pack my rifle in case they drop theirs, break a scope or somethin'. Anyhow, my hunter shot his ram and he fell. The other two rams jumped up and everbody was quiet and then they settled down and this guy took my rifle and he laid the other one down. We had two rams there. The ol' Doc Clair, I think that was his name, he got pissed off at me because we left next morning and he'd came out after we left and he didn't get to see the sheep. What really hurt 'im the worst was that both years, I'd got better rams than he did! And he was upset with me because I hadn't waited around for him – hell, I didn't know he was comin'.

My hunter got the better ram, but the local guy got a good ram and he was real damn happy with it. He didn't know anything about sheep huntin' and he admitted he didn't know anything. You know, when he had his rifle leaned up agin the back of his truck and backed out over the top of it, run over it, it tells you a lot.

At that time, John Bessett had a real fancy damn travel trailer and his son, Malvin, had got drawn for sheep. John said that we should take that trailer – he couldn't hunt with us for the first few days, but he said he'd catch up with us. I hunted this Malvin for several days and, Christ, he was little better'n a basket case! The first sheep I got a shot for 'im, a hell of a nice sheep – I know several hunters that'd give me $10,000 for that sheep – I got 'im down behind a rock and got 'im all rested up and everthing. And, Christ, the sheep wasn't 125 yards off! And he missed! The ol' sheep broke to run and he shot three more shots at it and didn't get it. John showed up about then. I told John, I said, "Now, goddamn, this kid is just fallin' apart when he gets to shootin'. We're gonna hafta quit trophy huntin' and just get 'im any legal damn ram we can get!" I told 'im about this one he'd missed.

So we're huntin' and John's with us then. We found this little ram; he's plenty legal but not anywhere in the world was he a trophy. I got Malvin a-shootin' at 'im and, Christ, the damn sheep wouldn't run, he'd just bounce around there. Hell, I think he had 17 rounds left in his pocket and he shot them all up! But in all this shootin', he'd wounded this ram with a ricochet! And it turned out he had one shell left. I told 'im, "Hell, there's no use you shootin' the damn thing 'cause, hell, you'll miss it again. I've got my .45 and I can sneak around and get a close shot at 'im, 'cause he's wounded, and finish 'im off." That wasn't, you know, the real proper thing to do. While we're discussin' what to do, Malvin shoots this last round into 'im and finishes 'im off. He was just fallin' apart, but, hell, I've seen him kill jackrabbits at 150 yards! And miss a big 'ol sheep, broadside, at 125!

I had practically the same thing happen to me on a javelina hunt. This was a lawyer and his son. They booked me for a guide on a blamed javelina hunt. I took 'em out to the old ranch and before I got there I see these javelina up here on the mountain, so we made a stalk. Both of 'em had a box of shells and I got this ol' kid lined up on one and one shot – killed his javelina! Then the ol' man starts shootin' at the other one. By god, I hunted 'im all day and he ended up, just before we got in to the ranch, shootin' up the last of his damn ammunition! 39 Rounds! And he'd wounded a javelina with a ricochet! I saw the ol' javelina go down into an old mine tunnel. We went up to the mine tunnel and there's the blood trail goin' down but the only thing we got is my .44 magnum pistol. I told 'im, "It's just half a mile down to the ranch. You just watch this hole and I'll go down there. There's a .22 in that house there and we'll go back in there and you can finish it off with the .22." Well, I got the .22 and it'd been layin' there so long, and all messed up, and it wouldn't shoot! I said, "The only thing we gotta do is, go in there with this .44 magnum." I had sense enough – we packed his and my ears with Kleenex – and we get in there and this ol' javelina is backed right up there in the back. He's about 10 foot from us and he's a-chompin' his jaws. The lawyer got up there with the pistol and fired away and there's just a ball of fire went up there into that hole and back over the top of us! Christ, that javelina really got excited and was chompin' his jaws then! I said, "Well, you're gonna hafta get closer!" And he's reluctant to get closer! I'm behind him. I always stay behind my hunters when they're shootin'. I got him by the the seat of his pants and the back of the neck and I hiked 'im up there where the ol' pistol was three or four foot from the hog and he touches off. The fire rolls back over and course, we had our ears packed so it didn't hurt our ears. He killed his hog and we drug it out.

That was the two animals we had to finish off after a ricochet.

Another father and son I had out after javelina – it was a windy kind of a day and I found these pigs and they was down in a draw. They're 75 or 100 yards. I had this kid shoot and he killed his pig. One shot. The old man started shootin'. This kid, I guess he hadn't realized he'd killed a pig and he started shootin'! And killed another one! The old man's still a-shootin and I said, "Jesus Christ, man, stop shootin'! You've killed a damn pig! Your son's killed a pig so quit shootin'!" He said, "I killed a pig?" I said, "Christ, yes, you killed a pig!" We went down there and showed one of the pigs that he'd killed and, hell, his son had killed both of 'em! He don't know to this day that he didn't kill that pig.

This is another javelina story. I was huntin' with my cousin with bows and arrows. We found some pigs and we stalked up on 'em. These pigs, they never did stop; they was just trottin' out single file. I shot at this pig and it looked like the arrow went thought his bristles. We went over the hill and I got a shot at another pig and I seen the arrow stayed in him. Then there wasn't anything to shoot at and my cousin never got a shot – he was a little too slow. We headed over the hill where this last pig that had the arrow in 'im went and when he got there, he was layin' right along side the first pig that I'd shot! The arrow had went behind his shoulder and it went all the way through and it looked like the arrow went through the top of his bristles. Then the other one stuck in 'im and I knew I'd got him and we trailed 'em up there and, Christ, I'd got two pigs then! My cousin, he just put his tag on it and that's the way I got away with that deal. It was a damned accident – I just thought that arrow went through his bristles and I've had it happen before. But it had hit him, hit both lungs.

This story is about Ed and the Number One Coues deer. It happened down on the Solero Ranch. He was 17 years old and they went huntin'; they'd hunted all day and along in the evening, they're comin' back to camp. Ed, now remember he's just 17 years old then, and this buck jumped up and he killed it! You know, it turned out to be the world's record Coues deer – still the world's record – and hell, he told me at 17 years old, he'd a-been just tickled to death to shoot a spike!

Ed, he told me what all hunters know anyway, that most of these trophy heads – people just lucked into 'em. Ed hunted for years after that, hunted hard, and I don't think he ever killed another buck that even made the record book.

Elk Hunting

My first elk hunt that I killed a elk – the first one wasn't too long after World War II. This Lloyd Harris was a good friend; I'd met him workin' for the Park Service in 1940. Up until the time he died a couple of years ago, we was the best of friends. We decided to go elk huntin'. By god, we got all packed up and I had my horse and he had his horse and we trailered up and we got up on top of the mountains; I don't know where it was exactly, it was up on the Rim somewhere. We knew where we wanted to go and it come a goddamn little snow storm and Christ, there was about four inches a-snow on us! We come by a forest cabin and Lloyd, workin' for the Forest Service, says, "Stop here and see if my key will open this place up. This is where we're gonna spend the night!" Hell, his key worked! We staked our horses out and fed 'em and Christ, they had bunks in there and we rolled our beds out on the bunks and we had quite a lotta food in there and firewood and everthin'. Hell, we eat their food and spent the night with the Forest Service.

Next morning we went on over to where we were gonna hunt elk and hell, we saw cow elk but we never could find a bull. We was ridin'; we weren't doin' any walkin'. Then Thanksgiving Day come along. We decided we'd walk and see if we couldn't maybe jump a bull out afoot. Lloyd told me, "We've been seein' these wild turkeys and poults, you know, Ollie, you get a chance to shoot one a-those poults, shoot it! We'll have a turkey dinner tonight, being Thanksgiving." And Lloyd was a good cook. I run onto this poult runnin' up about 30 yards up in front, up the hill. I shot with my rifle and I cut his neck off right at his body. I picked that turkey right there and cleaned 'im all up and took 'im back to camp. Lloyd come in and goddamn, he fixed up dressin' and everthing and stuffed this turkey. He had a 14-inch dutch oven, one of the thick ones, and that bird fit down in there just fine. He dug a hole there by the campfire and put coals in the bottom of it and set this dutch oven in there and put a bunch more coals on it and covered it all up. He drug the fire out over the top of it and we're havin' a drink or two and here come the game warden in. He looked all around and said, "You know, I'm checkin' these here elk-huntin' camps. It's Thanksgiving and some of 'em are liable to kill a turkey. I'm figurin' on catchin' one or two of 'em and arrestin' 'em." Lloyd, he's better at talkin' to game wardens and he says, "Well, there's a lotta turkeys. Hell, we've been seein' turkeys ever day. But we didn't think we oughta kill one for a turkey dinner." That game warden was practically sittin' on that turkey. Hell, he was sittin' there drinkin' coffee and it was right under his nose! So he had a cup of coffee with us and left.

When it was time to open up the fire, it was startin' to get dark and we didn't figure there'd be any more game wardens. He opened this deal up and this turkey is cooked and all the dressin' and hell, we had a real nice Thanksgiving turkey and threw all the bones in the fire. They burned up and we stirred 'em up in the ashes good next morning where they weren't showin'. That was one of the few times in my life I ever poached. There was a time or two in my lifetime when it happened.

I went huntin' with John Bessett up on the Indian Reservation there. On the Fort Apache. We hunted there several days and one afternoon we glassed across the canyon and there's three bull elk over there and one is a *big* bull. We got over there and these elk run down through there on a ridge a-ways and I shot at this big bull. I saw his hind leg fly up and it broke his hind leg up high in the hip. The bullet had went on up through and up into his lungs and it got down in this here clump of pines and I think there was a few of these Quakin' Aspens, too. Ol' John, he shot at this big bull and along about that time, ol bull, he just fell dead! I got a shot at the next biggest one and I wounded him. Course, John thinks to this day that he killed that, but when I looked 'im over I seen he had only one bullet hole and that's where that hind leg had flopped up. So I knew I'd killed that one. But I never told John and he don't know it to this day, but if he ever reads it, he will.

Anyway, I started trackin' next morning, trackin' this wounded elk up and this damn bear got it, trailin' it. You'd find where this ol' elk would lay down and then this damn bear'd come up and scare 'im off. I trailed this damn elk for a long ways. I never did ever see the bear but I finally trailed this elk up on a ledge. It was kind of a ledge that run around there and I'm a-trailin' there and goddamn! This ol' elk jumped up, right there in my damn face! I can remember his eyes now, they're in the shadows and they look red! He come my way, he had to to get out a-there and I shot 'im. He fell partly ways over this damn bluff but his horns hung in under a tree and he's just a-hangin' there. So I went back to camp and we got our two mules and we had some kinda pack horse and we went back with 'em. We got up there and I had to chop this ol' elk's head off and it dropped off this bluff. We quartered 'im up and we both had our elk and we come out, you know, successful elk hunters! I was more successful than John was, but he didn't know it!

So that was my first elk hunt where I actually killed an elk.

Elk Hunting in Arizona

One early winter I went on up to Flagstaff on a late elk hunt. I had a neighbor there in Happy Valley who was a pilot – Mahlon Mackenzie. He went up with us, he drove his truck up there and when we got there, we were going to rent an airplane and fly over the area where we had this special bull permit. We flew all over the place and we'd see these elk tracks in the snow and trail 'em up and, Christ, we covered that area pretty well. In a couple of hours, we saw one good bull and a spike or two. It turned real cold so we stayed three nights in Flagstaff; the temperature was gettin' down around 26 below. Then it kinda warmed up so we went out and camped and I know the first morning in camp we had a thermometer and it was 18 below! We didn't have cots in those days; we were roughin' it. We had a tent and a floor in the tent and we just slept in our bedrolls on that floor. I know it was cold enough that my bedroll froze to the floor because that ground was probably frozen a foot thick or so where we pitched the tent on it. We started huntin' and there was about ten inches of snow on the ground and I saw three grown javelina up there in the snow. I watched 'em, it seemed like they're doin' fine and the temperature'd been down to 26 below and 18 below that morning. I'd been hearing about the javelina down south that'd been freezin' to death and, Christ, they had somethin' else wrong with 'em that was killin' 'em. I think they found out later that it was some kind of flu virus. But right there where I saw these javelina there was a township marker, so I wrote down all the number on it. When I got back, I wrote a letter to the Game Department tellin' 'em about this marker, exactly where it was and about these javelina foolin' around in ten inches of snow when it had been 26 below in Flagstaff for three nights in a row and 18 below in camp. I thought it was information the Game Department would be interested in but I never did hear anything from 'em; they probably thought I was lyin' or didn't know what I was doin'. That's one thing I like about the Game Department – you can't tell the bastards anything. And a lot of the stuff they do, they're doin' it with young college boys. They might know how to get around in their hometowns but bring 'em out here in Arizona and turn 'em loose out in the desert and they're pretty helpless. I guess I'd better lay off the Game Department. I hate to criticize 'em because years ago, when they first had a Game Department, the men would run around with a cowboy hat on and Levi's and a denim jacket and most of 'em never even packed a pistol. Now, they've got these guys packin' a can of Mace and a big pistol strapped on and then in uniform. I don't know why they have to have all this hardware on 'em – they're not dealin' with criminals. They're just dealin' with misdemeanors. I've lost interest in the Game Department under these circumstances.

George Parker Lion Hunt

This story is about a lion hunt I made with my good friend, George Parker, who is probably one of the better hunters in the world. He has hunted everywhere, and he has hunted on a limited budget. But has always managed to get in on the good places and makes a real hunt.

He started out tryin' to get a lion when he was a kid, probably, I think he said about 10 years old. One of his uncles was a government hunter, and ever chance he'd get he'd go out with his uncle. But as luck would have it, his uncle never did catch a lion when he was along.

Now, George and I got pretty well acquainted. I'd always heard what a bastard he was and how hard he was to get along with. I never did cultivate him and he never did cultivate me, but we'd meet from time-to-time around at these sportsmen's functions and we'd visit a little bit. I knew George's sister real well, dated her, went out with her a time or two between her marriages. She'd been married several times. George has, too. Finally, George and I got acquainted enough that he told me he wanted a lion real bad. He told me he'd been huntin' or had his eye out for a lion for 52 years. A long time to try to kill a lion. He says, "I figured that sooner or later in my deer huntin' I'd run onto a lion. I had a sheep hunter out one time and we run onto a lion and I let the client shoot it. I've regretted that – I could've killed it myself!" I told 'im "Let's keep our eye open for a good tom lion that's a-runnin' somewhere, and we'll see what we can do about catchin' it."

This went along for several months, and George called me and said, "Ollie, I've found the biggest lion track that I ever saw in my life. And it's right down here in Amado in my front yard." I says, "I'll get things squared away up here, and we'll come down and see what we can do about catching it." "Ollie," he says, "this thing's track is so big it could be a jaguar."

This was in the early '70s. I forget exactly which year it was. I went down, and we made our hunt. On the first day, we made a few circles in there, and cut all the sand washes we could. I wanted to see the track, and we finally found its track in the sand wash on the Solero ranch. I got down and checked it out, and I said, "George it's not a jaguar. It is a lion, and it's one of the bigger lions I've saw." He said, "How can you be so sure that it's not a jaguar?" "Well'" I says, "George, I'm no authority on huntin' jaguars, nor on jaguars' tracks, and I've only saw 'em in the mud in Venezuela. They track different than a mountain lion. They're so much heavier in the front and narrow behind. The front tracks is wider than the hind tracks, and the hind tracks will be along the side of the front tracks. Generally they overstep a lot with their hind feet, and they'll be slightly in front."

"A lion steps with his hind foot in the front track, when he's walkin' along. But I have saw where a lion walkin' down a sand wash will overstep a little too, but generally their hind track is right in their front track. You have to have it in wet sand where you can see that it is off just a little bit. It won't be exactly in it, but awful close." "Well," he says, "I remember that and you're right; it's a lion track." We didn't catch it that trip.

We fooled around and we went down there several times and didn't catch it. One day he called up and he's about half excited! He said, "You know, ol' Clay Howell went down there with Westenburg and they caught a nice tom and they think it's the big one! But it's not; I saw it and it's not the big one! But the word's out and we're gonna hafta get down there and get busy and catch that lion!" Well, it was Easter time and Sunday's comin' up. The day before we'd found where it'd killed a calf. I called the dogs off it 'cause it was in the afternoon and I didn't want the dogs to do too much barkin' around 'cause it was a fresh kill and it was all covered up. We got back there next mornin' and, goddamn, the dogs hit the tracks. I had two young dogs and two older dogs and these two young dogs went one way and the two older dogs went off up the draw. I told George, "I'm gonna whip up ahead of these dogs and find out what track they're on. They may be wrong and those pups may be right!" When I got up there in front I could see the big lion track – my two old dogs're right. Christ, we trailed that thing for a long ways there and got into these Diablo Mountains. They're rough! We got in 'em as far as we could ride and then we had to tie our horses up and follow 'em a-foot. We got way back in those mountains and I'd gotten ahead of George and the dogs were down on a bluff a-bayin'.

I went down there and, Christ, there's a ledge there and there's a hundred foot drop off! I looked around there and, hell; right there in my face is this lion! The dogs were barkin' right in his face! They wasn't over two feet from 'im! The old lion would hiss and slap at 'em and when the lion would hiss, they'd back off. The lion couldn't catch 'em and they was pretty smart old dogs anyway to be caught by a lion his size. I backed off and yelled at George, "They've got this lion caught!" When he got down there I told 'im, "Now, he's right in front of the dogs. If you're not careful, you'll look over 'im, because he's right there close!" Sure enough, George is lookin' over the top of it. And about that time, that lion came outta there! Right over George! That's somethin' you have to be careful of when you're huntin' lions in the bluffs – they might just knock you off! I've been jumped over once or twice myself in these rocks. That lion dove off in the canyon and came out on the other side. George got a runnin' shot at it and it was runnin' full tilt, but he wounded the lion. It went on over the ridge. When we got over there the dogs had it bayed down in the bottom of a canyon and there was a bluff there that dropped off maybe 10 or 12 feet. This lion's in there and both a-the dogs was right up in his face! The lion reached out there and drug Lucky in and bit her on the back of the head! Hell, she dropped. I thought she was dead. I told George, "Goddamn, you're gonna hafta kill that lion or I'm gonna kill it!" He jumped around to where he got a shot at its neck and he killed it. He clipped the skull but it didn't ruin it for the measurements. Anyway, the lion fell on over the bluff and the two dogs went right out over the top. George had his birddog, Bandit, with us and he went off down there and he's a-chewin' on the lion. George, he's pretty proud of ol' Bandit, workin' on that lion! But he didn't have a damn thing to do with catchin' it.

And my Lucky dog, she came to in just a little bit and got down to chew on the lion, but she was deaf after that. The lion must've done somethin' to her eardrums. I kept on huntin' her but she never could honor the other dogs unless she could see 'em. She couldn't hear 'em; she couldn't hear anything! Years later, she got breast cancer and that did her in.

Anyway, it's Easter Sunday by then. We gutted the lion out and cleaned everything we could out of it. We got dry grass and dried all the blood and got it in the shade. We had quite a damn walk back to the horses. After we'd looked at this lion we saw that he'd been in a fight 'cause he had some pretty good fresh cuts on 'im. We were sure it'd happened at the kill and the two younger dogs had trailed the other one. They might a-caught it, but they was back at the truck when we got there. We come on in and, Christ, it's dark by the time we get home. The next mornin' we rounded up a mule and went up and packed the lion out. We waited until it'd dried out maybe 20 hours, everything cleaned out of it you could clean, and it weighed 136 pounds. I figured if we could've weighed it live weight, it probably would've gone 150, maybe 155 pounds. The skull made Boone and Crocket and it's the only lion I ever caught that made Boone and Crocket! It went to a real good guy – George, 'cause he wanted a lion real bad. He's got a world of stuff in the record book – Arizona Record Book, Safari Club Record Book, Boone and Crocket.

Elmer's Deer

This happened way back, before I was married. I was talkin' to my Arkansas brother – he was livin' in Tucson then, in South Tucson. There was a guy out there by the name of Elmer that had half-a-dozen or so cabins on his property that he rented out. My brother said that him and Elmer was goin' deer huntin' the next mornin'. I says, "Hell, I'm not doin' anything tomorrow; how about me just comin' along?" I had a deer tag and deer season had come on and it was about the first or second day of it. I got out there and I met my brother and Elmer and we got in Elmer's pickup. We went out somewhere in the Santa Ritas, I don't remember just where it was, but we got up to where they wanted to go deer huntin'. I had my old .25-.35 saddle gun with me. We got out and I hadn't been to bed yet. I'd been out prowlin' around all night, had about a half a hangover. I got my .25-.35 outta the scabbard and it's all rusty and the lever's not workin' right and they don't have any gun oil. I got Elmer to raise the hood up and I got the dipstick out and oiled my rifle up. Then I see over there, wasn't a quarter-mile, I see a nice spot where the sun was a-hittin' it. Alvin, my brother, and Elmer, they took off deer huntin'. I headed over here to this sunny spot and I laid down and went to sleep! About 8:00 o'clock, I heard shootin'. It woke me up! I look out there about a half a mile away where this shootin' was comin' from and I see a real nice little – maybe better'n average – white tail buck comin'. And I just got a-hold of my rifle and I waited 'til he got up there about 150 yards, comin' right to me, but at maybe 150 yards, he stopped, lookin' back and I killed 'im. So I gutted 'im out and drug 'im over to the car and hid 'im in the brush. I didn't put my tag on 'im.

I found another sunshiny spot and did some more sleepin' and about 2:00 o'clock, they come in. They hadn't saw a deer; they hadn't done anything. I'd gotten a can of water and washed up my hands and everthing. I told 'em, "I got a nice little buck out here that I haven't tagged. I don't want 'im. One of you guys can have 'im if you want 'im." Well, Elmer wanted 'im. He went out there and tagged 'im and put 'im in the back of his pickup. We come back and we got to Elmer's place where my brother was stayin' and, Christ, everbody in the neighborhood had to come and see Elmer's deer. And I still believe for ten years before that and ten years after that, everything dated to the time that Elmer killed the deer!

That was the only deer that'd ever been killed around there and Elmer killed it!

Sam Levitz and George Parker

George Parker and Sam Levitz, they went to Alaska one time to shoot Rocky Mountain Big Horn Sheep. Sam, he did a lot of huntin' and was a good hunter. I hunted 'im; I caught both him and his wife a lion. Anyway, George and Sam was up there and they was huntin' together and they found this huge Rocky Mountain Ram and Sam told George, he says "You're the big sheep hunter. I don't have to have a ram that big; you take him. He'll go good with your collection." So George killed 'im and then he had all four sheep species in his trophy room and all good ones. All over 42 inches – I think they average 44 inches.

Sometime after that George and Sam went down in Mexico huntin' jaguar with Dale Lee. George says, "You know, I was in real good shape then but I had all I could do to keep up with Dale down there in those swamps. He'd start out leadin' two or three hounds and they was wantin' to stop and pee or take a crap and he just drug 'em along! I was still havin' problems a-stayin' up with 'im!" This particular day they caught a really nice jaguar in there and George wanted that jaguar in the worst way. But with that previous hunt with Sam in his mind, he says to Sam, "You let me shoot the big ram, so you shoot the first jaguar." Sam killed the jaguar and they didn't get another one!

I hunted jaguar with George several times after that and we never got one. There's two things George never done: he never killed a jaguar and he never shot a black!

The Abe Dogs

After I got my cowdog, Ike, I bought Abe. I bought him from a guy, I forget his name, but he'd worked for Dale Lee down in Mexico. He'd gotten a bitch and she'd had pups and he was sellin' them pups for $35 apiece. I bought this hound pup, hell, he was only about six weeks old. This was before I quit construction. I hauled 'im around a lot in the car; I'd tie 'im up under the pickup in the daytime when I was out on the job. He got to where he liked to ride; he was a nice dog. Bein' outta Dale Lee's blood line, I knew he probably had potential, so I decided I was gonna make a lion dog out of 'im. Hell, I didn't know anything about lion huntin' – don't know a whole lot more now – anyway, I figured the way I'd have to train 'im. I'd hafta trap a lion, then turn the lion loose and let this cowdog and this hound pup (by that time he's a year old or so) trail it. By god, I set me out some traps. I wasn't havin' any luck a-catchin' one. God, I caught coyotes, I caught fox, I caught a blue jay and I caught a bobcat.

This bobcat is quite a story. A friend of mine that worked with me there in Tucson – a dirt man, he put in streets and curbs and all that sorta stuff – he went along with me the day I caught the bobcat. This bobcat's layin' back under some brush, hung up on this four-foot trap chain. He started crawlin' in there and I says, "You'd better be goddamn careful about crawlin' in there; that damn bobcat is liable to jump on you!" Hell, he didn't believe that! 'Bout that time, that ol' cat come out and "Wah!" right in his damn face! Damn, if he'd a-been six inches closer, he'd a-clawed 'im up! Boy, the worst cuss word he could have was "Shit a goddamn!" and he said it and was backin' outta there! And he got his pistol out and killed that bobcat!

Abe got some kind of a lung disease and he's only, hell, he's not but a little over three years old! I took 'im to my vet and he even got the University to help him and they run a lotta tests on 'im and it was some kind of a lung disease, I guess like Valley Fever. He kept a-gettin' worse and worse. I'd let 'im come on the house and lay there in the house – it was cool. I got back there from work one evening and he wants outside; the dog, he just wanted out. So I let 'im out and he just walked right over to the dog pen and visited there with the other couple a-hounds I had and Ike. Then he come back, got in the house and laid down and died! I don't know whether he went just out to see those dogs before he died, but I think he knew he was dyin'. So that was the end of Abe I.

That was the only two good dogs I had. I started 'round tryin' to buy a dog from all the lion hunters and no one would sell me a dog. Old, what was the name of this guy in Safford – Sewell Goodwin?, No, Sewell's friend, Ted Ferguson. He had two old dogs, they was good dogs, and he said he'd sell me one of 'em for $750. I told 'im, "I'll just take both of 'em!" That was fine; this was all on the phone. I went over to pick up my dogs and he said his wife wouldn't let 'im sell 'em! So I missed out on that.

Then I got Abe II. John Myrmo had this litter a-pups, and there's a guy up in the Superstition Mountains – a pretty good lion hunter – that give him a dog, a female. He had 'er out coon huntin' and he caught several bobcats with her! Then she had pups. He'd bred her to a black and tan hound. He had a half a dozen of these here pups out in that pen and he wanted to give me one of 'em. I went out there and I looked these pups over and hell, they all looked alike to me. But this one little ol' dog, he come up there, he just sit down there beside me and looked up at me and I told John, "Hell, I think this damn dog's picked me out! I'll take him!" So he tied a string around his neck so we'd know 'im when he was weaned. That's Abe II! He made a hell of a dog! I think he was one a-the best dogs I ever owned.

I caught several bear with Abe II. He was scared to death of a bear. Boy, when he'd hit a bear track he'd just *stop* and the ol' hair'd come up on his back; then he'd take the track. This Don Carr, he had a ol' worthless hound that he'd brought outta Arkansas and the bastard was trashy! But he would run a bear. I caught with Carr's dog, but I had to lead the bastard, hell, I couldn't keep 'im offa deer – they didn't have shock collars in those days. When ol' Abe'd start a bear track I'd turn him loose and hell, I caught at least four damn bear with 'im. I'd caught quite a few lion with this Abe II and huntin' up in the Catalinas he got his damn hind foot stepped on by a horse and it mangled up one of his toes – it was in terrible shape! I took 'im to the vet and the vet cut the toe off! Christ, he done fine. They went along and he got somethin' in one of his front toes and Christ, he was tough! I caught two, three lions with him just packin' that one front foot! He was a nice dog! After a couple a-months, the vet looked at that toe and says, "Hell, the only thing I know to do is just cut it off!" He already got one toe cut off and he's doin' alright, so I left the dog there with him. I still remember that damn hound, he's just lookin' at me and he didn't wanna stay there – he wanted to come home with me. I left 'im there and they took his toe off and sometime later he died! He didn't ever come outta the damn stuff when they put 'im to sleep. So I lost him!

Then the third Abe dog was a little spotted dog. He was just a mediocre hound. He never was a real good dog. But he was a good strike dog, you know, he was a little more'n a pack dog. And I don't remember what happened to him, but I lost him.

Then I got Abe IV. Christ, he was a real, real good dog! Layne knows him; he's hunted him; he's caught lion with him. If there's ever a damn strike dog, that was him! Christ, he'd just take off! But he'd never be more'n a quarter of a mile from you. When he hit a track – I don't know how he knew it or anything – but anyway, generally, ever time he's on the right end of it! The first lion he caught was three days before he was nine months old. We're huntin' in the Baboquivaries; they hit a track and they trailed it off down past some bluffs and brush and trees and outta the end of it I saw somethin' run through there. I thought it might a-been a lion but the hunter I had says, "No, I saw it. It was a deer." Anyway, Abe IV, he took that track and up and down and back up we went! The other dogs fell in behind 'im and when we went up on top, he was the second dog back. One a-the good lion dogs was ahead of 'im. They hit a trail and they trailed down there for, oh, three or four hundred yards. And

Abe, he took off down a little draw there. These other hounds started slowin' down; they was on an old track; they'd run over it. We hear Abe a-barkin' down there; Christ, he's a-raisin' hell and this client I had says, "What's he barkin' about?" I said, Aw, hell, he's bad about barkin' at cows; he's probably got 'im a cow down there!" Hell, come to find out, he's got a damn lion caught on a bluff! I told this guy, "Now, you stay right here and I'll go gather up these other dogs and bring 'em back." I'm comin' back and when I cross this draw, hell, my dogs just run! Down the draw they went! By this time, this damn dude, he'd climbed up on these rocks and he took three shots with his pistol at this lion and the lion jumped off and got away! By then, by the time I found what he done I could hear these dogs barkin' treed. We went down there and they got this two and a half, three year-old tom treed in one a-the oaks in the canyon! Up just about 20 foot. He had to kill it with his pistol, so he got a rest there with his pistol and shot and the lion come down! Christ, there's a ruckus takin' place then! Finally, the lion died and I gutted it out and hell, the dogs had killed his lion! The bullet went up under his shoulder and right down under his shoulder blade and out. That's all. It never had got into where the lion lived. The dogs had killed it! But I never told this guy the dogs killed his lion!

By that time those dogs was hot and I went up there and put 'em on this track and hell, they was covered with lion piss and everthing else – blood. They couldn't trail it. Well, that was all right with me 'cause hell, I had other clients. I was huntin' that country later on and caught her for someone else.

Abe IV caught 64 lions before he died. He got run over. Someone deliberately run over 'im and killed 'im! They're comin' up in the right side of the road and he's on the left and they swerved in and hit 'im and knocked the dog about 30, 40 feet. I could see the blood where he hit 'im and there's blood up along where he was a-layin'. Whoever killed 'im did it deliberately! I thought a-lotta that dog. He was a hell of a dog. Layne didn't think we'd ever catch another lion without 'im! That dog was on the bottom of the canyons; he was on the top of the ridges; he was always lookin' for lions! He'd hit a track, you know, and he'd be away from the other dogs and hell, he'd invariably be right!

That's been my experience with dogs. When they're all together and they hit a track, and they all just take off the way they're goin'. And if that's the way the lion is goin', they're on the right end. Damn, if the lion's comin' the other way, they're runnin' the backtrack. And in this country where I hunt, it's hard to see a damn track! Maybe you'll see a scratch and you'll know they're right or wrong. But a female lion – there's no way you could tell which way they're goin'.

But that was the end of my Abe dogs.

Donated Lion Hunt

This is a hunt I started several years ago. Every year I donate a three-day lion hunt to the Safari Club to be auctioned off at their fund-raiser. I'd kind a-wanted Rena Rias to buy this hunt and I talked to Chuck Westenburg and told 'im if any a-the local people'd buy the hunt, I'd add a couple a-days to it and give 'em a better chance. And I was sure he'd buy the hunt for her, or I wouldn't a-offered to give a couple more days.

It turned out that Rena bought the hunt herself. Paid a good price for it. And come time for me to take 'er out on the hunt, I'm a little apprehensive. She's a real lady, and I'm wonderin' if she's able to make a lion hunt, in rough country and bad country that you gotta go through. Chuck told me not to worry. "She's tough." Well, I found out that she *is* tough, physically and mentally. And a good client! If all my client's were like her, I'd a-been a professional guide. With people like her, it's a pleasure to hunt.

We went out to my old ranch, and we hunted for five days out there. We trailed several lions. And caught a fox. That was a disappointment to me 'cause I wasn't sure what they'd treed. But when we got there, it was a fox. Rena never complained. A lotta clients would a-really give me a hard time 'bout lion dogs catchin' a fox. But, anyway, we made the hunt, and a good hunt. But was unsuccessful. And I told 'er "Don't give up. I'll take you out again. Some rancher will report a kill." Or that somethin' would come up that I'd need someone, and I'd call 'er. She says, "Okay, because I really want a lion." And she's deservin' of a real big lion, and a good lion.

Things went along for several months, and Layne Brandt, a friend of mine, has some hounds of his own, and he borrows one or two of mine once in a while. He wanted to take off this Sunday, and go up in the Santa Ritas, and make a little hunt. There're quite a few lion in there, and I know there's a good possibility we might catch one. So I called Rena and told her that Layne and I was goin' huntin' there the next day, on a Sunday, and if she wanted to come along to meet me at the Green Valley Post Office at 6:30 a.m., and we'd go on over to Layne's and leave out from there.

Well, I got there at 6:00 o'clock, and she's already waitin' for me. She's ready to go. It'd snowed some the night before, and we go up into Box Canyon, near the top of it. We parked up there, and turned the dogs loose. We started across country, and we'd hunted, I'd guess a couple a-hours, and the dogs hit a track. They went off in West Sawmill Canyon, and went clear down in the bottom of it. We couldn't get off in there so we come back down the trail about a mile and a half, and rode out where we could hear off in the canyon where the dogs went. We couldn't hear anything, but back to the south of us, about on the same level, and the wind had come up, and we could hear some dogs barkin'. They just stayed in the same place. I told Layne and Rena, "Hell, those dogs aren't movin'." So we went back to trailin' 'em. We followed the trail back for about three-quarters of a mile, and quit the trail. We climbed up in the saddle, and about a quarter of a mile from us, Blackie, Sport, and Abe got this lion treed. There was no way you could get in there on horseback. Too rough.

We tied our horses up, Rena got her gun, and we started off down in there. It was kinda treacherous goin'. There wasn't any big bluffs or anythin' to fall off of but you could slide off one ten foot high and get yourself skinned up pretty bad if you're not careful. I broke off a pole, a "Moses Stick," to help me along. Rena was usin' her rifle. Layne, he's a-makin' it on his own. I'm in the lead. We get down in there and the tree this lion's in is a big old juniper, and it's about half-dead. The lion's on the far side of the juniper. We can't see 'im from the uphill side. So we circled around and we could see in the side, about 30 yards there, we get up closer and I could see the lion's head. I showed it to Rena, and she had to shoot off-hand. I get my "Moses Stick" out there, and she rested her rifle on that. And I'm holdin' it, too. 'Bout that time, ol' lion kind a-raised his head up a little bit and exposed his neck. She shot immediately. She's a good shot. I heard the lion hit the ground, hard. And down the hill the dogs go! The snow's slick, and these dogs hit that lion and started slidin' down the mountain. They're tuggin' on it, and it's just goin' down the mountain!

Rena says, "It's gettin' away!" "No," I says "it's dead. You could tell by the way it hit the ground. It's just slidin' in the snow." The dogs was draggin' at it, and finally it lodged against some brush. And we went down there, and it's a huge old tom. Big, and I would a-loved to a-weighed it. I know it weighed over 140. Layne and I had to skin it out. Christ, there was no way a-packin' it out. No way to get a horse in there. So we was gonna hang it up.

The snow was meltin' and the ground underneath was frozen. We couldn't stand up enough to hang this lion up where we wanted to. We slid it off to a spot in a kind of a draw, and there's a stump there. We get this lion behind the stump, and skinned it out there. It took us about 45 minutes to an hour to skin it. Layne packed the skin out. I started packin' Rena's rifle out. She just walked off and left us. She started out, and we were rimmin' around. Layne's packin' this lion hide, and it's tough goin' for 'im. I was havin' a lotta trouble with my legs. It was really tough on me. We got about halfway out when Rena come back and took the gun.

We climbed on out to our horses. I still had some dogs down in Sawmill Canyon. We could hear 'em after we shot this lion. Blackie pulled out and went down to 'em.

Layne took the lion hide and went back to the truck. And we was goin' down in Sawmill Canyon and gather up those dogs. There's a road that comes up it and goes out and hits the main road, and Layne would come by and pick us up. We got down to the dogs, and they're on another lion track down there! We rounded 'em up and pulled 'em off of it. By the time we get out to the road, it's startin' to get dark, and we went up maybe a mile. Rena's feet got cold, she got off the horse and walked – but she never whimpered about it. I've had some of these men hunters who've hunted all over the world and call theirselves international hunters. If their feet would a-been freezin', they would a-wanted me to build a fire and I don't know what else. Or maybe got a helicopter to airlift 'em out. But not this little gal. Just toughed it right on out.

We met Layne, loaded up our horses and the dogs, and come on in. This was one of my more enjoyable hunts. This lion couldn't a-gone to a better person than Rena.

Newspaper Hunting Report

In 1978, a *Tucson Daily Citizen* newspaper staff writer for hunting and fishing decided to write an article about Ollie for the weekend edition. He made several attempts to contact Ollie, who wasn't very keen on the idea at first, but the man finally showed up unannounced at the ranch one day. At that point, Ollie agreed to be interviewed. He says now that perhaps he'd had a few drinks before the interview. The following is the article as it appeared in the *Tucson Daily Citizen* on Saturday, February 24, 1979:

"Lowest in the ranks are the mealy-mouthed types, the Casper Milquetoasts. Then you come to the ones who have enough guts to open their mouths once in awhile to do more than let food in. Then you get to the ones who aren't afraid to stir up a little controversy. Then you come to the kind of people who are blunt, upfront, candid, outspoken.

Somewhere far beyond that point you'll come to Ollie Barney.

Barney is 60, white-haired, crusty, profane and, well, bulky. At 6' 2" and 230 pounds, he has the beer belly of a pro football addict. ("I was born with a curvature of the spine. It just protruded out a little bit.") But he's not. He's a lion addict. "It's just like dope," he says, "The withdrawal symptoms would kill me if they were gone. I'd just pine away and die."

He is also, say hunters around here, one of the best, if not the best, of all the lion guides in the state. He thinks like a mountain lion, says one hunter. Questioning Barney's knowledge of lions, says another, "is like asking Jesus Christ if he knows anything about the Bible."

Beer belly or no, Barney is capable, they say, of walking the legs off anyone in rugged, cross-country mountain hiking. And he is also, his wife Beryl says, the most honest person she has ever known. "I met him after I moved here from Wichita (in the early 1950's)," she says. "Everyone I knew back there was so phony. There isn't anything phony about Ollie."

"Phony" is definitely not the word you'd use to describe someone who, after his Tucson house had been burglarized repeatedly, put up a sign that said, "Anyone who gets caught robbing this house will be killed immediately. I'm willing to take the consequences. Are you?"

Barney, who now lives in near-isolation with his wife in a ranch in the Happy Valley area east of the Rincon Mountains, says he never got any takers on his offer. "I didn't have to shoot 'em, but I damn sure would have." You don't doubt it. He adds, "The only person who ever got excited (about the sign) was my insurance agent. God, it got to him. He thought it would run my liability up. But he's an old fuddy-duddy. I don't see his reasoning at all. If they got me for premeditated murder, it wouldn't have been any skin off his butt. I guess it's because I would have stopped paying him premiums."

Barney says he has taken between 95 and 100 lions since 1964 and claims to have, depending on how you look at it, a 50 or a 75-80 percent success rate. Of all lion tracks he starts following, he says, his dogs catch the lion 50 percent of the time. But he promises his clients, who pay him $750 for eight days of hunting, because if at first Ollie doesn't succeed, he'll try, try again.

"He has dedication, stick-to-itveness. He hunts to succeed. If you can stay up with him, keep your mental, physical pace up to his, you will get one (a lion)," says local hunter Jim Englemann.

If you want to go hunting with Barney, stand in line. He claims to have a waiting list of 10-15 people and a backlog of 2-2 ½ years. If he thinks the wait will be too long, he just won't take any more names. He gets letters from people who want to hunt lions from as far away as Wyoming, New York, Connecticut, Nebraska and Washington. Hunters say that from seeing a set of tracks, Barney can tell if a lion is male or female, large or small, young or old. One hunter recalls Barney taking nine lions in a section of the Catalinas, where not only had no lions been seen before, but where local ranchers had never even complained of losing calves.

"I don't know a lot about lions," Barney grins mischievously. "Ahh, I know a little bit about these things. It takes a momma lion and a poppa lion to make a baby lion. The gestation period is 92 or 93 days. I know they eat deer, cattle, javelina and colts, not rabbits and squirrels like the preservationists think. I know they don't prey of weak infirm animals that are gonna die. They're adult lions. They eat adult deer."

Seated underneath the heads of buffalo and antelope he shot in Angola, Barney sips a bourbon and Coke and credits his success to persistence and good dogs. "They'll make you or break you, these dogs...I've heard that every man's entitled to one good woman, a couple of good horses and a couple of good dogs in his lifetime. I've had all of 'em. I don't have one now (a good dog) but I've got some that will kill a lion."

He values the four dogs he keeps in cages outside his adobe ranch house at $1,000 apiece, based on the amount of dog food they eat and the time it takes to train them. Three or four years of twice-a-week sessions, some 6 hours long, some 18 hours, he says, are needed to teach dogs what to hunt and what not to hunt. He says he uses about 5 of every 10 dogs he trains, although only one of them is good.

Dogs that chase after sheep or javalina or deer, he says, "you give them to your friends that want a pet." If he can't find an owner for a dog, he says, he shoots it. "I can't let them starve to death. I've never let one starve to death."

How many have you shot?

"That would be giving away a trade secret. If I tell you how many I'd shot, I'd have the humane society and all the preservationists after me. But I'll say that I've got a few dogs who never made it home in every mountain range around here."

Preservationists are among his least favorite people.

"All these goddam Defenders of Wildlife don't know what in the hell they're talking about. I'd give 'em a swift kick in the (male sex organ). They're forcing their goddam stupidity on a lot more intelligent people...these goddam environmentalists, the bastards will lie to you. The masses of people as far as wildlife are concerned are stupid. They can't separate fact from B.S."

174

He tells of a hunting trip into the Catalinas in which he ran into a hiker who asked him what he and his party were doing horseback.

"Hunting mountain lions," says Barney.

"I thought lions were extinct in the Catalinas," says the hiker.

Says Barney, "I took her over to my horse, where there was a lion we'd shot and I said, 'what do you think this is? This is a lion.'"

He grins.

"The next day I went up and I caught another one, but I let it go." Offhand glance. "I had a few dogs who needed some exercise."

He's not particularly fond of the U.S. Forest Service either, because they cut down the number of cattle he could have run on his land. Or the National Park Service, because they allowed timber and duff to build up in the high country to prevent forest fires. Barney, who believes some of the duff should be burned off, says deer, unable to get to their food, have fled into the low country. Lions, who feed on deer, have followed, spread out over more acreage and are harder to catch, he says, even though there are more than there were when they were bountied.

Or for Mountain Bell, which refuses to build a phone line to his house, located 18 miles in from Interstate 10 on Mescal Road, because it is too far away from civilization.

But he does like mountain lions. "Better than people, I really do. They've got the innate intelligence that's been bred out of most people."

He's lost about a dozen calves to lions over the years, but unlike many ranchers he doesn't get disturbed about it. "I'm still ahead of them," he chuckles, "I've eaten more goddam lions than they've been eating calves."

"The only damn predators I can't cope with are the damn forest rangers. I can kill a lion, but I can never get a permit to shoot a forest ranger or a backpacker. My father (who raised Ollie on a ranch in Happy Valley) would have shot one of them hippies on the trail. I can't do that. Well, my conscience wouldn't permit me."

Dr. Stephenson

I got a bad vertebra; it's a problem I've had I guess all of my life. I get to doin' some hard manual labor and sometimes it causes the muscles in my back on the left side to spasm and draw up. Christ, there's been times when they hit me and I hafta have people take me home and put me to bed. To get up to go to the bathroom, I'd just hafta feel my way around the wall. This Dr. Stephenson from Yakima, Washington, was a real noted bone specialist and surgeon up in the Northwest. Supposed to have been the best one up there. He hunted with me for javelina; made 13 hunts with me. He told me, "If you'll come up to Yakima this summer, I'll operate on your back and straighten it out."

Beryl and I went up there; we went up on Highway 1. I guess this was when the hippies was migratin' south. Christ, they was in all these wine samplin' joints and they was layin' along side the road – you had to be careful how you pulled off or you'd run over one of 'em. One or two of 'em had a shotgun on their cycles and several of 'em I saw was packin' about an 18-inch chain. I didn't argue with any of 'em or start a dispute. This had to be in the 1980's sometime.

We got up there and this ol' Doc Stephenson was a rough talkin' ol' guy. He took me down one morning to get X-rays. He said, "I'm gonna take you over here to a Filipino X-ray technician. He's the best in the area." We went in there and saw him. Doc told him, "Take an X-ray of his lower back. I want every picture you can take." Then he said, "And I don't want a damn bill for it, either!" Doc took those X-rays and Christ, I got a stack of them must be half an inch thick, a bunch of 'em. Anyway he took 'em back into a little office, a cubbyhole of some kind, and was in there for a long time; Christ, it seemed like an hour! When he came back he said, "Ollie, I can't help you! And don't let anyone else ever cut on your back! Don't let 'em take any X-rays 'cause I'm gonna give you these and you got ever damn X-ray they can take!" Then he told me, "You shouldn't have ever been in the Army! You're 4F! You've got a vertebra there that's deformed. Some time or other, you cracked that vertebra – the crack shows up in the X-ray. A piece of shrapnel has knocked off a piece of it. You're just gonna have to learn to live with it!"

And then he wanted to know how I'd cracked that bone. I told him about the time I was helpin' Mac MacKenzie, Malcolm's dad, roundup and a critter ran off. I roped it and the damn thing got on the fight and turned around and charged my horse! The rope was tied solid and somehow my horse got over the rope and got to pitchin'. There was finally a little slack in the rope where it went across my leg and he threw me off! I landed on my back on a rock about the size of my hat and I know that's when it happened.

After the X-rays, he took us around the area and looked the place over. He took us up to a fruit stand one day to get some fresh fruit. There was a lady there who was a complete stranger to him and she had bought a couple of lugs of peaches. She'd opened her trunk and was gettin' ready to load 'em and he said, "Lady! I'm not gonna stand here with my thumb in my ass and let you strain your ovaries loadin' them peaches!" She let 'im! She didn't seem to get upset about it; she let 'im load the peaches! That was the way he talked!

He had several arguments at the breakfast table with this new wife he had. One morning they was arguin' about somethin' and she said, "Damn you Doc! If you had any nerve, you'd divorce me!" He told her, "Goddamn you woman! If I had any nerve, I'd kill you!"

Another morning, they got in an argument and Doc said, "Woman, what the hell have you got to bitch about? The allowance I'm givin' you and the erections I'm gettin' don't give you a goddamn thing to complain about!"

The first year he brought her to Arizona was the third time I'd hunted 'im. We were huntin' for javelina again and saw some in the bottom of a canyon. They was rootin' around pickin' up these winter acorns. He had her lookin' at these javelina through the scope. She's got the rifle up there and he said, "Are you sure you got those crosshairs right on the shoulder?" She said, "Yes, Doc, I have." He kept on and I see that the rifle was off safety and he got his finger down on the trigger and his thumb on the back trigger guard. He asked once more, "You absolutely positive the crosshairs're right?" She said, "Doc – they're right!" So he touched it off! Goddamn, it killed the javelina deader'n hell and the scope came back and hit her in the eye! Didn't draw blood but it hurt her and she gave him a good cussin'. I told my local game warden about it and, goddamn, he was gonna write me a citation for lettin' someone else kill Doc's javelina! I said, "Bob, I wish you'd take me to court on this! Goddamn it, when I tell my story they're gonna laugh you outta court! There's nothing, nothing in those regulations anywhere that say you can't let someone hold your rifle and aim it as long as you're pullin' the trigger! The guy that pulls the trigger is the one who kills the pig and Doc definitely pulled the trigger!" Well, he digested that a little bit and forgot about givin' me a citation.

The first time I took ol' Doc Stephenson huntin' was after he wrote me a letter. He said he'd heard I was a good javelina guide and that he'd been down huntin' outta Phoenix, I think three times, and never got a javelina. He really wanted a javelina and asked if I could absolutely guarantee him a javelina. And what would it cost. I told him I normally charge $200 for a three-day hunt. But if you want an absolutely guaranteed hunt, it'd be $300. When he wrote back he said he was takin' the guaranteed hunt. I picked 'im up in Tucson and took 'im out to the ranch. We weren't 20 miles down the goddamn I-10 towards Benson and he said, "Now, all

bullshittin' aside, what are my chances of gettin' a javelina?"
I said, "You're probably gonna kill one tomorrow morning."
He said, "Well, if it's that easy, why am I payin' $300 instead
of $200?" I said, "It's because you wanted it guaranteed!
Hell, I gotta charge somethin' for this guarantee!"

So we went out. It was before 9:00 o'clock and I spotted a
bunch of javelina. We tied up our horses and eased down
there and heard a couple of these boars fightin' down outta
sight! And here come a javelina sow by and, boy, he started
to shoot her. I pushed his rifle down and said, "No, don't
shoot that one. That's not the one. There's two boars fightin'
down there and we're gonna ease down there and shoot the
biggest one!" "Aw," he said, "that one's good enough for
me!" I told him, "Nope, you're not shootin' it!" So we eased
down there and sure enough, these two boars were fightin',
they'd run together and slash at one another and then they'd
back off. I saw which was the biggest and I told Doc to take
the one on the right. He shot and it was dead and hell, it's
not 9:30 yet! I took 'im back to the ranch and back to town.
Somewhere, Doc had met this Jimmy Wilson and he called
'im up and said, "This goddamn Ollie Barney is crazy! We
got out there and saw a good javelina and he won't let me
shoot it!" Jimmy got a little excited and asked, "Well,
goddamn, what'd he do?" Doc said, "Well, he wouldn't let
me shoot 'im; he said there's a better one down in the brush.
This one is a perfectly good pig and he won't let me shoot it!
But he took me down where there were a couple of boars
fightin' and he let me shoot the best one!"

In all, I think Doc hunted with me 12 or 13 times. I hunted
him for deer once and took him out for mountain lion once.
That lion hunt was on a windy day down on the Bear Valley
Ranch. There was a real nice tom that had a kill in there
somewhere. The dogs would trail it until they got up into the
wind and then they'd lose the track. His wife was along and
she's a-bitchin' all the way. The next morning I told ol' Doc,
"Goddamn it, if you really want to kill a lion, leave that
goddamn woman of yours home, in camp!" And we went
down to the horses and we're saddlin' up and the wind is
blowin' so bad then that he'd have to hold the blankets in

place while I put the saddle on. We're all saddled up about ready to go and here she come: where was her horse? "Well," Doc told her, "Ollie told me if I wanted to kill a lion to leave you in camp!" So we took off. We hit a track 'cause the tom had a kill in there some place. Those dogs ran that lion through some terrible bluffs and finally got it out on a ledge. Christ, clear to the bottom, it's probably at least 1000 feet, but there's kind of a ledge that stuck out about half way. We eased up there and I told Doc, "Now, goddamn it, if that damn lion comes back don't try to shoot 'im. You might kill a dog or fall off this damn bluff! You just drop down on the ground. We went a little further and he shot the damn lion and Christ, over it went! End over end! It hit that ledge below us and bounced off and went down into some oaks, outta sight. Doc said, "God, Ollie. Will we be able to find that lion?" I said, "Oh, we'll be able to find it." So we went down there and Christ, we had about a four foot crack that we had to hop over. I could do it then and he was in good shape and we got over and got his lion. We grabbed it by its front feet and back feet and threw it across the crack and got back to the horses. When we got back to camp his wife was still a little upset. "Well," he said to her, "it's just like Ollie told me: if we wanted to kill a lion, we'd have to leave you in camp!"

The deer hunt was another good story. He came out that year with his new wife, they'd been married a couple of years by then, and he had a nephew and his wife with them. The first deer we saw was a nice little three-point buck grazing on a bush. It was about 200 yards away and there was all the time in the world to shoot the thing, but it was too far. So this nephew started sneakin' up on it but the women were talkin' and Doc was arguin' with 'em and the deer finally run off! It picked up another little buck that was nearby and they ran through a saddle goin' over into the next ranch. I got up to the saddle and I told Doc and his wife to get off there and go over to the other ranch. There were quite a few hunters in there and I knew there'd be some shootin' takin' place. Those deer would probably come right back through this same saddle. So I told them to stay there 'til I got back. Damn, I got off up the way from there and when I looked back, here was Doc and his wife walkin' away! It's not two minutes after that, here come those two little bucks, hell, not 50 yards from where I told them to stay! I saw they'd quit and he went off on his own, so I went on and hunted this nephew. I come back and met Doc and, boy, he was all excited! He'd lost his wife! He couldn't find her! Christ, was he excited! I told him, "It's not far down to your horse. Let's get you back on your horse and we'll look around and find her." I started glassin' off down in this canyon to see if she's walkin' down there and I saw her. She's under an oak tree. She'd fell down and got her butt full of cactus and she's leaning over with her butt right up in my face, you know, with binoculars! It's pretty obvious that she's pickin' out these thorns. I handed the binoculars to Doc and said, "Look under that tree and see if that's not Elaine." He jerked down those glasses and said, "By God, that's her! I recognize her!" We went back to the ranch and at supper that night, he's got to tell everybody about her pickin' out cactus thorns and he recognized her. She got after 'im again over that!

Doc Stephenson came back every year for those 12 or 13 years. He killed about five javelinas then he quit shootin' 'em. They'd always bring two or three old people with 'em. Of course, they'd shoot javelina. This one time he said he had another doctor that wanted to hunt lion and javelina. I told him to send that doctor down a week or eight days ahead of time and I'd take 'im lion huntin'. But the doctor was late; he called me from somewhere in California and told me he thought he could be at my place the next evening. And Christ, he's only got about four days to hunt. I decided I had to take him to the ranch because we didn't have time to go where I wanted to. The first morning we were up above the ranch house maybe three or four miles in a big ol' canyon called Deer Creek. There's a flat there and ol' Blue, my top dog, hit a track and about the time he hit it, I could see it and he was on the back track. I started squallin' at 'im and got 'im stopped and turned around. This lion went up on the Rincon Mountain and the way the dogs went was through some terrible rough country. It was brushy, too. One of the dogs came back but we kept ridin' up and listenin' and the wind was blowin' a little bit – it was hard to hear. I made a big circle around 'cause I knew if I crossed the track the hound that was with me would pick the track up. I came around to a deep canyon and Christ, it wasn't 200 yards down there I could hear 'em a-barkin'. They had the lion up in a Ponderosa Pine. His head and most of his front shoulders was behind the trunk. I'd told the doc to shoot at the shoulder and he was lookin' through the scope and couldn't see the shoulders. So I told him to shoot in the rib cage. He did that and the lion fell out of the tree and run down aways and climbed up in another tree. "Goddamn," he said, "I missed 'im!" I said, "No! You killed 'im. Didn't you hear 'im when he fell out? The dogs is just chewin' on 'im down there." When we got down there, it was a good trophy tom, made the book, by the way.

One thing about this doctor that surprised me was that he kept up with me all the way. He was outside foolin' around and I asked his wife, "Where did your husband learn to ride? Hell, he's an accomplished rider!" "Oh," she said, "he plays polo." That sure accounted for his keepin' up with me!

Then we had several days so we were just messin' around, scoutin' for javelinas. Doc Stephenson and the rest got there and the doc was tellin' 'im about gettin' his lion. Doc said to him, "I told you you didn't need any eight days! Ollie gets 'em a lot quicker'n that! Got mine in two days!"

Ol' Doc Stephenson, he could get to be kind of a problem sometimes. You was always glad to see 'im and gladder to see 'im leave!

George Brown Lion Hunt

Tim Haas had made a deal with George Brown; George Brown had a couple of bear traps and Tim is collectin' 'em. So he traded Tim these two bear traps for a lion hunt. I went over there and hunted with 'em. They hunted one day and I went over the second day. Ol' Tim, he teamed up with George and I teamed up with Klump and we went out in different areas. They was close enough that you could make contact with radio. The first thing that happened with Klump and I was a big bobcat run across the road just as it was gettin' fair daylight. Boy, I'll tell you; off the road he went and turned the hounds loose! The hounds leave out on this bobcat and we get saddled up and they run this bobcat up in a crack. Johnny had a female dog there; he had three dogs and I had three dogs and this female got up there in that hole and the bobcat cut her up real bad! Ol' Klump got in there and got her by a hind leg and drug her out and shot the cat with his pistol. We took it back and threw it in the back of the truck. This female, she's bleedin' real bad. Ol' Klump, he fastened her up in the trailer and said, "I don't think we oughta hunt her, as much blood as she's lost!"

Later, we're a mile away from the truck and he turns to me and says, "These three dogs you got, what kind of dogs are they?" I said, "Hell, they'll catch a lion once in awhile. They're all right." He says, "Well, I'm glad to hear that 'cause that bitch I brought, she was my main lion dog. These other two dogs – one of 'em is a good bear dog but he's not all that good on lion. And that junk dog, he's not much good for anything." He wasn't a guy that would brag on his dogs.

So we climbed up on this damn mountain and there's about three or four inches of snow on the ground. The ground's froze underneath the snow. I see a blue tick hound up in the brush comin' down. "Klump." I says, "I didn't think we was that close to Tim and George." He said, "We're not. I don't know that dog." And we got up there in a little saddle and here's a guy on foot, he's got two or three more dogs and he's a-stompin' around in the snow. Course, our five dogs then, they go up there and they're all smellin' one another and a-pissin' on bushes. This guy says to Klump, "There's a fresh lion track in the snow comin' through here. I'm havin' trouble gettin' my dogs to take it!" And Klump asks, "Well, you don't mind if we help you a little bit?" He says, "Oh no, I'd be tickled to death to have you help." Klump says, "Well, if we catch it, we got a client that will have to shoot the lion." The guy says, "That's all right with me."

So Klump, he walks off up there about 100 yards and finds a track and whistles at his two dogs and they run up there. They stick their noses down in the snow and they start whimperin'. On the strength of that, my dogs got up there. I had a little red dog with me, it belonged to Layne and I, and it was a hell of a good lion dog but he was a little trashy, too. They just left there, those five dogs, three of mine and the two Klump had, hell, they just left on that track! And we're on the wrong side of a fence there so we ride up on top of a ridge there where we could get across the fence. We got across the fence and we could see these damn hounds down there about a half a mile and Christ, they're goin' out on a hot track and they're movin'! This little red dog's in front and ol' Klump turns to me and says, "Ollie, what kind of a hound is that red dog that's in front?" And all six of this guy's dogs is a-millin' around there with us – they didn't go! This guy's upwind there where he couldn't hear me and I said, "He's a hell of a lot better than this shit we got around here with us!" And ol' Klump says, "That's for damn sure!" We go off down the ridge there and Christ, it's steep and rocky and this snow and my mule didn't wanna keep up. He's ridin' this bronc mule and Christ, he just went off in there at a goddamn fast lope! And I got off and walked and led my mule down through this outfit and this damn frozen ground under that snow and I'm havin' trouble negotiatin'. I got through the bad place and got back on my mule and get down there on a little knoll and Klump's sittin' there on his bronc mule. He says, "Those dogs is treed down there." I said, "I can hear 'em!" They was about a half a mile off down there, right down in the bottom there. It turned out it was treed in a little hackberry tree, the last damn tree there was 'til they hit the desert.

Anyway, I asked 'im, "Did you get a-hold of George and Tim?" "Yeah," he says, "I got a-hold of 'em and they're on the way, but it'll be an hour before they can get here." After that, ol' Klump gathered up his bridle reins and shook his hand in the air and shouts, "Hooooweeee, goddamn, we've caught another cougar!!" And away he went at a run down that mountain! Me and this other guy, we just kinda trotted off down there. We get down there about 100 yards of the tree, there's Klump. "Goddamn," he says, "those damn dogs is really tryin' to get at that lion!" Layne and I had this little – well, she wasn't such a little dog but she was a young dog – called Sally. She'd climb up in this one tree and she couldn't quite reach this lion's tail. And she'd jump at it and down outta the tree she would go! And Klump says, "Boy, that dog of yours is sure wantin' to get a-hold of that lion! I hope she don't drag it out because if she does, they're gonna kill it right here on the ground and George won't get to kill it!" Then here come our other hunter, 'cause I'd gotten ahead of 'im, and Christ, he just rode up there practically under the tree and ol' Klump says, "Goddamn, I wish that bastard'd stay back! He's gonna jump that lion out and the dog's is gonna kill it!" And he called the guy and got 'im back off.

Finally, ol' George and Tim got there and Tim asked George, "George, you wanna take a picture of it in the tree?" He had his .30-.30 in his hand and he said, "I'll take a picture with this .30-.30!" He got off his damn horse and shot the lion. This guy's dogs, they never did act too serious. They run around the tree there and barked a little, but I didn't see any of 'em lookin' at the lion! They was just barkin' 'cause the other dogs were barkin'.

So Tim and George, they gotta go one way to get to their trucks and me and Klump gotta go another way to get to our truck. On the way back, ol' Klump says, "You haven't never told me much about your dogs." I said, "Hell, they're just hounds. They catch a lion once in awhile." He says, "Damn, they're good dogs! If you'd just hunt 'em more, you'd catch a bunch of cougars with 'em!" He was startin' to brag on 'em, especially that little red dog! That little red dog, he's a good dog and he'll hunt. But if you start back to camp too early and don't watch 'im, he'll sneak off and run a deer for the rest of the day!

Figure 17. George Brown and One of his Lions

Libertad, Mexico

George Parker come to me there one time and he says, "You know, I've got that hotel down there in Mexico, in Libertad, and these Mexicans is wantin' to take it away from me! All they want is that there hotel. I went down there and tried to burn it! I didn't get the job done!" I said, "Goddamn it, George, why didn't you let me go with you? I can burn the goddamn thing down." So we went back; we got a plastic five-gallon can of gas apiece. I told George, "You gather up some of your old Kapok life preservers and we'll get up in the attic and spread those things around and we'll pour one of those five-gallon cans of gas around on 'em! If you got some black powder, get one of Jackie's silk stockings and put it in there. I'll get 10 foot of blasting fuse and we'll put that into this here black powder and we'll lay that up by these gasoline-soaked life preservers. We'll come out and we'll light the fuse and leave! And I'll guarantee you – the place is gonna burn!" 'Cause we set this other five-gallon of gas there with these saturated life preservers.

When we come up there, there was a Mexican sleepin' outside there and another bunch of 'em around the front next to the porch, a-sleepin' there. This Mexican, he's a-sittin' up there on the edge of his bed smokin' a cigarette. Ol' George had give me a nightstick cut off one of his oars. He said, "Now, we're not gonna get taken here! If they catch us, we may have to rap one of 'm on the head or somethin'." There was several dogs a-barkin' at us and finally, this guy got his cigarette smoked and the dogs had quieted down. Course, George went in the back way and he knew where the scuttle hole was to get up in the roof. We got up there and set everything up, come out, lit our fuse and left. We drove out and kinda got up on a hill back there about a couple miles and stopped and turned around. The building was burnin' good; pretty soon the whole roof came down. George said, "We got the job done this time!"

We left and we got to a small border crossing, down farther than Sassabe, that didn't open until 8:00 am. We pulled out into the brush and camped for the night. The next morning, George told me, "Ollie, you know I really appreciate you comin' down. A lot of people would be afraid to do that." I said, "Hell, with you I'm not afraid to do 'bout anything!" We come out and crossed, no problem and come back. Course George had to go down to Mexico and buy a newspaper. They'd created quite a damn problem about this place a-burnin' down! And then, it wasn't wanted anymore and ol' George, he knew a couple of guys up in Alaska and he sold the five hectares of land that went with the hotel for $20,000!

Stan Corey and Gomer

This friend of mine in Tucson, this Stan Corey, he worked with me a lot when I was buildin' houses. He put in all the streets and the sidewalks, he got to goin' out with me, a-huntin'. I had a lot of fun with that Stan Corey! He'd went down to Nogales and he bought him a brand-new Mexican saddle; it was black, coal black. I had my hounds, two or three of 'em, tied up in the back of the pickup and he throws this Mexican saddle in there with 'em. I had an ol' black-and-white pup there called "Gomer". This pup, he had a ravishin' appetite! And when we got up on top of the mountain, Stan drags out his saddle and this silly pup had eat all the saddle strings off it, he'd eat the latigo straps off it and by god, we had quite a little problem gettin' his saddle patched up enough where he could ride! We used some of my piggin' strings and everthing. I assured 'im, I says, "Hell, you can buy more latigos and you buy some saddle strings and I'll put 'em in for you.". We went on and made our hunt.

We didn't catch anything, I didn't have the best dogs in the world then but they would catch a lion once in awhile. And this Abe dog, that was the first lion dog I had, you know, and eventually he made a real good lion dog. And about a half-assed bear dog! He'd run bear but you had to have somethin' with 'im that would put the bear up in the tree because he wouldn't never get too close to a bear. But he'd help the dogs trail 'em and when he'd run across a bear track he'd just stop right there and all the hair on his back'd bristle up. The other dogs'd get around 'im and then they'd take off trailin' this bear. We caught several bear with 'im.

But we come back to his place after ol' Stan a-gettin' his saddle eat up. I kept my horse there – he had a little corral and some other pens and a milk cow and a milk pen calf or two – and we're standin' there talkin'. Stan had some old pet Rhode Island Red hens and ol' Abe, you know, he's right there with us. This one ol' hen, she saw Stan and me a-talkin' so she come a-cluckin' over towards us and she got out there about 20 feet and he saw ol' Abe a-watchin' 'er and he says, "Get her, Abe!" And by god, I tell you, he had that chicken killed right now! I started to kinda get after and chastise my dog a little bit for killin' his pet hen and Stan says, "No, Ollie, I sicced 'im on her, he done just what I told 'im to do. Don't whip 'im for it! Besides, Ann'll just make chicken and dumplins out of 'er."

It's funny how I come to get that Gomer dog. Someone called me up on the phone one evening and they had this here hound pup that had come from Dale Lee's stock. He was wantin' to find a good home for 'im. I went and picked him up and god, I had all kinds of problems with 'im, but I kept on a-huntin' 'im. Then he finally got to where he was workin' a little bit; he'd work with the dogs and look like maybe he was trailin' a little bit and the bastard would bark treed. Things went along, you know, and then he started gettin' up front and wasn't trailin…hell, he was just runnin' in front of the dogs. He'd maybe go up one canyon and come to a fork and the other dogs would follow him for a quarter of a mile or so and they'd stop and come back down to the fork and pick up the track. He'd done this with me several times and I didn't wanna kill 'im – that's before I learned how to handle hounds – so I give 'im to Doug Baker.

This dog come from Dale Lee's original stock. It'd been bred; it was the offspring of some of 'em. Hell, these damn dogs, if you don't hunt 'em regular they'll breed all that damn hunt out of 'em, I think. To have good dogs, you gotta breed the best and these dogs that we're huntin' with now originated when they started lion huntin' here in Arizona 100 years ago, breedin' the best to the best. Hell, they've all got different kinds of blood in 'em; I think if someone really got interested they could register 'em as a lion huntin' breed.

But anyway, hell, ol' Doug Baker made a pet out of 'im; kept that ol' dog 'til he was dead. And Doug tells a number of stories about the dog, about bear comin' through camp and ol' Gomer'd run up and get in the camper! Ol' Baker, he come out to the ranch with me and went huntin' with me. And he had Gomer, of course. We got on a lion track and, by god, Gomer pulled those dogs off of the track. About the second time they were all off the track and millin' around and I only had my pistol but Doug Baker, he had a .30-.30. "Baker," I says, "loan me that .30-.30." He says, "Well, what do you want the .30-.30 for?" And I said, "Because I'm going to kill that goddammed Gomer! I don't want to start shootin' at 'im with my pistol! I might kill one of my own dogs!"

Well, by god, he wouldn't loan me his .30-.30, but that was the last time he ever went huntin' with me and brought Gomer along!

Shoe Store Owner

This is a hunting story about a client who owned a chain of shoe stores. Another friend of mine there in Nogales was takin' the guy's wife sheep huntin'. And he'd got her a nice sheep. By gettin' her the sheep and takin' her huntin', he'd met her husband. And this guy wanted a lion and he wanted to know if this fella, this Mel Rogers, could recommend 'im a lion hunter. Mel says, "I know one of the best!" So he got my name and address from Mel and the guy wrote me a letter. He says, "I'd like to come out on a lion hunt, but I'm real serious about catchin' a lion. I'm willing to take the time." I wrote back and told 'im that I generally sold a 10-day hunt and about 90% of the time I filled 'em out on that 10-day hunt. So if he really wanted a lion, why don't we go for two weeks? That was fine.

Along before the time he was supposed to come, I get a phone call from Denver, Colorado. He says, "I've come into Denver and I've opened another shoe store here and if I come on down now, we'll have three weeks. How would that work for you?" "Well," I said, "if I can't catch you a lion in three weeks, no one can catch you a lion." He showed up and at that time I was doin' a little huntin' up in the Catalinas. We went up to the Old Control Mine and we camped there. Next morning, bright and early, we're up and out and we went on up the trail goin' outta the Old Control Mine, up there in the saddle. That's about a 25 minute ride. In this here saddle, the dogs hit a good lion track and I don't think it was more'n 15, 20 minutes, they had a lion treed! First day! First 45 minutes! It was a real good female lion and he shot it and he told me, he says, "Ollie, you don't know how pleased and how happy I am to get this lion, 'cause I definitely wanted one! But wouldn't it a-been nice if it'd been a tom?" "Well," I says, "you've got the time and I've got the time and if you've got the money, we'll just keep on a-huntin'." This is back when there was a bounty on lions and you could take two. So we skinned the lion out, fed the dogs all they could eat and come back home, took the lion skin and put it in my deep freeze.

We went back and I wanted to hunt on this Samaniego Ridge but it was pretty cold campin' up on top so we went up there and camped in Canada Del Oro on the road up to Charloo Gap. We're into the second day, then. I knew the trail at Charloo Gap you could take up and get on Samaniego Ridge. We went way up on Samaniego Ridge and on our way back, these dogs found a calf kill. I didn't let the dogs fool around on the track there; I knew if we come back early in the morning, that lion'd be back, in all probability. So we went back the next morning and the dogs took the lion track, trailed it up and started barkin' treed. There was a little mound of rocks there and an oak tree or two in it and they're barkin' treed, and we went up there, there's no lion. No lion in this damn tree! And I looked across and about 100 yards, a layin' out there on a limb on a Ponderosa Pine, lay this lion. Don't know why those dogs was barkin' treed, unless they jumped it outta there and he run over and run up this tree. Anyway, we were right behind 'em and I'm sure, in a little while, they would've found the lion. He shot it, and it's about 120 pound tom and a pretty lion! I've caught two of these lions in my lifetime that instead of this brownish color, they've got a bluish tinge to 'em. A beautiful lion!

That hunter was well pleased with himself! He got two lions and one of 'em's a tom. Everything's fine! So he went home and I got a letter from 'im three or four months later. He said he'd like to get a buffalo. I wrote back and told 'im in Arizona they didn't give nonresidents buffalo hunts out (they didn't at that time; I think they do now). But I wrote back and I told 'im, "I've got a friend up in Wyoming and they got buffalo up there you can buy. If you're real serious about killin' a buffalo, I'll go visit 'im this summer, or sometime along towards fall, or early in the spring and I'll buy a buffalo and I'll bring the thing back in the horse trailer. I'll turn it loose out at the ranch and we'll go out and hunt it down and kill it!" Never have heard from the guy since! I don't know whether he got to thinkin' that's how he got his lion or what! Anyway, I never have heard from 'im again.

That first lion I caught the shoe store owner was a female. I could see she'd weaned some kittens. There was another guy come here in the winter and I guess he had a lotta money because he had a motor home that he said cost 'im a quarter of a million dollars! He wanted to go lion huntin'. He told me, "You know, I'm not really interested in whether I get a lion or not. I just want to go on a hunt." I said that was fine. He asks, "Can I bring my motor home?" I says, "Well, where I wanna hunt, we can park it up at Canada Del Oro." And I'm thinkin' about these kittens. If he's not interested in killin', I'm pretty sure I can catch one of those kittens. We went up there and camped and went on up in the neighborhood of where I'd saw these kittens. About the third day, I hit a good tom track. We trailed it up to a calf kill and here at this calf kill was all three a-these kittens. They'd come in there, followed this tom in there – they was lookin' for somethin' to eat! And he'd come in there and caught 'em on that and killed one of 'em right on the calf; bit 'im right in the back of the head. He run one out there about 20 yards – killed it. These kittens, you know, they're about 40 pound kittens, and about 50 yards out, he caught the third one and killed it! Killed all three of those kittens on his calf kill!

I took pictures of 'em; he took pictures of 'em; we're coming back and he says, "Ollie, you know, I'd just as soon stop this hunt. I've found out all I wanted to know. I just wanted to see how it was done, see the dogs work. We've trailed it up to this calf kill and found where this tom lion killed these three kittens. I'll pay you for the full hunt and just call it off!" So that's what we did.

I guess I must've impressed the guy because, hell, for ten years after that, he'd come and he'd call me up and he'd take me and my wife out to dinner. The last time he come down he had one of these Jap cars that he'd bought and he took us out to dinner. I don't know what ever happened after that, whether he'd died or what, but I never did hear from 'im anymore. But he never did talk anymore about goin' lion huntin'. He'd found all he wanted to know – probably had a sore butt, too! He was real nice, a congenial guy. I liked 'im.

I'd liked to a-caught that big tom for 'im. I think that in another two, three days I'd probably caught it.

I never did go back to that calf kill. Back in those days, I was gettin' paid a couple thousand dollars for a 10-day lion hunt. Hell, when I was exercisin' my dogs around, I've turned probably six or eight lions loose that I've caught under those circumstances. And then I've turned a couple of kittens loose that'd only weigh about 50, 60 pounds.

Lion Hunter Humor

Here's three short stories I'm going to tell that kind of indicates that some of the lion hunters, or at least some of the better lion hunters, has got a sense of humor.

The first one is about Dale Lee. He was camped down in Sawmill Canyon in the Santa Ritas, and these two other lion hunters rode into his camp along in the afternoon. Dale was already in camp. They visited a while, sitting on their horses. Dale then said to them, "Well, get down. I've got some coffee here."

Dale had a tent – he's camped there in a tent. They got down, and Dale poured them both a cup of coffee. This one feller says "Dale, don't you have any sugar?" Dale says "Yes, I've got sugar."

He went in his tent, and come out with an unopened 5-pound sack of sugar. Dale tore the corner off of it, and the guy stuck his cup out. And old Dale poured in there about a half-cup of sugar, and run out about half his coffee. He says "You want sugar – there's sugar!" He never cracked a smile. He turned around, and took his sugar back in the tent. He come back and went on a visitin'. Dale never cracked a smile, said anything about the sugar. This guy he just set his half-cup of sugar and coffee down, and never said anything to Dale about it.

The next one is a story that Lloyd Smith told me on hisself. He was hunting over in New Mexico with a mutual friend of ours. He was a cowboy over there, and was hunting out of his cow camp. Lloyd said that it was getting up to the Spring of the year, fairly warm, and they had hunted and they got back in about 2:00 o'clock. They hadn't had any lunch, hadn't had a drink of water, or anything. They went into the kitchen of this mining camp, opened the refrigerator, and got two cans of Coor's out. He set the one down there at his place at the table, and set the other can of Coor's over in front of Lloyd.

Lloyd said, "Don't you have anything but scab beer?" This guy says "No," and just reached over, picked up the can of beer, and set it back in the icebox. And Lloyd said, "I went without a beer, but I sure wish I would have kept my mouth shut! That beer would have tasted good."

This last story is a story on Sewell Goodman and Ted Fergenson. Ted Fergenson is dead now, but he was a lion hunter that used to hunt out of Sassabee. He had farmed all over there, and made quite a little money. He retired, and that's all he did was lion hunting. If any of the ranches around had a lion problem, they called Ted up and he would go out and hunt.

This Sewell Goodman used to hunt with him a lot. Ted is real frugal. But he always had lots of groceries in his camp, and he eat well. So they say. I never did hunt with him.

One morning there, Sewell likes a little sugar in his coffee. He gets his teaspoon, and sees that Ted is a watching him. Ted didn't use sugar in his coffee. It was a luxury. Sewell puts three big, heaping teaspoons of sugar in his coffee, with Ted Fergenson watching. Ted said, "Sewell, do you realize that you put three big spoons full of sugar in your coffee?" Sewell said, "Yes, but I don't stir it!"

Joe Goff

Most of the people around the Tucson area and all the ranchers knew Joe Goff. He's got kind of a reputation, of bein' kinda tight when it somes to buyin' groceries. This particular night, I'm down spendin' the night with George Parker, drinkin' a little whiskey. Joe'd got a lion kill up there and he'd called my house and talked to Sherry – she knew where I was at down at the Parker's and give 'im the phone number. So he called me up and said, "I've got a fresh lion kill and I'd like you to come up and see if you can catch it." I told him, "Joe, I'm down here drinkin' whiskey with George and my horses is all out at the ranch. I got my saddle but I don't have a horse." "Well," he says, "I'll have you a horse ready if you can be here at my house at daylight in the mornin'."

I got up there and he was with Cowboy Blue, he called 'im. Blue was just puttin' the last shoe on a horse's hind foot. Joe got a pack outfit there, all packed up on a mule, ready to go. He said, "I've got a pasture up there with a little lean-to where we can spend the night. I got all the groceries; I got everything." So I put my saddle on this horse and we got up there and got to where the lion kill was; dogs took a track and eventually, after several hours, they caught a lion. It was a young lion, a female. We shot it and, course, we'd used up quite a lot of the day, so we go up to his camp. He's got a little horse trap right up on the side of the mountain. If a damn horse ever fell down, he'd roll clear out and over the top of the fence and be out! And he's got this little lean-to. He unpacks his mule and, hell, he's got four blocks of salt in there and three cans of Spam! And there's three of us 'cause ol' Blue, the cowboy, is with us. So that night we split a can of Spam. The next morning we split another can of Spam. Then we go back to this kill and hit another lion track. Goddamn, we trailed it around and around and finally got up on the Catalinas and right up under the observatory and the dogs treed! God, we went as far as we could a-horseback and I told ol' Joe, I said, "You and Blue stay here and I'll go up and shoot the lion." I went up there and found the thing treed and I shot it. I started back and I met 'em; they'd found a way they could get up there. By god, it's gettin' late, we're gonna hafta spend the night there! And we got one can of Spam! We hadn't been eatin' too much since we left and I doubt if I'd had any breakfast when I left the first day. Anyway, I said, "We better get back up there and get that lion. These dogs haven't had anything to eat!" So we went up and got the lion and got down there to his camp and his boy was along, too. Hell, that was four of us that was sharin' a can of Spam!"

Anyway, I cut all these tenderloins outta this lion – he had a little grill there – and I said that we're gonna eat some lion meat. Hell, I was startin' to work up a little hunger! We fed the dogs good. Hell, he don't have any salt but he's got a horse shoein' outfit, so I take a rasp and we go over to one of these blocks of salt and I rasp off some salt, salted our lion chops and we ate pretty good then! Hell, we didn't eat as much of that lion as the dogs did, but with four or five dogs and the four of us, we ate that lion completely up. The next mornin' we divided up this last can of Spam. I told Goff, "You know, we better head back to the ranch. I've been on this starvation diet now for goin' on three days and I'm gettin' tired of it!" So we get down to the camp and ol' Blue had been down on the San Pedro and he had a bunch of roastin' ears. So he cooks up these roastin' ears but he don't have any butter for 'em. He's got some shortenin' or lard of some kind so we put that on these roastin' ears, put a little salt and pepper on 'em and ate 'em all!

So I left and I'll tell ya, I went back one other time and I brought my own groceries!

I had another guy tell me a story about a time when he was a big ol' kid, 16, 18 years old, and Goff had some cattle to move. "Hell," he said, "it was all day long getting' 'em up to where he was movin' these cattle and it was too late to come back. The only thing we had to eat – ol' Joe had two or three little pieces of jerky in his chap pocket. So Joe give me a piece of jerky and I ate that. The next morning the jerky's all gone and I went home and that's the last time I ever volunteered to help Joe Goff!"

One of those times I come in there, when I had my own groceries, I got down to ol' Joe Goff's and Blue was there. He whipped up some water gravy and he had a cottontail he'd shot soakin' there in salt water. He cooked that up and he had a couple ol' cold, dry biscuits and we eat them. And then I've talked to several of these wetbacks that worked for Joe and they said that he'd just starve 'em out!

Several years ago he was havin' lion problems and he wanted me to come up and hunt and I told 'im I can't come up there and hunt for nothin'. So he says, "I'm havin' lion problems and I'll give you $500 for ever lion you catch on my ranch." And I said, "Well, the weather'll calm down here pretty soon and I'll come up." In the meantime, he got a-hold of another lion hunter and, I don't know who he was, but he was supposedly a good lion hunter and had good dogs. Down in the lower Alter Canyon there somewhere these dogs treed a lion and when he got up there these damn killer bees was in the tree and they was after his dogs and they was after the lion and they got after him! He outrun 'em and got back and durin' the night one of the dogs come in. He went back the next day to try and find his other dogs and there was four of his dogs and the lion and the bees had killed 'em! Killed four dogs and a mountain lion!

And ol' Joe, he owns about 2/3 of that north end of the Catalinas! They say he's in bad health now and his boys is runnin' the outfit. I've been starved out so I stay away from there! Never been back.

Fritz Selby Lion Hunt

Fritz, he'd talked to me about goin' lion huntin' and I'd gotten to the point where I needed a lion hunter. He's right there in town, in Tucson. I quizzed 'im a little bit; I said, "Selby, how well do you ride?" He says, "Oh, when I was a kid, I rode horses all the time." "Well," I said, "hell, ridin' horses is like ridin' a bicycle. If you ever knew how to ride a bicycle, you could still ride one. And that should work on horses, too."

197

So we went down to the King Anvil Ranch and camped there. I had a big, stout, grey-colored horse; I got 'im all saddled up and, course, Selby's legs is only about half as long as his back. He's real short legged. I had the stirrups taken up short. Christ, I led 'im over to a big rock and he got up there and he puts his right foot in the stirrup and raises up! And, hell, he's facin' the wrong direction! He can see that's wrong. So he come down and got his foot outta the stirrup and he done that same damn thing three things! I said, "Selby, goddamnit, try puttin' your left foot in the stirrup and see what happens!" Hell, he got mounted up then!

I got on my horse and we went huntin'. He asked lotsa questions and after the second day he knew about as much about lion huntin' as I did. We're goin' down this long damn ridge and we got a lion track a-goin'. It come on a little ol' drop-off there, about two foot, and him and those little ol' short legs a-sittin' up there – Christ, I never even looked back and then I heard a hell of a crash! I looked around and he's layin' on his face on the downhill side in the rocks! The damn saddle is up on the horse's neck and kinda over on the side a little bit. He got up and said, "I got bucked off!" "No," I said, "You didn't get bucked off. You fell off!" "Oh no," he said, "he bucked me off!"

That saddle was tight. And we had to loosed up the damn cinches to get it back in place. I got it back on and by god, we lost that damn lion up in the rocks. The wind had come up and we lost our dogs. I had a good young dog I called "Trash" and he'd barely got up there and a lion or somethin' had knocked 'im off the bluff and we lost 'im. I went back one afternoon to see if I could find 'im and there was buzzards flyin' around up there. I had a horse that needed to be shod so I sent ol' Selby over to the Elkhorn Ranch to get it done and to pick up a little groceries. We were just gonna hunt there for three days and then go to the Elkhorn if we didn't catch a lion. But, goddamn, this damn big tom that we lost that day – I wanted to catch 'im! Ol' Selby, he come back with the horse all shod and he was tellin' about talkin' to Bob Miller; he said, "I was tellin' Bob that you went and got off the trail and got into some pretty bad country!" Bob said, "Well, hell, that's nothin'! He rides them horses all the time where a horse can't even go!" Ol' Bob, he can tell a hell of a good story. He exaggerated a little bit.

I caught that damn lion, a tom. He was out on the edge of a pretty good bluff – goddamn, it must a-been a hundred foot drop. It was just a big rock that went out over the canyon. There was a big crack in it and this damn lion is down in the crack in a little ol' oak tree. Christ, them damn hounds was about to drag 'im outta that oak. I got ol' Selby in there with his .30-.30 and I told 'im, "Now, goddamnit, you be damn careful that you shoot that lion on the shoulder and don't break his skull. That's a hell of a good skull! Don't shoot 'im in the head; shoot 'im in the shoulder. He'll drop down." And Selby did. Goddamn, we're pullin' the lion up there and we got the horse out on the edge of this bluff. I'm too damn big to be packed out with me and a lion both so I got his horse and I tied this lion on. Christ, he starts tellin' me how to do it! And it's the first damn lion he'd ever saw and the first time he'd ever saw one packed out! It kinda pissed me off – I started one time just to let it fall off and let it roll off the bluff and tell 'im to go get it; he's on his own. But, hell, I thought, I can't do that. I'd just be a-showin' my stupidity and I don't need to do that.

I got the lion all packed up and I'm leadin' the horse out and we're comin' down this trail and he can look off down in the bottom there and see a short cut. He takes this short cut. I get down to the bottom of the hill and I unload the lion – it was kinda gettin' over to one side – and we could drive up to there in the pickup. No Selby. Noooo Selby. Goddamnit, I waited and I waited and finally I could see him comin' off this hill. He'd got into this real thick brush and goddamn cholla cactus and other damn stuff. Goddamn, I thought he was never gonna get down! He says, "Jesus, I got into terrible country!" I told 'im, "If you had the brains God give a pissant, you'd a-stayed with me! I've been down here for 30 minutes."

We went down and got the pickup and unsaddled the horses and went back and got his lion. He loaded his lion up in his truck and went back to town. The lion did make the record book, too.

My Bear Hunt

This is the story of my one and only bear. I got to thinkin' I oughta kill a bear. I figured the way to kill a bear is to get some bear dogs. And a guy give me a Rhodesian Ridgeback and I thought that would be a good start 'cause they, I found out later, all they want to do is play and fight. Anyhow, there was a guy over south of Wilcox who had a bear dog for sale for $150. Absolutely guaranteed! So I bought this bear dog, had this Rhodesian Ridgeback and I had my cowdog. I went down to the dog pound and I got another Rhodesian Ridgeback. Then there was a black guy – he advertised in the paper; he had a coon dog that he wanted to give to somebody, so I picked this coon dog up. With my two Rhodesian Ridgebacks, my bear dog, my coon dog and my cowdog, I went over in the Grahams and camped over there. I had John Bessett with me. We took our horses over and we went bear huntin'. Christ, I was havin' problems with my Rhodesian Ridgebacks 'cause all they want to do is fight my bear dog, fight my cowdog; they'd even fight when they was playin' among theirselves.

So I'm gettin' a pretty good pack a-bear dogs together. And this colored guy, he's had his left arm off just above his elbow, and he bragged on Teddy. That's what he called his coon dog. I went over there and we hunted a couple a-days and we weren't gettin' anywhere on this huntin' with bear dogs. I went by the dump up there and there's bear comin' in on this dump. John had brought some honey over so we put this honey in a can and we put it on our campfire and boiled it good and took this honey over to the dump. The Forest Service had dumped a load of paper plates and other things there so we poured this honey all over 'em. This bear was comin' in at night. I went up there and I got back about 50 yards from this pile of paper plates the honey was on. I got in my sleepin' bag and it was a pretty dark night; there wasn't much of a moon. I went off to sleep.

Sometime, pretty early in the night, I heard these cans a-rattlin' and I could just see the outlines of this bear. And it looked like he was pickin' up these paper plates and lickin' the honey off 'em. I couldn't see the crosshairs of the rifle or anything so I got all lined up where I thought I was about right and I had a .270 Weatherby rifle. I touched off a round and everything black 'cause the flash and fire and everthing blinded me! And this bear, he started squallin' and slappin' his hands and stuff around and here I am in this mummy sleepin' bag and I'm not in a position to run or climb a tree! Pretty soon the ol' bear took off down there and he's still a-makin' noises and snappin' his teeth and growlin'. But he got outta hearin' and I got outta that sleepin' bag and I rolled it up where it was under my arm and I went to camp.

The next morning, John and I went up there. We figured there oughta be a blood trail and I took my bear dog and I took ol' colored guy's coon dog and my two Rhodesian Ridgebacks and got up there. I showed 'em the blood trail. The cowdog, he's kinda followin' us, but these other dogs, they're not doin' anything! We got off to the side of the dump and here's a car drove up. Well, I didn't want this guy drivin' up in the car seein' this blood trail and what we done, so I fired my rifle off in the air about the time he got outta his truck and I hollered at John, "I just wounded a bear!" And this guy that drove up hollered, "I don't wanna be around here with a wounded bear!" And he gets in his car and he left!

We followed that cowdog down through there and got off down there about a quarter of a mile and this bear, he's a-layin' there under a little juniper tree and he's dead. He was shot in the hind leg and he just bled to death. So I had a 215 pound bear there and I tagged 'im and brought 'im back to Tucson. Comin' into Tucson, it was just a little ways outta the way to go by and show this colored guy my bear. I told 'im, "We caught this bear with your coon dog! He run this bear for several miles, run 'im down in a deep canyon and up the other side and treed 'im! Hell, we was a hour and a half, two hours gettin' around there! But this coon dog, he's right there a-barkin', he's got a lotta the bark all chewed off the tree with the bear!"

This guy had some of his other buddies around there and I heard 'im tellin' 'em, "All this time we been tryin' to make a coon dog outta ol' Teddy and he must a-been a bear dog all the time!" And the first free time I had, I took both my Rhodesian Ridgebacks down to the dog pound and got rid a-them – cost me $2.00 apiece to get rid of 'em. I took ol' Teddy with me out to the ranch and comin' back, what would happen but a bobcat run across the road packin' a cottontail! Well, I'll get Teddy on a fresh bobcat track. He got down there and he started trailin' the damn thing! But he never could move fast enough to make that bobcat drop that rabbit! But I kept ol' Teddy around for awhile and a carpenter from California come to work and he was wantin' a dog and I told 'im, "I got just the dog you want!"

So I give Teddy away. The only thing I had left for a bear dog – god! I forgot to tell you about that! While we're guttin' this bear out and lookin' around, this damn bear dog come down and got a sniff of that bear and away he went – run off! And, Christ, I spent the rest of the day tryin' to round up my bear dog! By god, he was gone! When I got back, I sent a note over to Safford to put a notice in the paper that I'd lost this bear dog. It wasn't long 'til someone called me up; they had my bear dog. I went over and picked up my bear dog and then I took 'im back to where he was guaranteed and I told 'im what happened. He says, "Well, I just can't understand why he didn't work for you, but my brother had 'im out and he wouldn't work for my brother! Apparently, he just works for me!" Anyway, I got my $150 back and I'd killed my bear! The only bear I ever killed in my life! I caught 12, 15 later on with my lion dogs but other people shot 'em.

Jack Marteney Lion Hunt

I'd caught my good friend Jack a lion several years before this hunt, a female, and now Labor Day was comin' up. He had a cabin up there in the Catalinas and he said we could go up there and hunt out of his cabin. So we went up there and we got out on the Samaniego Ridge. The dogs hit a pretty good lion track; they took off, trailin' around, and went out over the edge. Just right over the edge they jumped this mountain lion, a big ol' tom. They treed it right there quick! Hell, we wasn't 300 yards down the tree line and they had it treed there on a rock. I told Jack, "By god, you better not miss this bastard 'cause if he goes off that rock, we'll be halfway down this damn mountain. I don't wanna walk down there and I damn sure don't wanna walk back!"

He killed it and we packed it up on top. It was kind of a steep climb a-gettin' outta there and Jack, he's real heavy. Hell, he weighed 230 or 240 pounds. So we tied this lion on his mule and we're comin' up outta there, gettin' towards the top and we run onto a group of these tree-lovers, nature lovers, environmentalists, whatever they were. Anyway, some of 'em was packin' butterfly nets and they all had on tennis shoes. I run into 'em up front and this lady that seemed to be kinda in charge of the group asked me, "What are you guys doin' up here a-horseback?" I said, "We're lion huntin'." "Oh," she said, "lions here in the Catalinas have been extinct for five years!" And I said, "They have?" And she said, "Why, yes!" So I said, "I've got somethin' down here on the end horse we're packin' in and I'm sure it's a mountain lion we killed this mornin'!" She said, "Oh, I don't think so!" So I suggested that we go down and look at it. And it was down there a-ways in the brush and 'round the curve. And by god, sure enough, it's a mountain lion. It amazed her! She said, "Well, the State, I'm sure that's what they told us." I said, "Hell, I think this is 11 I've taken outta here in the last two years." "Oh," she said, "are they that plentiful?" I said, "They were 'til I started workin' on 'em!"

We packed it out and we run the thing on downtown and skinned it out and put the hide in Jack's deep freeze. I told Jack, "Hell, we got our horses and my trailer and everything back up on top of the mountain – why don't we go out huntin' again in the mornin'?" He thought that was a good idea. I said, "This lion, you know when we checked it out, we

203

got this fawn out of his stomach and they've got a fresh kill there. I just wouldn't be surprised if there wasn't another damn lion a-workin' up there. So we went up and we got down there, oh hell, a half-mile or so from where we'd hit that track and the dogs hit another track. Christ, they flew out there and it was a big pack of these damn coatimundi's! God, I started hollerin' at dogs and got most of 'em back and I had this young Abe dog – turned out to be one of the best dogs I ever owned – and I see him a-comin' up there. He's got a young coatimundi he's killed and he's packin' it with his head up in the air. I'm still a-hollerin' at dogs and he looked up and he saw me, never changed expression, he just opened his mouth and let this thing drop. Then he came on and drifted on in like he was as innocent as a hound pup could be!

We got our dogs all gathered and went on around the curve and, Christ, it wasn't more'n a quarter of a mile and dogs just took off! I said, "Jack, they're back on these damn coatimundi's." We kinda whipped up a little bit and I'm a-hollerin' at dogs and Christ, they're still a-goin'! And they treed up there, on a hill up there! God, I got my piggin' strings out and my rope and I was gonna tie up those dogs and educate 'em. I can't have 'em runnin' these damn chulas all the time. We got up there where we could see and they got this female lion treed! I told Jack, "Well, we can't whup 'em for treein' a lion!"

He was ridin' an ol' palomino horse I called "Alligator." Jack had him tied up just by the bridle reins and I tied mine up – I had some good horses then. We went up there and we poked this lion out of the tree and down the hill it started! That damn lion ran right under ol' Alligator's neck and I thought, "Here goes the bridle reins!" But the bastard never moved! He just stood there! The dogs went off together and treed this lion in another juniper tree. We poked it outta that and it run down the mountain and up a fir tree. I climbed up in it – fir trees, you know, they're easy to climb – they got all these limbs come out close to the ground. I got up there pretty close to this lion and she was gettin' real nervous and she jumped and went up and let a little squirt of urine out.

So I backed off and I got down and broke off one of the dead limbs about three foot long, about two inches in diameter, and a good sharp end on it. I told Jack, "You go up there and poke that lion out." God, she was gettin' pretty well up in the top of the tree and ol' Jack, he's easily amused and he's a-laughin' and he got right up under that lion. I said, "Jack, you're gonna hafta poke her with that stick if you're gonna get her out!" Goddamn, he's a-laughin' and he poked her and she let out a squirt of this lion piss and hit 'im right square in the mouth! God, he's a-spittin' and the lion, she just went down the other side of the tree! Goddamn, he's a-spittin' and a-gaggin' and a-cussin' me; he said, "You knew she was gonna do that!" I said, "I didn't know it, but I was hopin' she would!"

He got the cat piss out of his mouth and was gettin' down outta the tree and the dogs have treed down there again. This is gettin' over some pretty bad bluffs in there and we went down and she was up in another fir tree. I told Jack, "I don't think you'd better go up there and poke her out. We better leave her here because next time they're gonna be off down in country where we can't ride. We'll just sit here and rest awhile and let the dogs bark at her. After they've barked for 20 or 30 minutes, I think I can talk 'em into leavin'." That's what we did. We got to talkin' to the dogs, tellin' 'em what good dogs they were but we just didn't want that lion. Jack thought we oughta leave her here and catch her someday with one of his boys.

So we hunted two days and caught two lions where they'd been extinct for five years!

Johnny Klump and Tim Haas

Johnny Klump and Tim Haas were young fellows and they got into this lion and bear huntin' and I'm here to tell you that they were *good* at it! They were as good as there was in the country at the time. This Klump, I'd hunted with him several times over a period of time and he was a real nice guy, kind of a hillbilly type, talked like a hillbilly. But he had a good brain and he could figure things out. He'd started with just a bunch of ol' worthless dogs and he'd whipped 'em up into shape where, hell, he could catch bear and lion with 'em!

He had one problem, though. Ever time he'd get a good dog, he could sell it for $3,500 or $4,000 and he'd sell it. And then Tim was a-huntin' with 'im and he bought several dogs and between the two of 'em, they had good dogs. But Tim, he wouldn't sell a good dog so that way they always had a good dog or two around the pack. They were very successful and apparently the Game Department, their local game warden over there – the way I can figure it out – he'd got to thinkin' they were *too* successful. Someone did; might not a-been the local game warden. Klump had caught the local game warden a nice lion and some of the ranchers around there suspected this game warden was doin' a little poachin'. He was real successful with a bow and arrow and some of these ranchers where he was a-huntin', they'd heard rifle shots in there a time or two before he brought out a good deer. It was stuff he was supposed to kill with a bow and arrow.

This is mostly hearsay from me because I didn't even know the warden. But anyhow, they sicced a couple of federal agents on this Klump and Haas. And the feds hunted with 'em for two years and they'd caught 'em both bear and lion. Then the agents, they was tryin' to get something on 'em! So this Tim, one of the hunts, got sick; he had the diarrhea in the worse way. He had to stay in camp and while he's in camp they got this Klump to let 'em kill a javelina out of season. And they went off on a elk hunt and Tim, he couldn't go 'cause he had this diarrhea real bad. This one agent, he was always real helpful, Christ, he'd pour 'em coffee and everthing.

Tim got over his diarrhea and went up there on the elk hunt. God, they're glad to see 'im and this guy was a-servin' 'im coffee and the first thing he knew, he's got the diarrhea again! I knew a doctor real well and I asked him about that. I said, "What the hell is goin' on here?" He says, "Well, they're givin' him Crotin Oil in that coffee!" Anyway, they didn't have any more luck gettin' 'em in bad.

Finally, this good friend of mine and Tim's, this George Brown, had picked up a jaguar, hell, it was 15 years or so before this time. George, he likes leather and god, ever time he got around leather, he'd buy some. There was a leather shop down in Mexico and he went in there and they had this tanned jaguar hide. He bought it and he brought it back and back then, it was perfectly legal. Then he got to be such good friends with Tim and he wanted to do something for him, so he had a rug made out of this jaguar hide and he give it to Tim. Hell, a perfectly legal hide! And Tim's got it in his livin' room there, draped over a couch. One of these agents saw it and he told Tim, he says, "I'll give you $6,000 for that hide and my huntin' partner would like to have one, too. If you can come up with another hide, he'd pay $6,000 for it." Well this Klump, several years before that, he'd caught and killed a jaguar in the Dos Cabesas. Several people had saw it and several people had pictures of it. The Game Department got after 'im and he denied it, never would admit it and they couldn't prove it! At that time, it was a misdemeanor for killin' a jaguar in Arizona and he could of paid a $750 fine and they'd a-took the hide away from him and that would of been the end of it. But the Game Department hadn't forgot about it.

So they sold these two hides – they hadn't collected the money on 'em because they hadn't delivered 'em yet. These two agents was outta Colorado, one of 'em was a Japanese, and I was at the trial when they tried 'em and everthing. I'll tell you, bein' a Japanese and a crooked, no-good bastard, my trigger finger got to itchin'! In the courthouse, there wasn't anything you could do about it!

Anyway, they called up from Colorado and was talkin' to Tim and told 'im they were real busy and couldn't make it down but they could meet him over in Albuquerque, New Mexico. They could bring the two jaguar pelts up and one of 'em, Haas, had his, somewhere or other, had a life size mount of it. And they took 'em up there and boy, as soon as they got there, they arrested 'em! They tried 'em for this "Crossing the State Line" – they got 'em on the Lacey Act. Both of 'em went through the trial and hell, the both of 'em got two felony charges out of it and Tim, he's absolutely innocent! He hadn't never done anything wrong but he's still got these two felony charges against 'im!

I've known that the bastards was tryin' to suck me in when I was doin' a little sheep huntin'. I got several letters from people who really wanted to kill a sheep but they was so busy, was there someway I could get 'em one. I filed those letters in the wastebasket. The only problem with Tim and Klump – Klump, he didn't have a dime. All he was makin' was a little horse tradin' and cow tradin' and his huntin' and he needed the money. So they sucked 'im in on this killin' a desert sheep for $8,000. They went up there somewhere along the Arizona – New Mexico line where they was tryin' to establish a new herd in there. There was a pretty good ram in there and this agent knew this little herd in there and it's way outta the place. He went in there and this agent, they poached this ram! The agent shot it and then they arrested Tim and Klump for guidin' on an illegal sheep hunt! They settled that deal with the Game Department; it cost 'em a bundle of money! But when they got the felony counts, it was on the jaguars. It was a rotten deal on the Game Department and the federal agents, settin' those two boys up, tryin' to ruin their lives and make criminals outta absolutely honest hunters! Like I said, I'd hunted with 'em off and on for 10 years, eight years with Tim and 10 with Klump. Tim would help me on hunts and all the hunts I was on, I never heard him ever say anything about doin' anything illegal.

I was with him one time and it was out of season on bear huntin'. We come by a cow and there was a black bear there, a full-grown black bear, and the dogs got after it. They worked real hard to get the dogs away from that bear and they wouldn't even let 'em tree it! So I know that basically, they was good, honest boys but they were a little too successful to suit the Game Department!

Oaxaca, Mexico

This story is about the time George Parker and I went into Mexico to hunt jaguar. We wanted to go to the south and hunt on the Isthmus of Tehuantepec, which is the narrow part of Mexico just north of Guatemala. George, he knew the head Mexican Customs man and this Customs man, he had a brother down in Oaxaca, just north of Tehuantepec. The brother was a two-star general in charge of the Army in Oaxaca. George knew how to handle Mexicans, spoke passable Mexican, so he bought a liter of good scotch and a carton of American cigarettes. After we got into a motel, George called this general up and invited 'im over. He come over and George give 'im the cigarettes and he was real grateful for the American cigarettes. Then George opened the scotch and we all had a swig. By that time they'd introduced theirselves and George is tellin' 'im what he wanted to do. Down in this Isthmus of Tehuantepec, under the control of this two-star general, we had to have permission from him to get down there – and that was durin' the time, or right after, they'd discovered oil down there on the Isthmus. He give us both letters of introduction and his permission to be down there. George wanted to get to the town of Oaxaca and the state of Oaxaca and see some of those old ruins up there and the ol' general loaned us his staff car with his driver! Boy, we go down the street, you know, and I'm a-sittin' back there where the general sits and it's got these red flags up there in front with the two stars on 'em and boy, these Mexicans is comin' to attention! We're ratin' pretty high! We went up and went through the ruins and they're a story by theirselves; they're real interestin'. We come back and turned our staff car in.

The next morning we went down; we had to go through the Army checkpoint to get on the road south. Boy, when those Mexicans holler, "Halt!" even if you didn't understand Mexican, you'd come to a halt and click your heels together! We got in and they were haulin' pipe, they'd bulldozed a road down in there, and they was haulin' pipe down in there for these oil wells. And, ever 15 or 20 kilometers where there was water, they was establishin' farm sites for Mexican families to move in. Ever one of these camps had an ol' vieja (old woman) there and a younger girl to cook for these workmen. This's durin' the Santas Semana (Easter) weekend and, course, there's not a whole lot goin' on. George had cautioned me to stay separated all the time – don't ever get close together – George was about half suspicious of the people down there and he had a good knowledge of how to take care of himself. He said, "I don't want you talkin' to anybody 'less they talk English. You just listen and they might think you don't understand Spanish and you might get tipped off on somethin'!"

They had a State Policeman in ever one of these camps and we both had a rifle and a pistol, but with these orders from this general, we weren't molested or bothered in any way. About the end of the first day, 'cause we was eating in these camps, this ol' vieja head cook asked George, she says, "Your compañero, your partner, he never talks!" George says, "Well, he's a priest! And he's on vacation. And when he's on vacation, all he does is hunt and drink whiskey!"

Course that created a problem! They had several families there that had five or six kids that never could afford to get married in their church. They was wantin' me to marry 'em! Through my translator, I had to explain to 'em that I didn't wanna get in bad with their priest; 'cause if I'd go to marryin' 'em and they'd lose out on this money, I'd be in bad with their priest and I wasn't gonna to that! So that got me out of the marrying business, but it wasn't long 'til they was wantin' to give confessions! George says, "We gotta get in on that; we might stumble onto somethin' pretty good, takin' these confessions!" I told him, "George, I don't know how to cross myself! And takin' confessions, I'm bound to be a point there somewhere where I have to cross myself." And, hell, George didn't know how to cross himself either! So we had to back off on takin' confessions. All I did was sit around and eat and hunt and drink whiskey.

Then we moved on down to the next camp, spent a few days there, and nothing happened there 'cause word had proceeded, you know, that I was a priest. These viejas was feedin' us pretty good; they was takin' care of us. And we got down to the third one and that country down there was all limestone and jungle. George and I had took a trap apiece down there – we figured that if we couldn't find a jaguar to shoot, maybe we could trap one. And this Mexican down there that was pretty much the head of that camp, he claimed that he'd hunted jaguar, he was an authority on huntin' jaguars. He took us down on this here creek, down through the jungles and there was places you go over some of this limestone country and you could hear water runnin' around underneath the limestone, some kind of a stream in this limestone. We got way off down in there about five or six miles and got into a bunch of howler monkeys. We shot two or three apiece of 'em there for jaguar bait. While George and I were gatherin' these monkeys up to set our traps by, this Mexican got busy up in a tree building a manikin. I said, "George, you're not gonna sit up all night in a goddamn manikin on a chance a jaguar will come by, are you?" He says, "No, hell no, you're goin' to!" I said, "Bullshit, I'm not spendin' the goddamn night up here on the chance of a jaguar comin' in – that's what we got these traps for!" So we set our traps and we come back.

The next morning, George had been visitin' with this guy, and George says, "We got a problem! This guy's real busy and he can't take us down to look at the traps. You think you could find your way down there?" I said, "Hell, I spent damn near four years in the jungle; I can go down there and check our traps." Well, that was fine. We took off and I noticed that we're bein' followed down there about two, three miles. This guy's followin' us and when he saw that we'd located 'em, he just melted off into the jungle. George says, "You know, that bastard wants to steal those traps! That's the reason he can't get back down. They think that flatlanders from the States don't know anything about the jungles. But I'll fix him." We went down and checked our traps and when we got back, this guy asked George, "Did you find your way down there?" George says, "Oh yeah, my priest here, he spent four, five years over in the South Pacific fightin' Japs. All they used him for, 'cause he was such a expert on the rifle, they'd send 'im around in back and get in around where these Japs was, empty his gun in 'em, kill four or five of 'em

211

and then sneak back out. There was an island up there that had about 3,500 Japs on it but they didn't know what they was. So they send him and a couple week's groceries and 1,000 rounds of ammo to go in there and harass these Japs. Gave 'im a radio to contact when he was ready to come out. When he shot up all that ammunition, he got radio contact and they took 'im out. He killed so many Japs – that's how come him to take up religion! He got to be a Catholic priest!" Well, needless to say, we never had no more problems with that guy!

In this village where we was camped, there was two big sinkholes. One of 'em there, where they was gettin' their water, we went down there the first evening and filled up our canteens. I put Halazone in mine and George says, "Well, why are you puttin' Halazone in there?". I said, "Goddamn it, I don't trust any water in Mexico!" He says, "Well, you saw all them fish in there, it's down there 20 foot in the ground and there's nothin' wrong with it." I said, "Well, it's got a soapy damn taste to it." "Aw," he said, "your imagination's playin' tricks on you. That's good, pure water!" I said, "You'd better Halazone it!" The next day we come in and this other sinkhole we come by, which was above the one we're gettin' water, these Mexicans in there was washin' all their clothes! That's where the soap was comin' from!

It went on and in another day or two, course by then we was huntin' by ourselves, we come in past lunch time and we went in our tent and laid down and took a nap. When I got up, I was hungry! So I went up there to this ol' vieja; I got to visitin' with her and I got a good lunch from her. I'm visitin' with her and pretty soon she finally asked me if I was sure enough a priest. She was a little suspicious. I told her, "No, I'm not a priest. This guy I'm a-huntin' with is the damnedest liar you'd ever want to meet. He absolutely cannot tell the truth! That Chevy pickup he says is his really is mine. What he is, he's a Sonora Mexican. I met him three years ago down there deer huntin'. He's got a little goat ranch way out west of Hermosillo. And I've hunted with him and he's a likable guy, even though he is a damn liar. We've been friends ever since and every year we make a hunt together."

By that time, I'd told 'em pretty much who George was. I went back to and I never said nothin' to George. Next morning there we ate and George was visitin' around. Pretty soon ol' George turned to me and says, "Ollie, these Mexicans act like they know somethin' I don't." I says, "Well, they do!" He asks me, "What have you told them?" I said, "I told them who you are. You're a Sonora Mexican. You've never but once or twice was in the United States, into Tucson when you were a young man. And you got a little goat ranch out there, way out west of Hermosillo!" "Damn you," he says, "we had such a good thing a-goin'!"

By that time, we were pretty much ready to come back. Course, we stopped at all these places on our way back and Christ, everybody knew who George was then! I didn't get the respect I had as a priest, either. We didn't kill any jaguars, but I did spend 10, 12 days as a Catholic priest – one who didn't know how to cross himself!

Figure 18. Arizona Big Horn Sheep

Jack Marteney Sheep Hunt

I had hunted Jack a whole lot. I'd started out lion huntin' with 'im. He called me up one evening and wanted to know if I could take 'im lion hunting and I said that I could. He says, "Ollie, you know what? Why don't we have a cuppa coffee and talk this over? 'Cause after you talk to me, you may not want to take me huntin'. And I may not wanna go huntin' with you!" So we had two or three cups of coffee and talked it all over and, hell, he's the nicest guy. I did a lotta huntin' with 'im after that and I did get 'im a lion. I ended up, over the years, catchin' 'im three lions.

Eventually, he got drawn for sheep, so we went down in these sheep mountains and, Christ, we worked our damn butts off. We finally found just a mediocre ram and he shot it. We worked around, got the Jeep and packed it into our camp. Then we got to drinkin' whiskey. We drank a whole damn liter of whiskey and then we come home. Both of us drunker 'n a lord. How we didn't have an accident or somethin', I don't know. I guess I was born under a lucky star and I think we just got back on my luck.

I caught him ever damn thing in the Big Ten but a wild turkey. We were huntin' up on the Fort Apache Indian Reservation and we run onto a turkey and he wanted to poach it, but I wouldn't let 'im. That woulda made 'im his Big Ten, but I told Jack, "By god, we're not poachin' this goddamn turkey up here with these damn Indians! They're payin' attention to what's goin' on up here! We'll get caught sure as hell." A good friend of his took 'im up later, somewhere, and got 'im a turkey.

Layne Brandt

Layne and I didn't know one another but we had a mutual friend – George Parker. George told me one day that I should get acquainted with Layne, that he's "a good son-of-a-bitch." I said, "You're sure he is?" He said, "Oh yeah! I know 'im well." So we met one day there at George's house, had a drink or two a-whiskey. I liked Layne. This was in the summer and I was doin' a little huntin' on the McGee Ranch, goin' one day a week up there. I asked Layne if he'd like to come and he said he would. We'd go up and make our one-day hunt. We messed around and used up, hell, maybe a month; hunted four or five times together. I asked Layne, "You really interested in killin' a lion?" "Yeah," he said, "I am. I killed one years ago with Clay Howell, but I'd like to kill another one." So I told him, "If you want to kill a lion real bad, we're gonna hafta go somewhere else 'cause there's nothing around here that's lookin' too good!"

The next time we went out we went way over on the Santa Ritas, kinda over on the north end of 'em there. We got up on a big ol' limestone ridge, headed north on it and went probably half a mile and the dogs hit a track. Christ! Away they went! We trailed 'em and, Christ, they finally headed off east, crossed a big canyon and went down another canyon. I got out kinda ahead of the dogs to see if I could see the track and, hell, they're trailin' it backwards! Well, in another half a mile we got the dogs all stopped, turned around and went back. Layne said, "You know, we don't have Drifter with us!" "No," I said, "hell, we haven't had 'im. He took off somewhere else. We haven't had 'im after these dogs turned east." So we went back and when we got back up on the ridge, up off to the northwest down there on the bluffs, we could hear ol' Drifter treein'! We rode down there where we could see 'im and, hell, he's got a big ol' tom lion out on a ledge of rock! And, of course, by that time these other dogs was all a-barkin' at 'im. We got down there in about 75 yards and Layne got off with his .30-.30 and shot the lion. It fell off the bluff and, Christ, there's a whole string of these bluffs. We had to ride back, hell, half a mile before we could find a place to get off. Then when we got off, we had to climb back up under the bluffs. Course, the damn dogs was already there; they're a-maulin' this lion and a-pullin' 'im closer down the mountain to us. We got up and told the dogs what good dogs they were and got that lion up in front of Layne's horse and packed 'im on down to the trailer. That was the first lion that Layne and I caught together. As I remember, he was a record-book tom!

Then Layne, he had one of his farm managers move down to Mexico, to Colonia Juarez, Chihuahua, Mexico, where his dad had a little farm. The father was gettin' in bad health so the guy quit his job and went down there to work with his dad, to help him. Layne said that we oughtta go down there and go huntin'. They're supposed to have lions down there. We loaded up our dogs and crossed the border there outta Douglas. Course, these Mexicans, they wanna know what we're doin'. We didn't tell 'em that we're goin' lion huntin'; we said we got a farmer friend down there and the raccoons are into his corn patch. He wants us to bring our dogs down there and catch some of these coons. That satisfied the Mexicans; that was fine, we was just goin' down there to help a friend.

We got to Colonia Juarez and I had a friend in the Army, a Mormon boy, who was raised down there and he had a brother who was still alive. So we looked up the brother and visited him, told him how I knew his brother, was in the Army with him. "Yeah," he said, "I lost my brother down there – never did ever find out exactly what happened to him. We were told he was bayoneted." I said, "Well, that's wrong. He was killed with a machine gun. In the Philippines. We'd been there for about 10 days. We went in there with a full company of around 200 men and we were down that morning to 27. I was wounded the day before, so I wasn't there, but one of the guys who'd survived the thing told me about it when I got back. They'd sent him out on a patrol to check something out and he come back and he told the Captain there was no way we could get in there – it was just infested with Japs and we'd all get killed. The Captain told him, 'Sergeant Johnson, that's our orders. Advance in there.' So Johnson just turned around and told the 27 men, 'Boys, come on. Let's go get killed!' They went in there and got pinned down with a machine gun. And he crawled around where he could see the gunner on it and he shot three Japs off that damn machine gun. Then his gun went empty and then a Jap got on it and killed 'im."

To get back to our story, after we left the brother, we went on off to this ranch. Layne's friend had a cowboy workin' there who had a lever action .22 rim fire rifle; it was the only gun we had. We got up to a big, deep canyon with lots of Ponderosa Pines down in the bottom. The dogs got out on the edge of a ledge and they started trailin'. They trailed along for probably half a mile and they went off in the canyon. They jumped a lion down in there and run it off in the canyon and treed it on one of these big pines. We had to go around for, god, a mile, mile and a half, before we got to a trail that went down there. We got pretty close to where these dogs is barkin' treed. This friend of Layne's and the cowboy, they couldn't stand it any longer; they just let out on a lope, run down there. Pretty soon, this Mexican cowboy come back. He said, 'Senor, los perros tiennen dos liones en la pina!" (Mister! The dogs have two lions in a pine tree!) And away he went again! I got down there and, Christ, here's a nice female lion layin' out there on a limb. I looked all over that damn tree and I couldn't see any more damn lions! So I asked the vaquero, "Donde esta la otra lione?" (Where's the other lion?) He shouted, "Es muy arriba en la pina!" (It's higher in the pine tree!) God, I changed position and I could see about six inches of his tail a-hangin' down there.

The friend of Layne's, he took the .22 and shot the one off the limb. The cowboy took the gun and run around and shot the other one. Now I know that there's been a time or two in my life when I've went off and left a lion a-sittin' in a tree – shoot one and think that was it! I know one case where I'm really sure that happened. I had a good friend of mine named Dave Miller who was huntin' with me. Going in, the dogs treed a lion in one of these blamed pinons and it was real thick and right in there I know I saw a tom lion a-sittin' in that damn tree. I've saw enough damn lions that I generally recognize a tom lion when I see one! We got down there and, hell, it's a female lion sittin' there layin' on a limb. He shot it and we gutted it out and tied it on behind his saddle and come out. If there was someway of provin' it, I'd bet a hundred dollar bill that we went off and left a tom in that tree!

The Cincinnati Hunters

Clay Howell, he called me up and told me about a hunter...give me his phone number, his address, said that he wasn't gonna hunt 'im and if I wanted 'im I could have 'im.

And Jimmy Engle sent hunters to Clay Howell and Clay Howell was a real good hunter, a real honest hunter. He caught quite a few lion there in the Santa Ritas, in fact he caught enough to build his house with his lion money. He give me this guy's phone number and I called the guy up; I was needin' a hunter. He was to meet me in Tucson. I wasn't pickin' 'im up at the airport, he was gonna get a room there and then he'd call me up from where ever he was stayin' and I'd pick 'im up.

When it was time to pick 'im up in the afternoon, I went to his room and he wasn't there. I went into the office inquirin' about 'im and one of the guys in there said, "Hell, he's out at the pool, asleep."

Figure 19. Ollie at the Elkhorn Ranch

So I gathered 'em up and took him down to the Elkhorn. God, I took 'im out the next day huntin' 'im and he's a basket case! Hell, he couldn't walk and he couldn't ride and Christ, he was a burden! I fooled around with 'im there and tried to keep 'im up and I had 'im on a good horse, but damn if he didn't get brushed off or fall off! Finally, the third day we hit a good lion track. I had about three young dogs and one old dog I was huntin' that day; ol' Tiger, I called 'im. They trailed this lion way back up on the mountain up there and we got up there and they got this lion treed down in a little deep wash in a oak tree. Just one damn oak all around there. This lion's right up in the top of it, layin' there. We tied our horses there and walked down there and we're about 40 yards from this lion in the tree. Christ, he couldn't see 'im; he couldn't see 'im! He had a .30-.06 Remington pump-action rifle and he couldn't see it. The dogs is runnin' around this tree a-barkin and a-leanin' up agin the tree and that ol' Tiger dog, he'd chew a little bark off the tree. And he can't see it. I said, "You see that oak there?" "Yeah, I see it," he says. "You see the very top of it?" I asked. "Yes," he says. I said, "You just go down in there and you'll see a dark object in there. This lion's head is on the right end of it." "Oh," he says, "you mean the lion's in the tree?" I said, "Yes, he's in the tree! You see all them dogs 'round under it, all four of 'em there a-barkin' at 'im! Barkin' up in the tree! You get over on the right side of that object and you put a bullet in 'im!"

And he shot. Ended up, he shot nine times! And all these dogs, you know, the bullets a-hittin' out there and flashin' rocks around, they'd all went off and hid! Crawlin' under bushes and brush and stuff and after the ninth shot that ol' lion just hopped out and down the canyon he goes! I thought to myself, "Jesus Christ, I've lost my damn lion!" But one ol' black-and-white pup I had, he climbed out and he took after that lion and a-course, all the rest of the dogs fell in behind 'im. They went down there a quarter mile or so and treed 'im in a big oak. I tied the horses back and walked 'im down there and that ol' lion, he's pretty cooperative, you know. I got 'im up there on a level with this lion in the tree and he's not more'n 20 feet. I said, "Now goddamnit, don't miss it!" "Oh," he says, "I can't miss; I only got one shot left!"

"Goddamn," I said, "you make damn sure you kill it!" And he shot 'im and the ol' lion just wilted right there – didn't fall outta the tree. He started runnin' over there, started to climb up the tree. I said, "You come back down here! I'm goin' up and get the horses and get my rope and then I'll climb up there and I'm gonna put this rope on this lion and knock 'im out and let 'im be a-hangin' there. Then these young dogs can bark at 'im and help 'em start treein' a little better." I got up to the horses and I hear that lion hit the ground. And I looked around and he's up in the tree. Goddamn, I have to come back and get the damn rope on him and let him down on the ground!

That same morning ol' Bob Miller (owner of the Elkhorn) was goin' into town and the guy had ordered two of these half-gallon jugs of whiskey. I got my hunter in the truck and all loaded up and he says, "I ordered whiskey!" I says, "Did you pay Bob?" He says, "Yes." "Well," I told him, "hell, just leave it…Bob likes that brand of whiskey." I took him back to town and got rid of 'im.

It went along there for three or four years and a judge in Cincinnati called me up. He wanted to go lion huntin'. He wrote me a letter; he didn't call me. He wanted to go lion huntin'. I told 'im, "I'll take you. How well do you ride and how much experience have you had in ridin'." He wrote back and he said that he hadn't had much experience in ridin' but why did I have to know how much experience he'd had ridin'? I wrote back and told him that I gotta know what kinda country to take you in 'cause if you're an inexperienced rider, I gotta keep you outta the real rough, bad country. And he wrote back and he says, "You take me where I got the best chance a-huntin'. I'll suffer the consequences." I decided I'd take 'im out to the ranch; there were a few lion around there yet. When I got to the airport to pick 'im up, I picked up his gun and I picked up his baggage but no Cincinnati judge! I got to checkin' on him and he'd missed his plane up in Denver, Colorado. And they said we'll have 'im back on the next plane; it'll be about an hour, an hour and a quarter. And he come in and *he's* under the influence! I got 'im loaded up and he said, "My secretary says you're gonna catch me a lion. Everbodys sayin' you'll never get a lion. But I'm goin' with you. My secretary says I'm gonna get a lion and I'm gonna get it on my birthday!"

We went out and the first morning he's got a great big ol', long single-action .44 magnum, made in Germany. He asks, "Should I take this along?" I says, "No, I want you to pack your rifle." He had a Remington .30-.06 pump. He said, "Well, I'm gonna take my pistol anyway." Hell, first day we ridin' along and he's behind me and he says, "Stop!" Then he got off and picked up his pistol. It'd come unsnapped someway or other and he'd lost it. I got 'im back in that night and next morning, he asks again, "You think I oughta bring my pistol?" I says, "Yes, by all means, I want you to bring your pistol." He says, "Well, yesterday you didn't want me to bring it!" I said, "Hell, you're gonna lose it and after you leave, I'll go back and find it!" And then he told me the history of the pistol. He said that there was a thug there in Cincinnati that was goin' around these bars and whippin' people. He was a big, husky guy and he'd whip a guy. He was in the bar there one night and he got this pistol out and started an argument with someone that was a little rougher then he thought. The other guy knocked 'im off the barstool and stomped 'im to death! I'd looked at this pistol and the serial numbers was filed off of it. He says, "I tried the guy for murder but the jury, they found 'im innocent, which they should have! It was three, four years back and I'm goin' on this hunt and that pistol's layin' down there in the evidence room – no one'd ever claimed it. I just went down and got it!"

So we made that hunt and he didn't have the pistol to lose; he had it hangin' on a nail in the tack room. But we did hit a lion track and god, they trailed it way up on top, nearly on top of the Rincons. It's about 5:00 o'clock and this ol' spotted hound that I had, Blackie, he's got that lion treed down there in a deep canyon. Hell, there's no way a-gettin' there before dark. Some of these other dogs that was with me had give up and some of 'em was still trailin'. I told 'im there was no way we could get to that lion; we better go back.

I'd had ol' Homer, the caretaker there at the Heart, meet us at the ranch. We'd left from the Heart. Goddamn, he's not there! So we start over to the Heart and hell, it's a eight mile ride. And it's already dark. We got down about a mile and a half and we met ol' Homer. He'd been over and waited for us, we didn't come, and then he'd gone back to the Heart to see if we'd come in there. We weren't there, so he's comin' back. Christ, by the time we got back and eat a little bit and got to bed, it's probably 11:00 o'clock. The next morning is Thanksgiving Day so I told him, "Over here in the next canyon, Miller Canyon, I see a lion track come through there, a female, ever once in awhile. We'll go over there and make a short kind of a token hunt 'cause the dogs is tired and you're tired." That was fine and we got over there and opened the gate and my damn dogs across the creek opened up! I got in through it and got the gate shut and got back on my horse and hell, they didn't go much over a quarter mile and they treed! We went up there and they got a real nice female lion treed. We shot it out with his rifle and we brought it back to the ranch and hell, we're back to the ranch 'bout 8:30. It's Thanksgiving Day, Beryl's a-cookin' a Thanksgiving dinner and he got ol' Homer and they went to town to get some wine. And when they get back, both of 'em had got a snoot-full a-this wine.

So we had Thanksgiving dinner and Homer and them had to drink some more damn wine. I didn't help 'em on their wine; I had a drink a-whiskey or two with 'em. And then he told me how come he picked me to go huntin'. He says, "You remember (and he named the guy, I've forgot the name now) this salesman. You caught him a lion. And he's an alcoholic, drunk, helpless, but he's a good salesman. A whiskey salesman. He told me about catchin' this lion with you and I figured by god, if you could catch him a lion, you could catch *anybody* a lion!"

So that's how I got this Cincinnati judge. He told me he was a hangin' judge. He says, "Hell, I got more people in prison back there than any other judge!" And it turned out just like his secretary told 'im: she says, "You're gonna catch it on your birthday, on Thanksgiving Day!"

The Backtrack Lion

This lion story happened a number of years ago, when I still owned the ranch. The road was washed out and I left my truck at Malcolm's place. I borrowed a horse and rode over to the ranch; I'd go out weekends and ride. I'd left my pistol in the truck.

I went out ridin' that day. I'd branded a few calves and I found one of these calves that I'd branded the week before in a sand wash, a lion had killed it. I'd brought two or three dogs along with me, to kind of exercise 'em. This is along past noon and the dogs wanted to take the track but I didn't have any gun so I called 'em off. I rode all the way back to Malcolm's and got my pistol and rode back to the ranch. The next morning I got up early and I got up to this calf and it was just startin' to break daylight. The dogs, they sniffed around and they bow-wowed and the calf was uncovered and pretty well eat up. The dogs took off and went up on the hillside and they come down and went up this main canyon, Deer Creek, and they come to Sycamore Canyon and they went up it. They're travelin' at a pretty good rate of speed and I could see a scratch ever so often comin' down. Then I could see a track comin' down. And then I realized that these dogs is on the backtrack. I never had luck catchin' any lions a-runnin' a back track! So I whipped up then and tried to catch 'em but I'd fooled around too long and I was too far behind 'em. They got up to this Sycamore Canyon where I had a trough and a water and they took a little side canyon. It went off to the east and climbed up on this big ridge where it come off the main mountain, the Rincons. I see four cows run outta this saddle there and they had baby calves.

My dogs, they went on over the hill and so I'm a-checkin' these cows and calves and I got up on top of the ridge I hear these dogs barkin' treed down there about a quarter of a mile. I had to ride on up the ridge about a half a mile to find a gate to get in there and I see where this lion had come off a-the main mountain down a old Forest Service trail. I see his big ol' tracks and where he'd scratched ever so often. I went on down where they had this big tom treed and I shot 'im with my pistol. Then I loaded it on my horse and on a

223

steep hillside, that was all I could do. I went back to the gate and come down. So I'm followin' this trail, this old Forest Service trail, and it goes down, not to my ranch but the next ranch north of me. I could see where this lion had went down this here trail and I could see where he's comin' back. And he'd got back up there where these four cows was with these baby calves and he was probably sittin' there on his haunches, lickin' his lips, figurin' which one of those calves he was gonna kill. And the dogs jumped 'im right there!

I'd gutted the lion out and hell, he was full of calf meat so I knew I had the right lion. That's how I figured out how I caught 'im goin' on his backtrack! I've never ever had that happen before and I never really think I ever run a lion off a-one of my calves he was fixin' to kill either! I think he was a record book tom, as I remember, but I was just glad to get 'im off a-the ranch!

The Game Wardens

Game wardens are supposed to be real knowledgeable, but some, I think, have a lot to learn. I had one game warden check me with a mountain lion – it was a real nice tom. He wrote in his little book and he made his calculations on the weight and age and then he lifted up the hind leg, looked and he pronounced it a female! I never corrected him on the deal, but I thought, "This young man has a lot to learn if he don't even know how to sex a mountain lion or a tomcat!"

And then another game warden, up north, a real conscientious game warden, he went out lion huntin' with a lion hunter up there. They caught a lion, but it was after dark. They had a flashlight and he shot this mountain lion after dark with the flashlight. Usin' artificial light and shootin' animals at night is illegal, only one that you can shoot at night with an artificial light is a raccoon. After he'd shot it, and slept on it all night, he realized that he'd committed a violation. So he wrote himself a citation! Took care of that and paid his fine! He took exception to even seein' a gum wrapper dropped in the field. He was by the book!

This other game warden – he's still alive and if this ever gets in print or anything and he reads it, he'll know who it is – he come out to the ranch; it was when they was surveyin' their deer population. I had a real good population of mule deer on the ranch at that time. I had four or five hounds and I had all of 'em so we got ready to leave I turned 'em loose. "Ollie," he said, "tie those damn dogs back up! I want to count these deer; I don't want these hounds a-runnin' 'em!" I told him, "Well, these hounds don't run deer; you don't have to worry about that."

On the north boundary of my ranch, there was a mountain ridge that we called Fox Mountain. We got up just about to the top of that and, accordin' to his count there was 17 does and fawns. These hounds went right up in the middle of 'em and they got their noses on the ground and pretty soon, they opened! "Ollie," he shouted at me, "you told me those hounds don't run deer!" "Hell," I said, "you see 'em runnin'? They're not runnin'. Those hounds found a lion track!" "Aw," he says, "they're barkin' at them deer!"

"Goddamn it," I told him, "I know more about my damn hounds than that! They're not!" And they went out of the deer, got up on top and then there's a trail that run on top and they headed east on it. We had to go around about an extra 300 or 400 yards to get through a gate and get on the other side of the fence on this trail. I got up there just beyond where the hounds come out on top of the mountain and over under a juniper I see a big tom scratch there, goin' the right way. I got past that – he hadn't saw it – and told him, "Goddamn it Bob, these dogs is a-trailin' a tom lion!" He says, "How do you know?" I says, "Can't you tell by the way they're barkin'?" He didn't have any comment on that, but I assured 'im it was a tom! We trailed the thing, I guess three miles, and on some bluffs that must a-been 300 foot high and right up on top on a little ledge, here sat Mr. Lion. A damn nice tom. And he wanted to kill it with his pistol. He could a-shot it with my rifle from down below, but no, he climbed around up there. It took him 15 or 20 minutes to get up there and then I see 'im sneak out with his pistol. He shot and that ol' lion just jumped out into space! He went for a 100 foot or so and hit a ledge and then just tumbled down and hit in these little saplin' oaks that was 15, 20 foot high with real think underbrush all around them. He crashed down through those oaks and run outta there and ran down the mountain about a quarter of a mile! How those dogs got down there so quick, I don't know, but they treed it out on a big rock, or rather, they bayed it on this rock. He's gettin' his pistol out and I said, "Bob, you put that damn pistol back and use my rifle to kill it, 'cause we've punished this lion enough! Hell, it fell out there, probably got some broken bones and it's bleedin' out of its mouth and nose!" So he shot it. We loaded it up and I says, "That's a record-book lion!" "Aw," he said, "I don't think so. It's not that big!" I asked, "How many damn lions have you looked at?" He said, "Well, not very many." I said, "Well, I'm tellin' you it's a record-book tom!"

We headed back to the ranch, we got this lion packed on his horse and he's walkin', leadin' it. We got about a mile or so down the trail and he realized that he'd poached this lion – he didn't have a lion tag! When we get to the ranch its maybe three o'clock and boy, he jumped in his government pickup and to Benson he went and bought him a lion tag. He come back and tagged that lion! Afterwards, he told Doug Baker that it did make the book but he never put it in the record book. But it was measured up to a record!

Sometime after that, we made a trip down into Mexico. This was a real education for me *and* him! The first night we drove until about four o'clock and stopped, built us a campfire and cooked us a little meal. His system of buildin' a fire was to dig a hole, shovel down about 18 inches deep and about that much in diameter and build a fire down in that hole. And then he had a little grill and a couple of pegs he'd drive in the ground with a cross on top. He'd put his grill on that and try to keep this fire going and cook on that. I told 'im, I says, "Bob, this is the stupidest damn thing I ever saw! Where'd you learn that?" He says, "Well, I learned it in the Boy Scouts!" I says, "Well, I'm gonna teach you what my dad taught me, how to build a fire. You get you three rocks, they don't have to be big, just about six inches in diameter or eight inches and spread them out and get an area in there about a foot or foot-and-a-half and build your fire in there. As the fire burns down, you can rake you some coals out for your coffee pot and over here you rake out coals for your fryin' pan and over here, you rake out coals for your dutch oven. You can keep your fire goin' and keep your coals a-comin' out and that's how you build a campfire to cook on in the hills." So we tried that and that's what we did the rest of the damn trip! He agreed that it was better.

The first night we cooked our evening meal and then we just drove on; it never got dark 'til about nine o'clock. This was in June maybe the 21st or 23rd, near what the Mexican's call San Juan's Day. So this first night we camped. Lotta ants down in that country and they'd have places cleared out about eight or ten feet – nice clearing. Ants is all gone to bed. That's where he laid his bed out. I put mine out in the weeds. God, next morning, just breaking daylight, he's got an ant problem! "Goddamn, Ollie," he said, "these ants is givin' me fits!" So he got up and shook his bed out and rolled it up. The next night he done the same thing. And the next morning, he's got a ant problem! The third morning he says, "Ollie, how come these ants never bother you?" I said, "Just being a poor country boy, raised up around ants and stuff, I learned not to make my bed out in their goddamn dens! Hell, I got mine out in the weeds! The ants is not botherin' me!" Well, after that, he rolled his bed out in the weeds with me!

We got on down there and it was San Juan's Day and we stopped in here and they're runnin' horse races in the streets there, you know. These Mexicans is drinkin' a whole lot and I'd brought my hound dog, Abe, along with me. There's a Mexican layin' there, passed out drunk, with his head up on the corner of a building and this Abe, what did he do but sniff around and then piss in his ear! All these Mexicans thought that was *real* funny! When we got through visitin' there with the Mexicans, we left and come into another little town. These roads comin' outta these towns down there – there wasn't any pavement; they're mostly just wagon roads. This one Mexican I was talkin to there, findin' out what road goes out. Bob, with a little of his high school Spanish, he's tryin' to talk. Pretty soon, this Mexican tells me, "Your compañero don't talk very good Spanish." Bob says, "What's he tellin' you?" I say, "He's tellin' me you don't talk very good Spanish!"

Anyway, when we asked how far it was to the next town and some of those people would say, "Tres dias via el caballo" (three days by horseback) or "quatro dias via el caballo" (four days) or just "media dia" (half a day). That was the way they judged distance down there. This particular time, the Mexican had to get out and show us which road went to the next town. On the way into this next town, we run onto a Yaqui Indian. This Yaqui Indian, he's a-gallopin' his horse down the road. When he saw us in the pickup, he stopped and his ol' horse had all foam lather on 'im. This Mexican's got a coke bottle full of bacanora and he was a-slobberin' at the mouth, pretty boracho (drunk). He offers us a drink, so I took it, I took a little sip of this bacanora – I knew enough not to drink too much of it. Bob, he shook his head no, and I said, "Bob, we're down here in this Yaqui country and it's very offensive when they offer you a drink or somethin' not to take it! So you'd better take a drink or it's liable to get us in trouble if you don't!" Well, on the strength of that he takes about three gurgles of the stuff. He was kinda light complected and in about 20 minutes he turned a pretty pink color and he's drunker'n a lord!

We went on and we got into a real pretty little town, about 18,000 people they told me. We're stopped in the cantina there drinkin' a beer and here come a young Mexican, looked like about in his mid-twenties, well dressed and spoke perfect English. He asked us if we were gettin' along all right and everthing. He had heard that there were a couple of white men in town and he had just come down to see if we needed any help. He's a state policeman. He'd been to some police school – I think it was in state of Washington or might a-been Oregon. That was where he'd got his police schooling. He was a policeman in the state of Sonora but was there visitin' his mother. After seein' this warden get drunk on that bacanora, I asked 'im, "Goddamn, where can we get some bacanora around here?" "Oh," he said, "bacanora is illegal!" Then he left but came back a little later and says that his mother had invited us to dinner. So we went and had dinner with 'em and I still got bacanora on my mind so we start scroungin' around for it and finally, he found a gallon of it in a cathouse! We bought it and one of the smart things we done on that trip – we had an empty whiskey bottle – nearly empty, so we drank what was left of the whiskey and filled this whiskey bottle up full of bacanora and put the gallon jug away where it wouldn't get broke.

We're nippin' along on that and sure enough, San Juan's rain come. And it did rain! I was wantin' to see this Novilla Dam they were buildin' down there at the time, but when we went through a little village I thought we'd better camp because we're gonna miss this dam. So we got just out of town and rolled our beds out and daylight come and here come all these Mexican workers. Some had their lunches in a lard can and some of 'em in a paper sack. Pretty soon a policeman come along and wanted to know what we was doin' there. "Hell, we're just camped out," I said. "We got drunk on bacanora and we just rolled our beds out here. Really, we wanna see this Novilla Dam. We camped kinda early 'cause we didn't wanna miss it!" He said, "All you gotta do is just raise up in bed and turn your head around and you can see it!" I did and there it was! Hell, it wasn't 300 yards, a great big old dam there! This ol' Mexican cop says, "Well, you're already in here, so if you wanna walk up and explore and check that dam out, it'll be all right." So we did.

The next night we were on the outside of Hermosillo. Over across the way there, about a half-mile, there's these red lights out there on these buildings. Bob wanted to know what they was so I told him they're Mexican cathouses. I says, "You wanna go over there and check 'em out?" Course, he did. We went over there and they had two classes there – they had the more expensive one for the businessmen and then they had the cheaper ones. We're out by the pickup and here's ol' Abe and he's a-standin' up, a-sniffin' and a-smellin' around and one of these whores come out and she wanted to drum up a little business. I told her we're both married and didn't want to have anything to do with whores, but I asked her what her price was. She says, "Three dollars". I says, "Well, you can screw that hound then for three dollars!" Oh my god, she wasn't screwing no dog!

Finally, we went back to our camp and bedded down for the night and drove on back to Tucson the next day. We didn't go to Mexico for any real reason; I hadn't been down through that part of the country before and I kinda wanted to see it. I liked Bob, helpless as he was.

Walapai Lion Hunt

I went back up to the Walapai Reservation one time to lion hunt with some Indians. After I was up there for a day or two, I found out what they wanted. They didn't want to catch a damn lion, they was wantin' to buy a lion dog! We hunted up there, oh hell, I guess it must a-been a five-day hunt. Them Indians took us around to ever damn place where you couldn't hit a good lion track. They didn't want me to catch a lion. But they did want to buy a dog.

One day we're right up on the edge of the canyon there and a damn big ol' buck elk, about a good six-pointer, he broke outta there, ever damn hound I had on 'im. They left! They didn't know what elk were – they thought it was somethin' to catch! Goddamn, they run that damn thing and we followed 'em around and, hell, they just left the country. That blamed elk, he just run a pretty straight line. We went back to camp and we got the pickup – unhooked the trailer – and we started huntin' dogs. Christ, we picked up a couple of 'em. The next day we went out and picked up two of 'em comin' back. They was a good 15 miles from where they started that damn elk. They was just runnin' the damn thing and ol' elk just went pretty much in a straight line. He's a-headed south! So I gathered up my dogs.

I had this whiskey salesman from Tucson with me. He'd hunted elk up there with them Indians and drank whiskey with 'em. He got along with 'em pretty well. We told 'em we wasn't gonna catch a lion up there and we come back. That was my only Walapai lion hunt and I didn't sell 'em a dog.

Tom Faust

Tom was the hunting and gun editor for, I think, the *Citizen* (*Tucson Daily Citizen*). He wanted to go lion huntin' real bad and I liked Tom Faust real well 'cause he told a real good story and he told it pretty much like it was. I thought at the time if I ever was gonna write a book, I'd get him to be my ghostwriter. He knows how to tell a story. I took him up on the Catalinas; we went down Samaniego Ridge and there, next to the mountain, Samaniego Ridge, they had a cabin down there in a place they called Shovel Spring. So we packed our gear in there on our saddle horses and made camp in there. Tom Faust and I, we started huntin'.

I hunted him pretty hard, 'cause that's the only way I knew how to catch a lion, to work at it. The first evening when we come in, he got off his horse and he just fell down and he crawled over to the door of the cabin and sat there in the door. He couldn't walk. He'd had polio when he was a kid and that was still affectin' 'im. We hunted two more days; didn't catch anything. Two more days and when he got off his horse, he couldn't walk; he'd hafta crawl over there and sit in the door while I was takin' care of the horses. Unsaddlin' 'em, gettin' 'em staked out with hay. By then, he could get up and help a little with fixin' an evening meal. The third morning, I told him, "Faust, you don't have to punish yourself this way. If it's too tough on you, we can just call the hunt off. And I'll give you your deposit back. I hate to see you punish yourself this way and I'll give you your deposit and we'll still be friends. I'll keep it to myself; I won't tell anybody." He says, "Ollie, I want a lion so damn bad I'll do anything to do it!" I said, "Faust, if you wanna punish yourself this bad, I'll damn sure catch you a lion and I'll try not to kill you! I think we've pretty well covered this

Samaniego Ridge and we're not doin' any good, so let's just knock the hunt off and let you kinda recuperate a little bit."

Well, he was agreeable to that. The next time I took 'im out, the next weekend, we went down on the Elkhorn Ranch, in the Baboquivaries. We got on a good lion track real quick and trailed it up on top of a big damn ridge, rough damn place, and the lion went over the top and down. We could hear the dogs treein' off down there about half a mile. There's no way to possibly walk in there. Don Carr was with me and I told Don, "You take my horse and Faust and go around and I'll go on in a-foot with the dogs, see if we can keep this lion treed until you can get Faust around there". I got around there and hell, by the time I'd got off down in there the lion'd jumped and they treed it again. I saw this lion when it treed and it was in kind of a damn pine, about 20 feet tall, not big, and I saw that lion just jump straight up and land on top of that damn tree. I knew a lion could jump, but I didn't know they could jump 15 or 20 foot right straight up and land on top of this damn little ol' pine like a bird! It was an adult female. I got over there and an Indian rode up. He told us, "You know, you guys aren't supposed to be huntin' in here." I said, "Well, we started this lion over on the Elkhorn and we followed the dogs over here." This Indian cowboy says, "I don't care about you huntin' in here. Hell, I hope you catch ever lion around here 'cause they catch a lotta calves. But down in the village we're out of, those damn officers and tribal council are gonna raise hell about it!" "Well," I said, "that's fine." And about that time, the lion jumped again and Faust and Carr was there with my horse and the damn lion was goin' back up towards the top of Baboquivarie Peak. We got up in there and the damn lion got away from the dogs and we gathered 'em up and come back.

When we're comin' back to the Elkhorn, there's an Okie, I forget his name, outta Oklahoma and he had some dogs. He was a tough damn guy, did a lotta huntin' on foot, followin' those dogs around on foot! And he had to be a tough bastard to follow those dogs a-foot, especially the deer-runnin' bastards he had! He never had a damn decent dog.

They were hot on a track, we could see 'em up there, the dogs were comin' and trailin'. They'd be trailin' damn good if they was trailin' a lion, but they was doin' kind of a piss poor job runnin' a deer, 'cause I could see the deer! We met Quimby (Bill Quimby, Outdoor Feature Writer for the *Citizen*) and this Okie and they wanted to know what we done and we told 'em we'd caught a lion and lost it.

Well, this Okie spoke up and said, "My dogs is workin' a hot lion track." I said, "The way they're workin', if it's a lion, they're gonna catch it. Better get to followin' 'em!" Faust and I went on and come back to camp; it was just a one-day hunt. I was huntin' ol' Faust just on weekends; I was huntin' 'im for half-price, wasn't chargin' 'im full price.

The next evening, Faust called me up and says, "This Okie called me up and they wanna make a wager. That they can catch a lion before we do!" And I says, "Faust, you know for the price I'm chargin' you, I'm workin' and you're workin' and I can't just take off and catch a lion before they do just to prove 'em wrong! But if they wanna make a damn wager, tell 'em to put up $500 and they're on!" Faust, he passed on the information and the next evening he called me up and says, "Ollie, they don't want to make a wager, they just wanna bet for funzies!" I told Faust, "Goddamnit, I don't bet for funzies! Those bastards wanna take us on in a competition, put up $500!" Next day, they couldn't put up the damn $500. They wanted to go back to the funzie bit. So I told Faust, "If they wanna go in for funzies, I'll tell you what to tell 'em. Tell 'em we're gonna give 'em a 30-day start with a damn calendar. And then we'll catch a lion before they do!"

So we waited our 30 days and hell, they hadn't caught a lion yet. I took him out to my old ranch and lo and behold! I got on a good damn tom track and god; we trailed it for about five miles. They bayed this lion up on a big bluff and we come out on top of it and we couldn't see the lion from where we were but the dogs were underneath us barkin' and I knew it was in there. I told Faust, "You're hurtin' and by god, I'll ride around and make damn sure they do have the lion in that bluff there where we can shoot it." So I rode around and goddamn, sure enough, there's this big ol' tom sittin' up there by a big ol' boulder. I motioned ol' Faust to come around and hell, it took 'im 30 minutes to get down there and here's this damn lion. He's sittin' up there and Christ, he's lickin' himself just like a house cat! He'd take his paws and rub on his face, unconcerned as hell! I told Faust, "Shoot him right in the chest! Don't break the skull 'cause this is a big lion!" Faust got his .30-.30 out and he got him a little rest there and he shot that lion right in the chest. He just sunk down right there! I told Faust, "Well, I guess we can't get into 'im from the top; we gotta get to 'im goin'up." So I climbed around up there and I took a-hold of that big rock and it moved a little. Then I knew I had to get around this damn rock and roll that lion out. I got up there and rolled it out and got down outta there without killin' my fool self or knockin' that rock off. This is the first day after the 30 days and ol' Tom, he's got him a Arizona record book lion. Christ, he couldn't hardly wait to get to town! Boy, he showed 'em that lion and, you know, the word was already out about our wager, givin' 'em that 30-day lead. And I'll tell you, them goddamn guys around there that knew about it, they laughed and teased that damn Okie so much about it that he went back to Oklahoma and no one's ever heard of 'im since!

Tony Don Sheep Hunt

Tony Don was a dentist in Tucson. He used to hunt with a Chinese farmer all the time. They both of 'em got drawn for sheep up in the Catalinas, north of Tucson. So ol' Tony Don, he got a-hold of me and wanted me to pack 'im up in there and hunt. I had three saddle horses and two pack animals. I thought, for three men, we could pack enough groceries and beddin' up there for a 16-day hunt with two pack animals. But we ended up with all five horses packed up! I didn't know Tony well, but I'd met 'im and I told 'im about the Chinese merchant I knew down in the south part of Tucson. Taft Lee. "Oh," he says, "I know that goddamn Chinaman." I said, "Well, I know 'im, but I don't know as I can call 'im a goddamn Chinaman!" He says, "I can!" It turned out they was related someway through marriage.

And then when we got all this here truckloads of stuff, takin' five horses to pack it up, I said, "Don, Christ, takin' an awful lotta equipment for just for a little sheep hunt!" "Well, Ollie," he says, "we're livin' in the land of plenty. We don't wanna do without, do we?" I says, "Well, I guess not!" So we packed up on these Catalinas and we hunted there several days. We was camped back up under a big ledge where it was dry and then it come a six-inch snowstorm. After that, it turned cold! We scouted that mountain pretty well; we'd find ewes and a few little sickle-horn rams and not very many of them and not too many sheep. 'Cause I was of the opinion that there wasn't more than 30, 40 sheep on that mountain anyway. There was reports that there was as many as 150 but I never believed it. The lions has eat 'em up now to where I don't know if they got any left. The Game Department has thought several times of restockin' it, but they're gonna hafta take the lions out before they restock it or they'll just be feedin' sheep to mountain lions! And that's not the way to go.

Anyhow, we hunted the full 16 days up there, covered the country and got real well acquainted. Ol' Tony Don, he looked at my mouth and when I'd got outta the service, I went to some horse doctor and he put a bunch of fillings in that was fallin' out. And I had some bridge work that was fallin' out. Tony Don says, "When we get through with this sheep hunt, you make an appointment with me and I'll straighten your mouth out." By that time, I was gettin' to like the guy real well.

Gettin' back to this snowstorm, this was the highlight of the whole damn hunt! We're up there underneath this ledge and it's probably 8:00 or 9:00 o'clock at night. Nights is real long, you know, you couldn't spend 10, 12 hours in bed, we got a little fire a-goin'. The reason we got a little fire a-goin' is because there's no wood around there! Christ, we'd be spendin' the daytime sheep huntin' instead of gatherin' firewood. This snowstorm come on and cold, goddamn it was cold! We was up in the pine timber. We're sittin' there one night by this little fire shiverin' and visitin' and pretty soon ol' Dr. Don just fell over on his back and just burst out laughin' and just kept a-laughin'. Finally, I said, "Goddammit Don, what is so goddamn funny about freezin' our ass up here?" "Well, Ollie," he says, "what would your friends think of you if they could see you up here freezin' your ass off with this little fire talkin' Mexican to two Chinamen?"

My opinion went a-way up on him 'cause, hell, he had a sense of humor. I went to 'im for years and he fixed my mouth up and the work he done is still there! He was reasonable. He was always glad to see me and he's always talkin' huntin'.

He got a back problem and he went to a doctor and they told 'im he had a disc problem and they could fix it. They cut in there and they cut into cancer. Christ, they sewed 'im back up and six months later, he's dead!

But that was a good hunt. For all our huntin', we never saw a legal ram. There was one other hunter up there and he never saw a legal ram. In 16 days nobody saw a legal ram. The sheep wasn't there! There was several guys had been up there and counted the same sheep over and over again. They give the wrong information. After I moved to Rio Rico, a game warden come to see me and said, "I've got a lion problem up in the Catalinas. The lion are startin' to kill these sheep. I'd like for you to go up there and do some huntin' and take some of them lion out." I told 'im, I said, "Christ, that country's so damn rough you can't ride in it and I can't take clients in there. But what I will do, if you can get some Game Department men and some volunteers to go up on the mountain and go out on all those little points and ridges, I'll go in there and turn my dogs loose. If they catch a lion there'll be someone up on the top that can come down and shoot it and come on off the mountain and we'll pick 'em up." He thought that was a real good idea. He took it back to the Game Department and they wouldn't have anything to do with it. They just couldn't be involved in killin' those lions. Public relations – it was just all wrong.

Walapai Sheep Story

It was a cold, miserable damn trip. I was huntin' this Buck Buckner. He had to have a Indian guide but he didn't wanna rely just on a blamed Indian guide. I'd caught 'im a lion and I think I got 'im a couple of javelina so he wanted me to guide 'im on this sheep hunt. Of course, he couldn't get me a license, but he could take me along as a kind of a swamper, or helper. We got up there and this here Indian guide he had was a alcoholic and he had 'im a helper and he had horses. They met us there at our camp on the reservation.

Buck leaves out with his two Indian guides a-horseback and left me alone in camp. My idea was to go out and scout around and see if I could locate some sheep. I'd brought my Abe dog, my pet hound, along with me. So, they get off a-horseback and I take off with my hound and my field glasses. I'm glassin' these big canyons and long about noon, I got off in this big, deep canyon – I don't remember the name of it – and there was an old Army camp down there. Here was Buckner and these two Indians walkin' around this old Army camp pickin' up buttons and whatnot. Old spent cartridges. Across the mountain there from us, wasn't a quarter mile, there was three rams. They weren't very good rams and they were rollin' rocks – I could hear from, hell, a mile away! They're so all engrossed with pickin' up their souvenirs; they never saw these sheep.

I was in ahead of 'em gettin' back to camp and the tent flap, about a foot from the bottom, was unzipped. I unzipped it more and in there, in one of the grocery boxes, was a big ol' skunk! It was right in the tent. And, fortunately this box was sittin' out there kinda apart. I had my rope so I got the tent flap all open and tied back. This skunk, he'd settled in and gone back to sleep so I dropped my loop over the box. Well, that woke the skunk up. I wait awhile and ol' skunk goes back to sleep so I pull the box about a foot and the skunk wakes up! So I quit. There in about 15 minutes, I had that skunk out in the yard about 10 foot, or out in front of the tent. I'd tied ol' Abe up 'cause I didn't want him in the tent with that skunk. That skunk finally wandered off and I watched 'im go off in the brush about 100 yards.

The Indians and Buck come in and everything's settled down and I turn the hound loose. What the hell does the hound do? He just takes that skunk track, trails 'im up and kills 'im and packs 'im back into camp! He's a stinkin' damn mess! I had a two-quart can of tomato juice – I'd heard you could kill that skunk scent with it – so I give ol' Abe a kind of a bathin' in this tomato juice. And hell, it did! It cut that skunk scent damn near to nothin'! This hound, you know, he's used to sleepin' on my jacket in the tent with me. He's a pet dog, a good hound.

Goddamn, and the weather turned cold! This Indian got on a drunk so they licensed me; I had to give 'em $100. I think I'm probably the only white guy that ever had a damn guide permit to guide for sheep on that Walapai Reservation. About the third, fourth day we saw what I thought was a good ram but Bucker, he's a Boone and Crockett measurer, and he's got to have a Boone and Crockett ram. This ol' ram's horns, they come way down and they'd broomed off real big, he was an old sheep, and I tried to get Bucker to make a stalk on him and kill him. Hell, he was plenty legal and these sheep permits is hard to come by. I understand he hasn't got one yet. Puts in ever year.

It turned colder and there was an Indian comin' around there choppin' ice off the tank where we was camped. And then it rained. And then it snowed. Christ, the wind blew and blew our tent down! The only thing to do is just, by god, cover up everythin' with our tent and get it weighted down. Then, we got in the Jeep and the Jeep was stuck! So we took the tent stuff off this dry spot and put it in the trailer and got it covered up. Then we winched our Jeep up on this dry spot. We fired that Jeep up and made a run for it – got up on the road and went on in a little village there and got a motel room. This Indian is a-sellin' us a room and he saw this hound. He told me and Buckner, "Don't let that hound in. You can't let him in." By that time that ol' hound had taken off to checkin' things out and I said, "Hell, we won't see that

238

hound 'til mornin'. But he'll be a-layin' under the Jeep in the mornin'." We got all settled down and pretty soon I hear the ol' hound a-whimperin' outside. So I opened the door and he got on my damn huntin' jacket and hell, he slept all night there in a warm motel room.

Then these Indians decided we oughta move up in the mountains. Christ, there was a good skift of snow on the ground then! We went on up these mountains there where we wasn't too far from the edge of the Grand Canyon. Goddamn, we pitched our tent and it's cold! With about six inches of snow on the ground. The only damn time that I ever tried to pitch a tent when it's so cold this damn aluminum frame is tryin' to stick to your hands! So I had to get the gloves on and we finally got it all pitched up. Christ, our water cans was all froze solid. The only way we could get coffee water or any water to drink was to melt snow!

So we started huntin' and there's a lotta wild horses up in there and a lotta wild burros. We'd glass these sheep across the canyon and around, we never could find a decent ram. They were all sickle horns. Course, ol' Buckner, he wasn't shootin' one of them. One night there, I had a pressure cooker we'd fired up and had a stew cookin' in it. Goddamn, I guess we had it a little too full. This meat and stuff had blew up and stopped this pop-off deal. It was plugged up and the first thing I know there was a crash and a bang and this damn pressure cooker just took off like it's goin' into orbit! It got up there and just spun around three or four times at the top of this tent and that goddamn hound made a dash for the tent flap – it was up six, eight inches – and outside he went! We ducked down and didn't get burned with any of that hot stuff 'cause most of it just hit around the top of the tent. When I finally wore that tent out it still had pieces of that damn stew glued to the top of it. We got it cleaned up and started another goddamn somethin' to eat; I don't remember what it was.

Finally, it got down to the last day of the season and what do we see but a fairly decent ram. He wasn't broomed or anything but hell, he was plumb legal. Easy shot. We could get the Jeep within a couple hundred yards of 'im. Buck wouldn't shoot the thing. Nope. He had to have a Boone and Crockett ram or nothin'. I told 'im, "Goddamn, you may never get drawn again Take it!" He wouldn't take.

Then the Indians broke a trail in there to help get us out. We come back to Tucson – no damn sheep. We should've killed that first one or, even as a last resort, Buckner shoulda shot that little one. But he wouldn't do it. Now, the man's an international hunter. Hell, he got a-hold of a bunch of money and Christ, he's a big hunter. But he still don't have a desert sheep. And probably never will! I'll bet he's regretted that!

"Wild Kingdom" TV Shows

I saw this guy from Mutual of Omaha, this Stan Brock they brought up from Belize, South America. Mutual of Omaha had been down there and made a movie or two with him, one of 'em 'rasslin' a alligator or a crocodile or some other damn thing. They were real impressed with this Stan Brock and they hired 'im! I helped 'em make a movie about ropin' a grizzly bear. They had this animal man that brought in a big, ol' black, fat bear and a mountain lion and a grizzly bear. The first thing, they turned the mountain lion loose and my dogs run it up on a rock and they made the movie. I had a little ol' dog, a pretty good dog, I called "Teddy." I tied Teddy up and one a-these cameramen asked me, "Well, how come you didn't turn Teddy loose?" "Oh," I says, "hell, you wanted to get pictures a-that lion on a rock and if I turned Teddy loose, he'd went up there and drug 'im off! Just messed the whole picture up!" This animal man says, "Aw, you worry about your damn hound! I worry about my lion!" I just stored this information away. A few days later they took this mountain lion and this guy led 'im all around, probably about a diameter of a quarter of a mile there and brought 'im back to the truck where his box was. But he didn't put 'im in the box. He walked on across the canyon and climbed up on a big rock to watch the dogs trail this lion up. They had three cameramen around takin' pictures of it and recordin' their noise. These dogs come into the truck and they looked up and that lion wasn't in the box. So they picked up his track and they trailed 'im across the canyon and here's this animal man a-sittin' up there with his lion and what did Teddy do but just jump up and drag 'im off! The fight started, hell, the dogs bailed in on 'im, and this lion man, he come down there and says, "Goddamn you guys, help me get these dogs off this lion before they kill 'im!" And we got 'em off and he got the lion back in the box. That evening he told me, "Ollie, you've got lion dogs!"

The next go-around, we turned this here bear loose. It was up in the pass between the Rincons and the Catalinas. They turned this bear loose and the first thing they did was run this bear over the mountain and down there's a canyon that runs into Tucson, between the two mountains. They run this ol' bear off down there in a water hole. This is about a three-year-old grizzly bear. He was real easy to handle but those dogs had 'im kinda worked up a little bit. I had my pistol on and the cameraman says, "What're you packin' that pistol for?" I says "By god, I'm not gonna let this goddamn bear eat me up!" We got our dogs off of 'im and this Stan Brock was gonna rope this bear. I had a horse I was a-furnishin' him to ride and he wasn't a race horse, but he was outta race stock, it took a race horse to outrun 'im. They turned this bear down kind of a little draw, fairly open, but they'd brushed out Mesquites and had them piled up and it was kind of a rough run down there. Goddamn, these grizzly bears can run fast!! First couple a-times he run 'im down there about 200 yards and missed the bear. And then the third time they come down there, he was to rope the bear and this Marlin Perkins, he was gonna heel the bear. And then they would tie the bear up and then they was gonna haul 'im clear outta the country because hell, he was supposed be killin' goats around there for some Mexican.

He roped the bear but there was no way Marlin could heel 'im so I heeled the bear and handed the rope to Perkins but you know, they cut all this out. It just showed Perkins comin' in with a rope like he was gonna heel 'im and then the next thing he's got the bear heeled, holdin' the rope. It turned out that ol' Stan Brock, he was gonna get down when they had

241

the bear all stretched out and tie the bear up where they can haul 'im off. He got down there and the first thing the horse got a little close and the bear just slapped that rope off his neck and then Marlin Perkins let 'im loose! And he got after Stan Brock! By god, Stan Brock has a pretty big Mesquite there and he had to run about 20 yards to jump and get up in that! The bear was just about to catch 'im! I saw the movie afterwards and I saw him course, afterwards. The bear'd slapped 'im in the seat of the britches and tore his britches clear down to his knee but he got up and got away from the bear. Finally, we got the bear back in his cage and ol' Stan Brock come down outta the tree.

Stan always went barefoot. He was ridin' barefooted. He was a pilot and when he got into Florida he went out to get cleared to get a license to fly in the United States. He got up in this airplane and pulled his shoes off – he was tellin' me this himself – and the pilot says, "What are you doin' pullin' your shoes off?" "Well," he says, "I learned to fly barefooted. I can handle the controls better barefooted. I thought that pilot was gonna get out! But he stayed with me and I got my license." Flew a plane and rode a horse barefoot. He used one a-them South American riatas made outta rawhide and they tied it in the ring in the flank cinch. Hell, he had about 40 foot a-rope, 45 foot a-rope. All that riata…Christ, it was a sight to watch him handlin' that bear! He was ridin' a good horse and he had to be one hell of a good rider to ride that horse down where he was 'cause they was *movin'*! He was for real. There wasn't no damn counterfeit business about him!

Winter Lion Hunt

This story is about a lion hunt I made awhile back for a client in Tucson that wants a lion real bad. I hadn't been able to get 'im one, so I called 'im the night before 'cause it was snowin' and I'd arranged for these cowboys to meet us. I'd come up about 10:00 o'clock if it quit snowin'. His calendar was so busy he just couldn't make it.

Next morning about 6:00 o'clock it was still a-snowin' a little bit here at the place. By 8:00 o'clock it'd quit. So I went on out to the ranch, and the two cowboys was waitin' for me there, so we drank coffee and shot the breeze 'til about 11:00 o'clock. I'd only brought two dogs, but it don't take a lotta dogs to catch a lion, 'specially in the snow, if they got any idea at all what they're doin.

We got up on the road in a 4-wheel drive pickup, and was drivin' around for about 30 minutes. We see some tracks across the road. They wasn't deer tracks, so we got out to look at 'em. They're about half-filled with snow, so we cleaned out several of 'em around there. They're lion tracks all right, and not just one lion, but a winter covey with three of 'em.

So I turned Blackie, one of my better dogs, out. He was poisoned here in the summer, and was still sick, but he still knows what he's supposed to do. He got out in the snow and, hell, he just started playin' up and down the road and rompin' in the snow! He didn't think we were huntin'!

So I turned Abe out. I showed 'im the tracks, and he wasn't interested in 'em either. He went playin' up and down the road with Blackie. But he come back in a little bit. He went over and stuck his nose in one a-these tracks, and started a-whimperin' and a-whinin' a little bit, and smellin' more of 'em. On the strength a-that, Blackie got up and stuck his nose in one of 'em, and he lets out a bellow and starts trailin' 'em.

I thought in the snow they'd trail 'em a lot faster than they did, but they trailed off down in a deep canyon about a quarter of a mile from us, and snow all over the ground about six inches deep, and on all the brush and trees. By the time those dogs got to the bottom of the canyon, you could barely hear 'em. Snow changes the acoustics of the country, 'cause if it hadn't a-been for the snow, you could a-heard those dogs plain. There was no wind. There was no reason for not hearin' 'em other than the snow dampin' the sound.

And this steep old canyon heads off to the south and slightly east, and hits the main canyon down there, and there's a road down there. So we circle around, and go down to this road, and no dogs had been through. And we listened, and after a while, up to the north, and way up on the mountain that we'd just passed, we could just barely hear Blackie. And then, in a little bit, we could just barely hear Abe. So, we turned around and started back.

Some a-the kids from the ranch there was up there playin' in the snow, tobogganin' on some of the smoother slopes in a tire. And we asked 'em if they'd heard any dogs. And they say, "Yes, just a little while ago there was two dogs went across that mountain," and pointed to the mountain in front of them. "There was two dogs makin' a lotta noise and trailin' fairly fast." Well, that sounded good. At least they was gonna try to catch a lion.

We get back up on the main road, back up to where we'd turned 'em loose, and we'd passed five hikers that'd been up on this mountain in the snow earlier in the mornin'. We saw their tracks a-goin' up. They'd gone up to a microwave station and turned around. We asked 'em "Did you hear any dogs?" They says, "Yeah, there's two dogs up there got a lion treed." Well, that sounded good, so we asked 'em, "Where was it?" They says, "It's up there in back a-the cabin, but we think the lion got away and left. The dogs'd quit barkin', and we couldn't see it in the tree anymore." It went out through the branches and they couldn't see it anymore. So they figured the lion had jumped and gone.

Well, I'm figuring if the lion jumped, the dogs was gonna catch it pretty quick again. So we got on back up and got to where we could see this basin and behind this cabin, and we stopped. Sure enough we hear the dogs up there barkin' treed. And they're right there behind the cabin. We went up there, and sure enough, they'd got this lion treed right there in a tree behind the cabin. And here was the tracks a-the hikers where they'd walked up and looked at the lion in the tree. And apparently the lion, he spooked a little bit. This tree was real thick, and there was another tree a-growin' up in it there, and the lion had just moved over on the other side of the tree. They couldn't see it. And the dogs, seein' all these strangers there, they apparently just quit barkin' momentarily.

I would a-liked to went back to a phone, call this hunter I'd tried to get the night before, and tell 'im I had his lion in a tree. But the Game Department passed a law this past year, and changed the rules and regulations to where it's illegal to do this. One a-these cowboys, he's got a lion tag, and he wanted to shoot a lion. He wanted a lion rug, so he shot it. It made a real easy hunt, and my only regret is I didn't have my client there. You can't catch people a lion if you can't get 'em out in the woods!

Lost Dogs

All lion hunters are bound to have a few lost-dog stories. There's one comes to my mind and it was huntin' up, again, in the Catalinas. I had a big – wasn't too big – but he was a good-sized black-and-tan hound called "Jack." We're up there huntin', me and a client, and we lost Jack; he just disappeared. We went on up there a-huntin' and I caught a lion for my client and then we come home. Beryl told me that there's a guy down in Phoenix that's got Jack. He had called up several days ago and he had the dog and, you know, she's had experience with lost dogs, too. When they called up, she'd get their name and their phone number and their address and the whole nine yards. So I headed down to pick up Jack. I found the guy and he said, "Yeah, I had 'im here several days, never did hear from ya. There's a colored guy that walks by here ever once in awhile and I give the dog to him." "God," I said, "you give a pretty valuable damn dog away to this colored guy!" I knew that if he was walkin' he had to be somewhere in the neighborhood. Jack was just an average dog, but one you didn't want to lose! Since the guy had to be around there in walkin' distance, I started drivin' around there. Pretty soon I went down a alley and I heard ol' Jack a-barkin'. He knew my truck! I went there and, hell, I was there in the back yard and there's a gate so I got my leash and I went in. Ol' Jack, he met me right at the gate; I put my leash on 'im and here come this here colored guy out of the back door and he's sayin', "Man, you tryin' to steal my dog?" I said, "No, I'm not tryin' to steal your dog. I'm just gatherin' up mine!" And he says, "That's my dog!" I said, "Listen. I know that this guy up the street, he picked this dog up clear up there out of the Tucson area, in the Catalina mountains. He called me up and I looked him up and he said he give it to a colored guy. So I knew it was around here somewhere so I started lookin' around and I found him! And I really intend to take 'im home with me." "Man," he says, "that's my dog." I said, "He's not your dog anymore. He was your dog for a couple a-days maybe." I'm a-reasonin' with him. So I told him, "You know, I appreciate your takin' care of 'im; you got some dog food in 'im and I really don't want to argue with you, but I wanna treat you right." So I gave 'im a ten-dollar bill. That took care of everything! "Now, man," he says, "I sure want you to take good care a-that dog, 'cause I sure like 'im!"

So I brought Jack back home.

The next time I had dogs end up in Phoenix; there was two of 'em. We were huntin' in the mountains up above Green Valley, the Sierritas. The pack, they got down off the mountain down in the desert and I could hear 'em trailin' around there and they weren't gettin' anywhere. I went down and started gatherin' up dogs. Christ, these two dogs; I couldn't find 'em! I hollered and I fooled around there and Christ, they're just nowhere to be had. So I come on back to the house – we was just out on one of these day hunts – and Beryl said that there's a guy who called and has your two dogs. And he just called on his cell phone. So I called 'im back and he says, "Yeah, I got 'em." He told where he was there at the forks of the road and he said that he'd wait for me.

By god, I got down there and he's there. "Goddamn it," he said, "I got to apologize. There was two of us in two vehicles and this one guy had his two kids along. They took up with the dogs and they all just left!" "Well," I said, "I got to get these dogs back. There's no catchin' up with 'em now. You say they have a 20- or 30-minute head-start. You give me your phone number and his in Phoenix and I'll come down there tomorrow afternoon and pick 'em up."

Before I left the next day, I called 'im up. 'Yeah," he says, "we got the dogs. We know we done the wrong thing. We'll meet you halfway. We'll meet you there at Pichaco at the Texaco station." By god, when I got there, here they are just pullin' up a little ahead of me. And they got my two dogs and they're apologizing about takin' 'em off and it was real decent of 'em, you know, to not make me drive all the way down into Phoenix to find 'em.

Malcolm MacKenzie Lion Hunt

I was at home relaxin' one day when Malcolm called me up. He says, "I've got a cow that come in, got a little calf, and she didn't bring it in this morning. I'm sure a lion caught it because yesterday I saw a fresh lion track up in the canyon." I told 'im, "Well, I don't wanna run down there for nothing; you just go out and find that cow. She'll be a-bawlin' and she'll be around the calf."

So he went out and his dog found the calf and the cow was right there bawlin' by it. He called me back and says, "It's covered up." So I loaded my mule and went down and spent the night with him. Malcolm lives just north of Benson, Arizona and has some land and cattle in the Little Rincon Mountains. We was out before daylight, where this calf was and the dogs run around there for, hell, for ten minutes; I was beginnin' to wonder if they was ever gonna get the track out of there. But finally they lined it up and they headed up into the Little Rincons and the roughest damn part of 'em! We lost the dogs but I knew which direction they was going so we kept a-rimmin' around through these damn rocks. Finally we could hear the dogs barkin' "treed" across the rough canyon so Malcolm, he took my gun and he went over there and this lion was up on a big rock in a crack. He found a way to get up there and he aimed at the lion but there was a big oak tree between him and the lion. Finally, he moved around where he could get a shot at it. He wounded the lion and it jumped off the rock and this Sally dog I had, she was right behind it. They went down into a deep canyon and these rocks, over the centuries, had rolled in there and there was cracks and holes all through it. I told 'im I'd bring the horses around, and Christ, I was forever gettin' 'em around. He thought I'd gotten hurt or somethin', so he come back a-lookin' for me. Just as I rode into this little valley there, he says, "That lion's up in the rocks there somewhere, but I can't find it!"

I says, "I'll go up there with you and we'll find it!" I started throwin' rocks down in all these holes and cracks and finally I got a growl out of one of 'em. It was way down in there – hell, it must a-been 30 foot down in there. Malcolm took the rifle and he started down in there and it was kind of a real narrow place to get through and he had some kind of phobia; he couldn't get in there! He could see these lion's eyes down there. I'm tellin' 'im, "There's a dog down there, too. Sally's down in there – don't shoot her!" And he says, "Well, you come get the rifle and you do the shootin'!" I shot and then that's when this lion went on down and got in this other little hole. So I took the rifle and I went down there and that damn lion was right in under me and there was a crack there about a foot wide, or narrower. I poked my rifle down there and I thought when I hit hair, I'd pull the trigger! And the damn lion grabbed my rifle, tryin' to take it away from me, and it's a-draggin' my arm down there! You can see this scar here and it goes clear up to my elbow! Malcolm was yellin', "Don't let it have your rifle! Don't let it have your rifle!" That damn rifle has some pretty deep teeth marks in the forearm and even some deep scrapes on the barrel!

Well, I finally got my rifle back out and, of course, I'm afraid to stick it back in there again. I couldn't see it so I told Malcolm, "There's a little flashlight down there in my saddlebag – we had that maybe we could see it." He says, "I'll go get it." While he was down a-gettin' it, this lion crawled up there where I could see it – it's back was broke;

I'd overshot it and broke it's back. I don't know yet where Malcolm had shot it, probably in the stomach because it was bleedin' quite a little blood around on the rocks. So I killed it, then. Sally's still down there with it; she'd jumped off about a eight-foot ledge. Malcolm got around where he could see her and he'd call her. She'd jump and he finally got her by a front foot and drug her out. We got back up on top and damn, down there she went again! This time she found the dead lion and licked the blood off of it. Then we had the same problem gettin' her out – she had to jump several times before you could get a foot and drag 'er out. She stayed out that time.

Ol' Drifter dog, last time I'd heard him when I left the horses, was barkin' treed. When we came back, he was still barkin' treed! I know he had a kitten up there treed and I never realized this 'til I called 'im and called 'im off. I know we went off and left a second lion there! And then we got back, hell, it was after dark when we got back and my butt was sore! Malcolm, he couldn't hardly walk next morning after that hike he'd taken. I got on home and Christ, I was ready to take a shower, and my drawers was stuck to my butt! I had to pull that loose and you know, that hurt a little bit!

Then I checked with the Game Department. This lady in the Game Department says, "Did it have spots?" I said, "No, I told you it was a female lion." She says, "Well, what did you do with it?" We couldn't get it out; it was up there in that crack, so I told her, "The rancher wanted the hide, so we skinned it out and he's got the hide." That took care of that. I suppose if they read this someday, they'll realize I violated the rule but the statute of limitations has run out by now. But I did take my tag and I threw in down in the hole – I didn't save my tag for another hunt. That's about as legal as I could be in that situation.

Patty Jones Lion Hunt

Patty is the lady who originally bought my ranch. She called me up one afternoon and she says, "I think I've got a lion kill out here." I says, "I'll be out in the morning and we'll check it out." I was out there in the morning and we checked it out. We went to this dead calf. I could look at its hoof and I see it was a calf that'd been born a little early and there had been a coyote around there, eatin' on it and draggin' it around. No sign it'd ever been killed by a lion.

So I told her, "As long as I'm here, let's go up to the Upper Springs. Hell, it's dry and if there's a lion in the country, it might a-come by and got a drink of water durin' the night." We went up there and sure enough, the dogs hit a track! Christ, they headed up into the worst damn country there was on that ranch. We got a-way up there on the damn peak and here's a fence that the Park Service had put in there. I generally carry a pair of pliers, so I cut the fence and we followed the dogs along for a mile. We got over on another ranch and, finally, the dogs is barkin' treed. We had a real problem a-gettin' down there to where the dogs was – and then we had to tie our horses and walk in there about a quarter of a mile. We got up on this bluff and this lion is treed about 100 yards across the canyon. I got Patty down behind a rock and coached her a little bit about how to shoot my rifle; told her to squeeeeeze the trigger and all those other good things. She shot and the lion fell out of the tree, wounded. Apparently, its back was broke because it couldn't run off. The dogs was around there a-maulin' it. I says, "Patty, you're gonna have to get off this bluff someway and go down there and finish it." Course, when she got up there the damn lion is still got a lot of life in it; it's a-snarlin' and a-growlin' and she's about half-spooked. I yelled, "Hell, don't pay any attention to it! Just shoot it! Put it out of its misery!"

So she shot and killed it. I had her check the stomach and no calf meat in it or anything, just old deer hide. So I told her, "If you want this here hide, you're gonna hafta skin it because I don't think I can get down there." Well, she says, "I don't think I'm up to skinnin' it." Then I told her, "Well, you'd better get your ass up here and just leave it!"

Patty was real happy with her lion and she wanted my rifle! I told her, "I can't give you that rifle when I get through with it because I've promised it to another guy. Hell, I'm a man of my word and you can't have it." But when she paid the ranch off, I bought her one of these rifles like Layne and I got and give that to her. And that pacified her! It was a Ruger .44 magnum. She went right down there where she was stayin' there at Malcolm's and killed a coyote with it about the third day she had it. And that endeared it to her more.

Drifter's First (Successful) Lion Hunt

A neighbor I had in Tucson called me up one morning and a rancher friend of his down towards the border, down in below Patagonia, had a lion problem. He wanted somebody to come down there and hunt it. I told 'im the only way I'd go down there huntin' is if I caught a lion on his place, I wanted $500. And that was agreeable! So Buck and I went down there. He showed us this canyon where he'd lost a couple of calves and was seein' a lion track from time to time. We headed up in there and got up there around 8:00 o'clock, maybe a few minutes before, and I know it was colder'n a bastard. The dogs hit a good track and trailed it for a couple of miles and got out of hearin'. When we caught up they weren't movin' so fast. They'd switched tracks some way or another and trailed this track nearly over to Parker Lake. We was lookin' down on it. The track was wore out and we called the dogs off and come back. We come back by where they'd switched tracks and damn, they was off on it again. Real hot! They got outta hearin' and we fooled around – it was gettin' pretty late – and we couldn't find the dogs. So we come on to camp and spent the night.

The next morning we got in the pickup and went around back into where we'd heard 'em last. Way off to the east, we could get a readin' on our trackin' collars. So we went back and saddled up our mules and headed over there. We got over there and checked the trackin' collar and, hell, they was clear off several miles from where they were. So we headed there and damn, they'd moved again, gettin' into all kind of bear sign. I know they was treed at least three different places that morning. I told Buck, "Hell, they're runnin' a bear!

Next time they tree, we'd better hurry up and get down there and kill this damn bear and end this hunt!" They treed way down in this canyon that drains off into Parker Lake. I can't recall the name of the canyon right now, but we got down where they were treed and they had this female lion up in a Ponderosa pine and she was too high to jump. Buck was anxious to get a lion so he shot and wounded it and knocked it outta the tree. It ran across the canyon and up another tree. This little Drifter pup, she's still with these dogs and you know, they'd started at 8:00 o'clock the morning before and this is 1:00 o'clock the afternoon of the next day! Buck shot the lion out of that tree and it hit the ground and run about 20 yards and folded up. That damn pup was right there and grabbed it by the neck and shook it! I was startin' to get a pretty high opinion of Drifter! A pup that would stay from 8:00 o'clock to 1:00 o'clock the next day with those old dogs! I don't know how many times that lion had been treed but I know it was at least four times. We brought the lion back to the ranch and the boy was there but the dad was off in town. The kid, he looked at it. We loaded up and come back. Sometime that evening the guy called me up and said he'd come by and pay me and he did. He come by and gave me five $100 bills. He said that if he ever had any more lion trouble, he'd call me back up. But I never have heard from 'im, so I don't know whether he's hasn't had any lion trouble or he didn't like coughin' up $500!

And that pup! She was less than a year old and ever since then, every lion she's been in on, she's either been up in the tree with it barkin' at it or she was achewin' on it when it hit the ground! She's not as good as her sister Liza, but she's only done a third of the huntin' – everybody's hunted Liza and everybody's caught lion with her. I think they're probably two of the best young dogs around that I know of – not because Layne and I own them! I'll even brag on a good dog that belongs to somebody else! And a sorry bastard, I don't care who it belongs to, I'm gonna tell 'em that too!

Brian Murray Lion Hunt

One of the easiest lions I ever caught was for our gunsmith, Brian Murray, who owns Murphy's Gun Shop there in Tucson. I was just gonna take three women out this huntin' season: Rena Westenburg, my daughter Sherry, and Denise Murray, Brian's wife. But when I called Rena she couldn't go; she was movin' her office. So I went over to the gun shop to see Denise and she couldn't go on that Saturday because she was going to the Concealed Weapon Permit class. Then Brian says, "Well, I'll go with you!"

Figure 20. A Successful Lion Hunt at the Elkhorn

We got down to the Elkhorn Ranch and since I like to hunt with some kind of a plan, I told him we'd head out south of the ranch house and stay headed south in the low country. Then we'd go up this Chiltipin Canyon and come out on top and then we're up above the ranch right along Lion's Kitchen where we can come on in. We got up there about 10:00 o'clock and I told him, "Hell, it's only 10:30 or so. Let's just give it the last mile; we'll take the trail out around to Vance's Trail and go down it, cross center Mule Canyon and around down through Nogales Canyon. Maybe we'll hit a track."

We hadn't gone far and the dogs treed this chula. Mexicans call them solteros, old males that's been kicked out of the herd.

I've got this one new pup and Murray's got a littermate to her. They treed and Murray climbed up to look and said, "It's a chula and both these pups was barkin' at it." I said, "Well, gather 'em up and come on back 'cause we're not huntin' chulas." Although, I think I catch more chulas than I do lions. Well, we went around under the Lion's Kitchen and nothin'. We crossed the center of Mule Canyon and along the ridge there, the mountain side, you climb up to a saddle right on top. I stopped to let my mule blow a little bit. I don't like to hunt too fast; I like to give the dogs a chance to sniff around. Liza and the two pups was trottin' right on up the trail. Drifter's smellin' around on the weeds and the bushes and I told Murray, "There's a ol' wore out lion track here." Liza, she saw Drifter smellin' so she come back and got to foolin' around in some mesquites, just sniffin' around and I told Murray, "Hell, it's a ol' wore out track; we might as well go on." I started off and hell, I hadn't gone 15 feet 'til Liza let out a real bark outta her and they headed off down in the canyon! It was a hard place to go off down in there and they was goin' aways under the trail, so we went on followin' the trail around and, hell, just down there a little ways, they're barkin' treed! I told Murray, "Hell, they've caught another chula!" We rode on around to where we could ride down in this canyon and I got bluffed down there and I heard this damn lion snarl. Now I've heard foxes snarl just the same and I told Murray, "Hell, they've caught a fox!" So we rode down and crossed the canyon and rode up to this tree where they're all barkin' treed. The two old dogs and these two pups, they're just really givin' up the head. We ride up under the tree like a couple a-big ass birds and hell, there's a lion sittin' in the tree!

Ol' Murray got off and shot the lion 'cause I didn't have a lion tag – I got one now, but I didn't back then. He killed the lion and when that thing hit the ground those two pups was on it, and the two old dogs, and they mauled it around. I'm still asittin' on my mule, so I told Murray, "Go down there and really pet them pups and brag 'em up. Let 'em know that we're pleased with what they're doin'!"

They couldn't a-trailed that lion 50 yards from where they first barked. I don't know if that lion was prowlin' around there and they just run into it or whether it was layin' under that tree and it just jumped up in the tree or whether it was in the tree – I don't know. But I do know it was the easiest lion I ever caught. But what I tell these younger hunters: don't go through the country so fast. Just poke along and let your dogs check these little draws and saddles. A lot of times when a lion just crosses a trail and if you're in a big hurry, the dogs will just walk over it and not find it. But it's pretty hard to convince a lot of these guys that, especially my good friend Buck. He goes through the country! He likes to put in a day! And get back after dark a lot of times.

My experience is when you're huntin' the country, pay attention to how these lions is travelin' through the country and hunt your dogs this way. They hit a fresh track, nine times outta ten, they'll be goin' the right direction. But when there's a kill around, the damn lion tracks are liable to be goin' any direction. Then you gotta kinda pay attention to what your dogs is doin' and try to find a track or a scratch. There's several times that I know when there's a kill in the area and they'd be on the wrong way and I'd turn 'em around – which generally is kinda hard to do, especially on a fresh track. If you've got dogs that believe in you like you believe in them, sometimes they'll listen to you and you can turn 'em around.

I've caught over 200 lions; I've turned a few of 'em loose. I haven't turned any loose lately, but I was takin' out clients and gettin' $2,000 for a lion. So when I was out just workin' my dogs and I'd have a nice lion in a tree, it was pretty hard to shoot it, knowin' it was worth $2,000 to a client! I've probably turned 10 lion loose in my lifetime – several of 'em was just year-old kittens that the client didn't want or I didn't especially want to kill 'em either.

Of the 200 or so, I've actually killed 194. I think when I get to 200 kills, I might just give Layne my dogs and quit! Sell my trailer and give my mule to him, maybe! This lion huntin' is gettin' to be work now! It used to be fun, but it's more like work now. I was 84 last January (2003). I did a little bit of lion huntin' when I was young and before I went into the service, but I never caught any. I trapped three way back then, but never caught any with dogs.

Jerry Shaw Down On The Farm

One Sunday Jerry and I went out huntin' on the FICO farm. He was going to Australia with me and John Bessett in September 2004 and I thought if I took him out on the farm a time or two I'd get better acquainted with him. Maybe I'd know more about how to handle 'im. So far, he'd been real enthusiastic and very easy for me to get along with. I'd just gotten an ID photo from 'im to send to Australia to put on his huntin' license, or gun permit. I asked to come out on the farm that Sunday so he met me at the Post Office at 5:00 o'clock. I was there about 20 to five and he was there about five minutes later.

He comes up with his money real quick and he's always on time, which I like. So we went out on the farm and we went by this one place where there's supposed to be some coyotes, but – nothing. We took a back road where we could shoot a coyote or a jackrabbit. We didn't see any coyotes but we did see a half-dozen jackrabbits. He missed four jackrabbits in a row and I got one shot at a jackrabbit and killed it. He decided it was the ammunition he'd just loaded up and maybe it wasn't just right. So he got another box of shells and killed a couple of squirrels with that; his shootin' seemed to be all right. We went on down where we always see coyotes and got in there just a couple a-minutes late – the irrigator come in there and run 'em out; run six of 'em right across the road in front of us. One on 'em stopped and Jerry took a shot at it but it turned endwise on 'im just as he pulled the trigger and he missed that. So we went around and looked at some more of the farm and couldn't find a coyote, then come back through this same place. A coyote pup run outta there but neither one of us could get a shot at it. He said, "I see a badger standin' out there!" I told him to shoot it. He asked, "Can you kill badgers here on the farm?" I said, "Hell, if you can hit 'em, you can!" And he fooled around; he's a little bit slow on gettin' his shots off, and the badger got away. I said, "Well, it's gettin' up in the morning now and we're not apt to see many coyotes. Let's go down on the southern end of this farm and let you shoot some squirrels. There's houses there across the river and a golf course and you'll have to use your shotgun."

I'd told 'im to bring his shotgun 'cause I knew I'd get 'im some shots at squirrels. We got down there at about the right spot and I told 'im to load up his shotgun but to keep that barrel pointed out the window! I don't like to be in the cab with a loaded shotgun! He did and we got in there and we made couple a-passes up in through there and he killed 22 squirrels with the shotgun. He run outta ammunition. I'd misplaced my chewin' tobacco and he's lookin' around and he finds a box of shotgun shells under the seat. So he had a new supply of shotgun shells.

There was a irrigator in there – we'd passed 'im several times – and he passed us and got ahead of us a-ways and slowed way down. He's lookin' off down in the orchard and I'm lookin' down there and I don't see anything. Finally, he stopped, pulled off the road and got out. I told Jerry, "Hell, he's got somethin' to tell us!" But he didn't tell us anything!

He pointed out in the field and I asked him what he saw but he didn't answer me. So I said, "Que vera?" He answered then; he said, "Gato!" I asked, "Que classe?" "Oh," he said, "Gato matea." So I told Jerry, "Hell, he sees a bobcat out there somewhere!" Ol' Jerry's got a real expensive pair of damn binoculars; 'round $1,200 or $1,500 binoculars, and he could see this bobcat out there layin' up right agin the trunk of a tree. I'd be damned if I could see it! It's down there a couple a-hundred yards and I said, "That's too far to shoot but you've got a lot of cover with these trees; why don't you try to slip down there and get a little closer." He took off with his single-shot Luger .22-.250 and pretty soon I see 'im get down in the prone position and fire off a shot. Then he got up and he a-motion' to me and I'm thinkin', hell, he's went off down there with one shell in that one-shot gun! I give this young Mexican a piece of a box of his shells and he took it down there. So Jerry's re-supplied with ammunition and this Mexican's a-pointin' and a-pointin'. Jerry didn't take his binoculars with 'im so he's a-sightin' around with his 8X scope. Finally, I guess he got this bobcat located and got off another shot and killed it and damn, it was a pretty nice bobcat! I drove around and run down through the rows where I could pick 'em up because, hell, by then they're 300 yards or so away. I got down there and he's got this bobcat killed and then he tells me, "With my first shot, I shot a stump!" I said, "Well, you didn't kill the damn thing 'cause it's already dead!" He had to admit that the stump was dead, but he had hit it! He really tried to impress me that he'd made a good shot on it.

By god, that's all I heard the rest of the day – about his bobcat. He said, "I've never done a lot of huntin' but this is the most exciting hunt I've ever had! Stalkin' a bobcat and killin' it!"

But it is fun to hunt with people who are enthusiastic.

The Monkey and the Jaguar

This was a hunt George Parker and I made down in Mexico *years* ago. We went down for jaguar and I never knew anything about jaguars and George didn't either. But I'd heard Dale Lee and some a-these Mexicans that had this gourd that they could get what they said was a jaguar call. So we're down there and we're moved out in the jaguar country and early in the mornin' I heard a jaguar – by god, right close! And I could hear another one away off, a mile or two. Just barely hear it. God, the two Mexicans we had down there for guides – they're sleepin' and George is a-sleepin' and hell there's a jaguar right in camp! I thought, by god, I'd better just get up and kill that bastard!

Anyhow, I'd brought a light that you put on your rifle and it had a mercury switch in it. As long as you kept your rifle sideways, the light wouldn't come on. But when you got in position to shoot, turn it upright, this mercury, someway or another in there, would turn the light on. And god, I got up and I put my light on my rifle and I start out there to where this closer one was and one a-the Mexicans, he woke up and he followed me out. He was tellin' me, "Señor, el tigre es muy lejos." (The jaguar is way off.) I tried to convince him that there was one here closer. No, it's just a jaguar – too far! I didn't believe the bastard.

I got around there where this noise was comin' from and by god, there's these monkeys a-scamperin' around in the trees. There was enough light that, you know, you could see one once in awhile jump from one limb to another. Just get the picture of it. I figured this jaguar in there was tryin' to catch one of 'em and that had 'em all excited. I kept a-lookin' and up in this one tree there was a black object and it looked to be about the right size for a jaguar. There was a little movement in it! I figured that was a jaguar! So I got down in a shootin' position and I turned my rifle up and nothing! The damn battery was dead and the extra one I'd brought with me was dead, too! Course, I didn't find that out 'til later.

Anyhow, I decided I'd take a shot at this black object. I shot and Christ, I tell you, the monkeys left! They just got outta there! But this black object up in there, it was still there! Pretty soon, I could hear blood a-drippin' on the leaves, so I knew then that I'd wounded my jaguar. So I got squared away and I shot in there again and it dropped out. I'd heard enough bear and lion fall outta trees that I knew I had a monkey! I didn't have a jaguar! I went back to camp and George, he wanted to know, "What the hell are you doin'?" I said, "Hell, I was out tryin' to kill a jaguar! All I got was a stud howler monkey!" They got a big kick outta that.

The next morning there was howler monkeys come in there when we was eatin' breakfast. I got my .45 and I told George, "I'm gonna shoot one a-them damn howlin' monkeys with my .45." I went out and I saw one of 'em that was makin' the noise and I got up 'bout 30 yards of it and I shot and it fell out – I'd hit it in the head. I drug it back and George, he told these Mexicans, "Mi compañero is a *good* shot; he just shoots most everthing in the head!"

Chapter Nine   International Hunts

Asia

  I 'm a little bit afraid that some of these "international" hunters, who're a lot more pure than I am, will probably not want to count it, but I honestly did go huntin' there for wild pigeons and I killed several of 'em. But my main huntin' there was scoutin'.

They'd get these Japs broke up there in small bunches and they're livin' out of these native gardens. My first sergeant, he give me way more'n my share of this here blamed scoutin'. They called 'em combat reconnaissance patrols. You found out all you could and reported that and if you found any Japs, it turned into a combat patrol and you killed all of 'em you could. I wouldn't take a full squad. I'd just take myself and half a squad and my two scouts. We'd circle these fields and gardens and we'd find where they'd come in and where they'd go out. I'd do the trackin' and the scouts, just in front of me, they was the ones keepin' their damn eyes open so we didn't walk into an ambush or somethin'. That's the way we worked it. Always we'd find these people, there'd be anywhere from three to six, sometimes seven who'd have a lean-to, camped there. They had a little fire goin', generally, and sometimes you could smell the smoke before you saw 'em. Other times you'd see 'em. When these scouts would see 'em, they'd stop. The way I worked it, they'd stop and point and I'd walk up and get on the right and the next guy behind me, he'd walk up and form a firin' line on the left. We'd just alternate that way until they'd discover us. Then everybody on the firin' line would just empty their guns into this blamed lean-to. And, of course, those scouts had tommy guns with 20 round clips apiece in them – there's 40 rounds – and us riflemen, we'd empty our 8 round clips. The damn country'd be so full of smoke in front that you couldn't see anything so we just split up; my side would go to the right and the other side would go to the left and then once in awhile you'd see one run out and someone would shoot him. That type a-shootin' was the only way you ever knew you killed one, is if they run off, one that hadn't got killed in the first volley of fire. Sometimes one of us would get to shoot one on the side. I'd get about two or three of those patrols a week. We ended up we killed a lotta damn Japs that way.

After bein' there, you know, I was there 27 months in combat in the Philippines and these islands off to the side New Guinea in there. That totaled quite a bunch of damn Japs. I don't know how many we killed but I was sure that my squad and myself and my platoon over the 27 months probably killed between 300 and 400. That's a lot of dead Japs, 'specially if you could get 'em all in one pile.

That pretty much explains the kind of huntin' I did in Asia. I consider it a real, genuine Asian hunt because, hell, it was dangerous game we was huntin'. By god, every once in awhile someone would get killed!

First Trip to Africa

The first trip I went to Africa, you know, I'd thought about this, but just thinkin' about it, I never figured I could afford it or anything. Then I got real well acquainted with this Jack Marteney. I'd hunted him quite a bit. I'd got 'im all of his Arizona Big Ten but a wild turkey and I had a chance to get 'im a wild turkey on the Indian Reservation but we'd a-had to poach it, and I discouraged that! Jack had a strong desire to hunt Africa. And he wanted me to go with 'im.

Charlie Askins had been over to Africa had a real good hunt. He come out from Texas and was visitin' George Parker and Jack Marteney got to talkin' to 'im. He talked this hunt up that he'd just made over there. He was sellin' hunts for the guy. And Jack got real interested and he told me, "Why don't we just go?" I talked it over with Beryl and she was in agreement. She says, "You oughta go to Africa and hunt!" We checked our finances and I could make it. This was in 1972 or 1973.

So we bought this 21-day hunt in Angola. And we got all of our stuff together and we took our elephant rifles and we'd hunted coyotes with 'em, we'd hunted jackrabbits mostly with 'em. We had 'em all tuned up and we ended up in Angola.

Jack and I flew into Nuevo Lisboa, Angola and we had a charter flight, 'bout 300 and some miles down to where they'd fought a little war there a couple of years before. They'd cleaned most of the blacks out a-there, they'd took 'em out, but the Portuguese had a army base down there and a airstrip. The army had black troops and white officers. We flew down in this charter airplane and the pilot, I don't know what nationality he was, but he was white. He didn't talk English and he didn't talk Spanish and what he talked, I don't know. Anyway we got in this little airplane and I'm a-sittin' up there in front and I could see the gauges of this Cessna; the one with the push-pull engines, one in front to pull and one in back to push. One of the manifold pressure gauges would go *way* up and then it'd come down to nothin' – come to think if it, there wasn't a whole lotta instruments in this airplane! But I see 'im and he'd have his watch out in his hand ever once in awhile, checkin' the time, I suppose, and a compass. When he got down there within what he figured was 50 or 60 miles of this strip, he starts zigzaggin' in and located his airstrip. He landed there and course, my hunter was there and took us into camp for a 21-day hunt.

The amount of game we saw there, it was unbelievable to me! We hunted there 21 days and on the average I know we was seein' at least 500 animals a day and sometimes more. Christ, in 21 days, you get to figurin' up there 10,000 to 12,000 head of game! Christ, I've done most of my huntin' in Arizona and Mexico – this was unbelievable! And then my first trip over there, I wasn't too interested in the little animals; I wanted to shoot the big ones. I got to kill my elephant on this trip and I'll tell you, I have no desire to ever kill another elephant. Shootin' this big elephant, my guide, he told me, "You might hunt elephant the rest of your life and you might get bigger ivory, but you'll never kill a bigger elephant!" I took measurements on 'im and near as I could measure his height, he was 15 foot high! And then I walked around 'im – it took me 25 long steps right up against 'im to walk around 'im. Then I measured his ear; from the center to his ear out to the end it's five feet! And he's got two of 'em! Add that together and that's 10 foot! And then across his forehead was 4 feet! When he throws his head up and throws his ears out, that's 14 feet and he's 13 foot tall – I'm a-lookin' at my .458 and I'm wonderin' now if this is a big enough gun! The first thing we'd found his track and his track was about the size of the top of a 55-gallon drum. We're a-trailin' it along here and this black, he wants to take my rifle and I'll tell you, trailin' an animal this big with tracks this big, and seein' where he'd reached up there about 20 foot and jerkin' off limbs as big around as I was, I'm a-thinkin', "Little as my gun is, I outta be a-packin' it!"

We followed 'em, there was two, this huge monster of an elephant and then there was a companion. And the guide had already told me, "I don't like to shoot elephants in the head 'cause the brain isn't much bigger than your two fists and ever time you gotta shoot 'em from a different angle and it's real easy to miss that brain. And then you might have to trail that thing two, three days. That's a lotta work! You've got solids and you've got soft point bullets, but you put a soft point bullet in the chamber and watch 'im. When he runs his foreleg forward, shoot 'im right in the heart. You shoot 'im in the heart, he'll whirl and start away. Try to break 'im down in the back. " I did just what he said – shot 'im in the heart and then put two shots in the back but they missed the spine. He got out there about 50 yards and he started gettin' weak behind and this companion elephant went up, run his tusks in under his flank and walked 'im along 'til he collapsed in the front. The young stood around there for a few minutes and Christ, I'll tell you, that killed all desire for me to ever shoot another elephant.

We'd been shootin' ever day and this guide was pickin' out good game and when I shot my buffalo – he pursued these buffalo in his Land Rover 'til he got to what he thought he got the best one cut out. Then he chased it and got to about 50 yards of it and said, "Jump out and shoot 'im!" Well, I didn't jump out! I just raised up in the Land Rover and shot him in the heart area, which is the only place I ever – I always try to break a shoulder or shoot any angle that'll get it in the heart area. This bull, he let out a beller of some kind and he went down. He's layin' there kickin' so I walked up a little closer and brain shot him. It turned out he was a real good buffalo. There's two ways of measurin' and he made the book by both ways. That's the only buffalo I've shot. I've saw several more shot since and they claim to be real dangerous. I've shot all the dangerous game in Africa, and I shot most of 'em on that hunt, and I've never had a problem. I've talked to these African hunters, international hunters, and they talk about all the dangerous game they've shot and I haven't had a problem with it – only had one lion charge and that was this hunt. I'd killed one African lion, I'd shot it in the shoulder with a 7 mag and he whirled around so I crossed to the other end with another shot and hell, he just went down and he was dead!

But Marteney, when it come around to killin' his lion, this Angolan hunter, he's a quarter native himself – his dad had come down there as an army officer years before and married a half-breed – that made him a quarter-breed. But hell, this was his 25th year of guidin' in Africa and he convinced me that he knew his business. So when we got ready to kill this lion for Marteney, he found the three tracks of these big lions in this sand that blew in from the Kalahari Desert. We were right on the edge of it – lots of white sand! These two blacks he had, the skinner and the tracker, they was kinda reluctant to trail these African lions up! And they'd lose the track and he'd get out and he'd point the track out to 'em and I guess he told 'em in their native language that he was tired of this damn nonsense and to trail 'em! So they're trailin' 'em and we're followin' along behind in the Land Rover and pretty soon they jumped these three big African lions, males. Boy, these blacks, they hopped up in the Land Rover and he started pursuin' 'em in the Land Rover. I don't know whether this is fair chase or not, but it's exciting!

Pretty soon they all stopped and whirled around and they growled. Ol' Jack, he was a-shootin' my 7 mag mostly because he had a .375 and a .458 – he had 'em sighted in for 100 yards and all the shots we was gettin' was a lot longer than that and he was undershootin'. So he was usin' my 7 mag. He killed the biggest of the African lions and then these other two stopped and they're workin' up kind of a mad spell and they wouldn't leave! So we just drove off and circled around for 30 minutes or so and come back and this one African lion, he's still there. And this third one, he'd left. We're circlin' around there and we're poundin' on top of the cab and firin' off a few shots and this damn lion, he's backed up there in some brush and ever once in awhile, he'd run out in the open there, growl and back up. I'm a-thinkin' in my little mind, "What in the hell am I gonna hafta bride this African guide to let me shoot that thing!" And I'm a-turnin' it over in my mind and finally he says, "Ollie, we either gonna hafta leave this lion here and lose 'im or kill that other lion! It won't be long and he's gonna charge and when he charges, you kill im!" I said, "Fine!!"

And in just a little bit, you know, there's no doubt about it – this is a charge!!! 'Cause boy, he roared and his tail come straight up and he come for us! I've got a 2 ½ power scope on my blamed .458 and he's out there about 100 yards and I'll tell you, he come about 50 yards before I got on 'im! I shot 'im right in the chest and he whirled around and I put another one in his rear end and he went down. He's just layin' there on his chest, dead. We walked all the way around 'im, gettin' closer and closer and finally this guide realized he was dead even though he was a-layin' there, not on his side, but layin' there on his stomach and chest with his head down on the ground. He told me, "Now goddammit, don't you tell *anybody* in camp that you killed this African lion! I killed it! It charged and I had to kill it to save my trackers and my two hunters!"

So that's the way it went. When it got to where we settled up, I had this smaller lion that I'd killed first and I kinda liked to get the hide and the skull of the big one. When I settled up with this guy, I give him a $50 bill. I said, "If you get a chance to change the tags on these two hides, I'd appreciate it." So we went down and we went through the pile of trophies and we put my trophies in my pile and we put Jack's in his pile. There was another hunter there and a couple of his men, and several onlookers, and my smaller lion skull come out and it went in my pile. My lion hide come out and it went in my pile. I can't say anything with the audience there and I just thought to myself, "Hell, it was worth $50 to kill that second lion!" But when I got the trophies back, he'd gone back there and changed the tags on 'em so I got my big skull and my big hide!

I'd killed a leopard on this same hunt, this was my first leopard. We'd jumped this thing drivin' around through the country and he run into a clump of trees in this kinda savannah deal there and off to the left there's a stream runnin' through there about 10 foot wide. They're poundin' around on top of the cab and fired off a shot or two tryin' to scare this leopard out. But that leopard didn't come out so they set the place on fire! Then the wind changed and the fire starts comin' back towards our Land Rover. The guide and his two blacks, they broke off a big limb and start beatin' this fire out. And while they're beatin' this fire out, the leopard jumped across that stream and he run out there and stopped right broadside! Jack was wantin' a leopard real bad, so I said, "There he is; shoot 'im!" And he couldn't see the damn thing! And he said, "Well, you shoot 'im!".

I got my .458 and I shot him behind the shoulder and I shot through both lungs there and he jumped up and run between two trees. There's a termite mound and kind of a hole there and he come around there and he's got his head down and he's gaspin' for life, you know. And he fell down and he kicked off in this depression. These guys was busy puttin' out the fire and they didn't see it. Tony, the guide, he asked me "What'd you shoot at?" I said, "Hell, I killed that leopard!" He says, "Where is he?" I said, "He's over by the termite den and kicked off in that depression; you can't see him." These guys was busy puttin' out the fire and they didn't see it. Tony got up on top of the cab and he's lookin' around with his binoculars and he can't see him. I said,

"He's there!" And Jack said, "Hell, he's dead!" Tony, he says, "Well, bad luck; too bad!" and he drove off. I thought he was goin' down to find a place to cross that stream and come back and pick up my leopard but they just kept on a-goin'. Them people, I tell you, are absolutely terrified of these leopards. So I lost that leopard; I never got 'im! I guess they were afraid he was wounded but Jack and I both knew he was dead.

A couple of mornings later they were takin' in all these animals I killed and makin' jerky out of 'em that they called bulltong and I heard a leopard out on the bone pile. I woke Jack up and said, "Goddamn, Jack, get your gun, there's a leopard out there on that bone pile!" We went out there and there's two leopards on it; I guess a male and a female, out there about 125 yards and Jack *could not see 'em*! Hell, they were just there! And he could not see them! I wouldn't shoot one of 'em because I'd already shot one in front of 'im and Jack's a guy you gotta be *real* fair with because he's absolutely more than fair. He'd always let me shoot the first animal; he'd say, "Show me how to kill it!" So I was gettin' to shoot most of the animals first and this time he couldn't see it and the damn things wandered off down into some low country and the trees weren't too thick. Hell, you could see a hundred or two yards down there.

The guys started crankin' up a vehicle; they had three of them there and they couldn't get any one of the three to run! They wouldn't start! Finally after about 20 minutes they got one started and they went out there to where I'd saw 'em and I told Tony, "They went right down through that valley deal through there." "Well," he says, "Milo (the tracker) says they went that way." So we went that way and, of course, we never did see 'em. And I never got another chance to kill a leopard on that hunt – and Jack Martiney didn't get a leopard on that hunt.

I think I shot 16 species and Jack, he shot about the same species. We killed the most desirable stuff, the big game: elephant, buffalo, lion, leopards, a lot of the plains game, the better ones. I had one chance there to shoot one of these little antelopes, one of the small ones. I can't think of his name. Ol' Tony said, "It's way up in the record books, shoot it!" I says, "I'm not interested in any of the little stuff!" Hell, there was only a $15 trophy fee on 'em, but I had a blockage in my brain; I was huntin' Africa and I wanted to kill the big stuff. He says, "Can Jack shoot it on your permit?" I said, "Yeah, if he wants it, shoot it!" He did and, Christ, that little ol' head had about 7½ inch horns, this little thing. And it went a-way up in the record book but I didn't feel bad about it because, hell, I wasn't interested in it.

Figure 21. Ollie's Trophy Room

In camp, they had beer we could buy and they'd put it on the tab. We'd drink a couple of bottles of beer ever day and then when Jack had killed his big lion we bought a liter of whiskey. We had a couple of drinks out of that and then ever evenin' after that we'd have a drink and the stuff wasn't a-goin' down in the bottle of booze, but it was gettin' weaker! The damn natives was sneakin' in there and takin' a snort out of it and then put a little water in it. Hell, we got down there and we had half a bottle of goddamn water. When we settled up there, we had a $800 liquor bill! $800!!! Christ, I don't think we had $150 worth but these blacks was drinkin' beer while we was gone and puttin' it on our tab! But we'd had a real good hunt and we didn't let this $800 liquor bill destroy our hunt. Cut in half, that was only $400 apiece, and we'd had a hell of a hunt. After that hunt I found out that if you hunt Africa once, you can't stop there; you've got to hunt it again. Now I've hunted it five times and still, I wanna go back one more time.

It was kind of a stormy day the day we were to come back; it was overcast and drizzlin'. We got to the airstrip and three blacks from camp had come along. One was supposed to be a tracker, one was a skinner and I don't know what the other was – a roustabout of some kind. We get out to the airstrip and course, these three blacks, they each got a sack of bulltong, which is jerky, from the hunt and they headed down to the Army camp to do a little tradin'. God, we was there and the airplane's supposed to be there and an hour passed and the airplane's still not there. Pretty soon, these blacks come back, our three and three or four soldiers and then there was another guy there. They was all talkin' to him, razzin' and givin' 'im a hard time and at a hundred yards I can see this guy's upset; he's fightin' mad! They'd stop and talk awhile and then they'd come on a-ways and this guy's real agitated. I finally turned to this guide and says, "I can see this guy's got a hell of a problem! You know what it is?" "Oh yeah," he says, "this guy they're a-razzin' there and he's all upset – last night he come back and one of these soldiers was in bed with his wife. He drug him outta bed and they're wrasslin' around on the floor and he's tryin' to cut the guy's throat with a real dull pocketknife. They pulled 'im off of 'im and stopped 'im from tryin' to cut the guy's throat and now they're tellin' 'im to just forget about this! Just quit worryin' about it! Because if he killed that soldier, he either gets hanged or goes to the penitentiary for murder for 28 years! So they're tellin' him the solution to the problem. They say to forget about killin' this guy and charge him – make him pay for it! And your wife – just whip hell outta her and make her wash it out and you'll never know the difference!"

Anyway, the plane didn't get in until the next day, when we finally left. It was the same plane we'd flown in on. When we come back outta there, he missed Nuevo Lisboa, by hell, 15 minutes, but he saw a landmark that he recognized and flew back into the airport and landed. Course, we'd missed our airplane. So he took off, I guess lookin for transportation or a place for us to stay. While we're sittin' in the shade of this plane I got to lookin' at this airplane and saw a big ol' knot about half the size of a baseball formed on one of his tires! Pretty soon, he come back and he motions for us to get in his truck, and he took us to this hotel and unloaded our guns and everthing and all of our equipment. And Christ, this hotel man, he doesn't talk English, so he motions for us to come along with him. I tried some English on him and he didn't respond to that, so I tried Spanish and, by god, he could talk Spanish! And a hell of a lot better than I could! He informed us there'd be a plane in there the next morning at 8:00 o'clock that we could get on and showed us a room and said he'd get us there in time to fly out. The next morning we got on our airplane and we were homeward bound!

Comin' back across the ocean one of the stewardesses got real friendly with us and she kept a-bringin' booze to us and both of us got about half drunk. When I got home I found out that I'd lost three of my hundred dollar traveler's checks. But I had the numbers of 'em so I sent in the numbers and in due time they sent me my three hundred dollars.

So that was kinda the highlights of my first African hunt.

Sometime later I got a letter from the huntin' guide – it turned out that the next time the pilot was flyin' in a hunter, an American hunter, too, he crashed the damn airplane and killed both of 'em! I guess Jack and I were two lucky guys!

Red Man Chewing Tobacco

I've never told this one story about when I was chewin' Red Man. This happened back when the war was goin' on in Rhodesia, Chuck Westenburg and I was over there – we weren't supposed to be, but we were. He was travelin' with one of the mercenaries they had there and I was travelin' with another one. In the Land Rover I had, we had three blacks that went with us, a tracker, a skinner and what the other one was, I don't know. But one of 'em was a big, husky black, and he was a-kind of a surly bastard; I didn't like him very well. But I was chewin' this Red Man and when I'd take a chew, I'd pass it around to these three blacks and they'd all shake their heads; they didn't have anything to do with it. About the third day I told this here mercenary I had, "You tell those blacks that this chewin' tobacco that I have, this Red Man, I don't like either. But it's a kind of a medicine. I chew it because it keeps my pecker hard!" So he told 'em and I took a big chew and put it back in my pocket. And this big surly bastard – he had three wives – and the next time I took it out and took a chew and passed it around, he took on about three chews, had a big wad in his mouth. This guy is black as tar but pretty soon this black started takin' on a purplish tinge and he's gettin' kinda nervous, you know, and squirmin' a little bit and pretty soon his head went over the side and he just urped up everythin' he'd eat! But he still had that wad in there! Then pretty soon, he just turned purple and, goddamn, he urped again and he got rid of that chewin' tobacco! These other two blacks, they got on his case and they're really razzin' 'im and I finally asked this here mercenary I had, "What are they tellin' 'im?" He said, "They're not tellin' 'im anything ... they're wantin' to know how hard his pecker is!"

Barnes-X Bullets

I've got a good friend up in Montana and he's goin' to Africa in June and he's heard about these Barnes-X bullets. He was askin' me and John Bessett about 'em, what we thought about 'em. I told him, "I think they're the best bullet made for big game." He says, "Well, will they kill a buffalo?" I told 'im, "I've killed two buffalo with 'em, and Sherry's killed three buffalo with 'em. And she killed her three buffalo with four shots... and the fourth shot the buffalo was already down and the guide told her to shoot it in the neck. As far as I'm concerned, it's the only bullet to use on buffalo! They're gonna want you to go to those solids. And they don't work!"

Figure 22. Ollie in South Africa with his Rhino (could not bring into the US)

I know that the solids worked when their daddy's was young and their granddaddy's was young and the soft-point bullets they had then, the expanding bullets, didn't work on that big game. They had to use solids. They're a real poor choice now. He says, "Well, load me up a couple of boxes of 'em." And I loaded 'im up a couple of boxes. Now he tells me that his outfitter won't let him use 'em! I said. "You tell that outfitter that you know an old guy back in Arizona that's killed buffalo with 'em and he'll bet you a thousand dollars a buffalo that, if you use your solids and he uses his Barnes-X, he'll kill 10 buffalo with less shots and quicker than you do with your solids. And if the outfitter doesn't like that bet, tell him that the old guy has a daughter that'll shoot half of 'em at the same bet! That oughta prove to him that the Barnes-X bullet is the best!"

I like the bet! I hope he takes me up on it 'cause that way, win or lose – I'll get to kill 10 buffalo for $10,000! That's a bet I wouldn't mind losing, but I won't lose – I'll get the 10 buffalo plus $10,000!

First Australian Hunt

John Bessett, Jack Marteney, and I made a trip in August and September 1980 to Australia. We was there for 30 days and traveled some 8,500 kilometers (5,200 miles) in South Australia, New South Wales, and in the Northern Territory. We went over there pretty much in the dark, not knowin' what to expect, but I had been tryin' for three years at the Safari Conventions in Las Vegas to put a trip together, without any success. So Bessett and I just decided we would go over there on our own and find out how things worked. At the last minute, Jack asked if he could come along, and we figured with three of us, we could cut down the expenses quite a bit. Also both John and I have hunted with Jack quite extensively and enjoy huntin' with him, so we said, "Sure, come along."

We did get some help before we left. Layne Brandt's boss, Keith Walden, at the FICO Pecan Orchards knew an Australian fellow in Adelaide, a Mr. Howard Michell, who owned a lot of property there and has a great deal of influence. Layne asked Mr. Walden if he would write to Mr. Michell and ask if he could give us any help when we got there. As it turned out, he was a great help. He knew a tour guide named Peter Shultz who owned two 4-wheel-drive vehicles and spent a lot of time in the Outback, taking payin' clients out and checkin' out the country. Later we were able to hire Peter to take us out.

When we arrived in Adelaide, Mr. Michell picked us up at the airport, arranged hotel accommodations, and took us out for our first dinner in Australia. He owned a sheep and cattle station and some extensive farms in New South Wales also, and he had permission from the Government to kill 4,000 kangaroos on his property. Now that sounds like a lot of kangaroos, but he had a lot of land – 98 miles long on the sides. I don't know exactly what that would figure into, but I

274

know it's a lot of sections of land. He had also contacted his foreman there and told him that he was lettin' us come up there to do some shooting.

Peter Shultz met us the next day on schedule and he had good equipment and a good camp outfit. We drove up to New South Wales and spent four days there huntin' the kangaroos, shot a number of them and shot a few foxes. They had a lot of foxes. They'd been brought in from England about 100 years ago for the English to enjoy their foxhunts. We also shot a number of feral cats. Bein' a cat-lover, I hated to shoot these cats, but Peter told us they was really a menace and very hard on the bird life. They were very big cats and very fat, so we could see they had all been eatin' well.

Leavin' there, we went out into the Flinders Range on a wild goat and wild donkey hunt. We never saw any wild donkeys but we did see their tracks. The country was overrun with goats though – goats of all colors: black, white, brown, silver and all shades of color in between. This was the most challengin' hunt we had in Australia. We think our white-tailed Coues deer here are shy and hard to hunt, but if we had Coues deer here in the abundance they have of goats over there, hell, even the kids could shoot them. But these goats had been culled for the last 50 to 100 years, and they have gotten smart and WILD! We saw them in bunches of from 3 to 40, and they were careful where they grazed so they never grazed into a trap of some kind where we could make a stalk on them. Also there was always a couple of old nannies on guard at all times and they could SEE! Talk about your mountain sheep being able to see – they don't have anything on these Australian goats. We did manage to kill a number of them, all long shots – about 200 yards was the average for a close shot. You might get a first shot at a standing goat, but after that, they were all runnin' shots, all very difficult targets and at long range. We had long-range rifles though, and we got our share of goats.

We come back to Adelaide then and put together a hunt to go up around Alice Springs, and hunt along the way and try to look at as much of the country as we could. After 3 days we come to the Simpson Desert, one of the last deserts in Australia to be explored. The French had come in there in 1962 and run some bladed roads in and knocked down the brush and porcupine grass so they could get through the country, and then drilled for oil. They never found any oil but they did find some Artesian wells. At one well – one of the better-known ones, although I can't remember now what its name was, the water comin' out of it was steaming! I asked Peter how hot it was and he said it was boiling. I touched the pipe there at the well and couldn't hold on to it, so I know it was hot.

At this same well, we found an Australian couple there from Victoria. They had been stranded there for two days, with plenty of food and water for another ten days, but only two or three liters of gasoline left. They immediately tried to get some gas from Peter, but he told them he only had about 200 liters left, enough to get us out of the desert and couldn't help them with gas, but he did have a two-way radio.

Figure 23. Ollie and John Bessett in Australia

276

He got it out, threw the antenna wire over some brush and was able to get a-hold of a friend of his that he always checked with before goin' out in the desert. He told the friend where this couple was and their predicament and the friend promised to be out there about 10:00 o'clock the next morning with some gasoline. It was about 176 kilometers from where he was, through terribly rough country with lots of water and swamps to get around, but he had been out there before and was sure he could make it. So we left them and I'm sure they got their gas the next day. They also intended to follow their rescuer out, because they had been wanderin' around out there for several days on their own and was completely lost.

We went on quite a distance, probably about 100 miles into the Simpson Desert and saw quite a lot of wild camels and the tracks of wild burros. The wild camels were not a real challenging game animal, but never havin' shot one and never knowin' anyone that had, and bein' as they were there, we each shot one apiece. The Australian government claims that by 1991, they intend to have all the wild horses, wild camels, wild burros, and all the buffalo eradicated, so we didn't feel too bad about shooting three of their wild camels.

From there we went on up to Alice Springs and saw our first Aborigines there, off their reservations. It's against the law for tourists to go on the reservations. You have to get permission from the Aborigines themselves, and Peter said that it was almost impossible to do so. I would love to have taken some pictures of them, but that was against the law, so we didn't try. We did cross a corner of their reservation going on over to Ayers Rock National Park and saw some of them at a mission they had there. They looked pretty wild to me.

We got to the Ayers Rock which is quite a curiosity to the Australians. Apparently, it is one of their more prominent landmarks and they have turned the area all around it into a National Park. Out of sight of the Rock, they've built a-lotta camping facilities and accommodations for as many as

5,000 people, several hotels and several motels. We tried their camping-out facilities and they were great except for the swarms of people there. It was impossible to get to sleep until after midnight because of all the noise and commotion, and then by 4:00 o'clock in the morning, they started gettin' up. People on tour seemed to be eager to get started early. However, our tour guide wasn't much for getting up early, but we managed to get him into the habit of gettin' up around 6:00 in the morning.

Figure 24. Ollie and Wild Boar in Australia

After our visit to Ayers Rock, our trip to Australia was pretty much over, but it might be interesting to tell about some of the side trips we made along the way. One of 'em was down to the Fink River which runs out into the Simpson Desert. A lot of the rivers in Australia never get to the sea – they just run out into a desert and make temporary lakes and dry lakes, but the Fink River was supposedly the oldest river in the world, according to Peter. Australia is the oldest continent in the world and the oldest know fragments of the earth's crust are found in the Jack Hills, and are supposed to be 4.5 billion years old. I don't know exactly how long that is, but it must be a long, long time. Anyway, down this Fink River it has all washed out, due to a 10-inch rain in 2½ days, which took in the whole of central Australia, and this river drains quite a lot of it. There were some palm trees in there, the only kind of those palms found anywhere in the world, and they were nearly all washed out. There was no roads left, but Peter managed to find our way out.

Signs of the flood were everywhere – I never saw anything like it. I tried to take pictures but it was just too big to get a picture of. The channel would go in between several hills and the water in the main channel would be 35 to 40 feet deep. We could see masses of debris in the tall eucalyptus trees that hadn't washed away, and it would be from a quarter-of-a-mile to 600 yards wide. Then it would back up in between the hills and it would be a half-a-mile wide, and out where the channel never gets, it would be half-a-mile wide and six to eight feet deep. Just lots and lots of water is all I can tell you.

We were there a month, like I said, and I never did learn to talk the language, which they call "*strine.*" We did catch on to a lot of their slang words, such as "*ute*," a pickup or a similar vehicle. They call their bedroll a "*swag*" and also roll up some of their personal belongings in them. A "*station*" is a sheep or cattle ranch, an Englishman is called a "*pawn*" and a basic Australian is an "*ocker.*" They call a sheep a "*jumbuck*," a rancher is a "*grazer*," and a prospector is a "*fossick.*" "*Dinkum*" means honest or genuine. A "*dingo*" is an Australian dog and a chicken is a "*chook.*" The back country is called the "*bush.*" "*Bonzer*" means great or terrific and they call a man a "*bloke.*" A woman is either a "*bird*" or a "*Sheila*" – and it seemed to me that the ones they call "*Sheila*" were always a little better-lookin'. And everwhere they stopped they had to get out the "*billy*," a container to boil water in for tea or coffee, and a water-hole was a '*billabong.*" Of course, any number of their words are self-explanatory, like a "*windscreen*" is a windshield on a car, the hood is called the "*bonnet*," and the fenders are "*mud-guards*."

We was all very impressed with the Australian people. They would invariably go out of their way to be helpful and they all loved to talk. They are very knowledgeable about whatever they do, but when asked about something they are not familiar with, they just are not able to help you. That's where I had my trouble with the Australians in Las Vegas, because I never could find out about all the costs and necessities about what I wanted to hunt for, and I like to have all that information before I jump into anything.

John and I and maybe Jack or my daughter, Sherry, plan to go back and hunt with him clear across the continent from Adelaide to Darwin – fly into Adelaide and fly out of Darwin to come home. We are gonna allow ourselves three weeks to make a hunt. Peter says it would take a week to drive across the continent and that would allow 2 weeks for huntin' along the way. I'm lookin' forward to it just as soon as I can get my daughter's consent and she can get her time off her job, we are gonna make that trip!

Venezuela

Ol' George Parker had been huntin' lion, he told me, for 54 years and he'd never killed one. He'd saw several out when he was huntin' but he always had a client or somethin' and they'd shot the lion. He'd even hunted with Sewell Goodwin when Sewell was a-ranchin' down there close to where he had his place. And no luck!

I got acquainted with 'im and he said, "Maybe we could catch a lion!" 'Well," I says, "we can try! But with your damn luck, we may not be able to do it!" Anyhow, this one night we're out in camp and we've got a little campfire a-goin' and George, he kinda believed in roughin' it. I believed in roughin' it, so we're sittin' around this little campfire, neither one of us got a camp stool or a chair, which I manage to have now. And we had a liter of whiskey and we're drinkin' that and talkin' and tellin' different stories. Along about the bottom a-this here liter a-whiskey, we got to talkin' about friends and gettin' in trouble. I just casually mentioned to George, I says, "George, if a friend a-mine is just half right, I'll go the full length a-the rope with 'im." Damn, he jumped up and he says, "Goddamn you Ollie, that's where you and I is different!" And Christ, his excitement damn near sobered me up! "Ollie," he says, "if he's a friend a-mine, I don't give a damn if he's right or wrong! I'm with 'im all the way!" And then he quieted down; he's all right. He was OK then – he got it off his chest.

That's the way George was, you know. Hell, if you was his friend, you was his friend regardless a-what you done. He only had two kinds a-friends: they was either a good son-of-a-bitch or a no-good son-of-a-bitch. There's no in-between.

I've actually hunted twice in South America – I guess really the first time I was in Latin America when I was in the Army. We hunted turkeys, spent a whole day doin' that but didn't kill any turkeys. Then one day we decided we'd go down to Venezuela and kill a jaguar. This is back when Goldwater was in the Senate. Barry and George was pretty good friends. So George writes a letter to Goldwater and he's tellin' 'im that we're comin' down there jaguar huntin' and to see his attaché down there in Caracas about gettin' us gun permits and a permit to hunt jaguar. In the due course a-time, here come a letter back from Goldwater. "George," he says, "there's no way that I can get you a gun permit; they don't give 'em. And besides that, it's agin the law to hunt jaguar down there!"

George, he read that letter and he digested it and he told me, "Piss on it! Let's go! Let's take our guns and when we get down there to the Caracas airport, they're gonna take 'em away from us, but hell, I'll pull some strings or do somethin'. We'll get our guns back." We get down there and Christ, first thing they did, they grabbed our guns. Wanted to know if we had any ammunition – course they knew we did – and they confiscated that. We had four dogs with us, too, but they didn't want to take them. We got a taxi and went to a motel; tied the dogs up on the lawn and went to bed. It was about 10:00 o'clock at night by then.

We're up bright and early next morning and got some breakfast. So he gets on the phone and he calls this attaché down there. He's not into work yet, he hasn't come in, and George, he didn't like that! He thought he oughta be on the job, hell, it was after 9:00 o'clock. So about 10:00 am, George calls again and the attaché, he's still not in! So George says, "Damn him, we don't need him! Let's get us a taxi and go see the general – he's the one a-runnin' things down here!" So he digs down in his duffel bag and gets a carton of American cigarettes out. The taxi takes us to the general and we get up to the door and the guard lets us in. Course, George, he's got a good vocabulary in Spanish. We go in to see the general and they say their howdy dos and everthin' and he introduced him to me and he gives 'im this carton of cigarettes. They visited a little while and finally the general says, "Well, Mr. Parker, what can I do for you?" George tells 'im, "We come down here to hunt jaguar and they confiscated our guns. We'd like to get our guns back and get a permit to hunt down here, to hunt jaguar." The ol' general says, "Is that your only problem?" George says, "That's all."

So he blows a little whistle and here come a corporal in. He tells this corporal, "Go get these guys' guns and get their ammunition. They're gonna hunt jaguar; they need that ammunition!" In a little while, here come our guns and our ammunition. The ol' general, he writes ol' George a little note; it's all in Spanish and I couldn't read it, but George says its permission for us to hunt and have our guns.

We went on and we made our jaguar hunt. No problems. We went to a ranch where there was jaguar. It was a big ranch we was on – they claimed they ran some 26,000 head of cattle – they'd cleared a lot of the jungle and it'd grown up into grass pastures. They had as good a cattle as I ever saw down there. They had 300 bulls that they'd brought outta Texas, cross-breed bulls, as good a-bulls as I ever saw anywhere. This ranch was kind of a little nation of its own;

282

they had their own schools, they had their own stores, had their own vet.

We never did kill a jaguar but we had one caught for about three hours there in a little clump a-woods. Where we was gonna hunt there was kind of a little peninsula that run out of the main jungle out into the savannah. There was a road cut through there for about, oh, no more'n a hundred or two yards and had about a hundred-yard clearing in there.

This one morning, someone workin' on this ranch, they'd saw a jaguar cross the road and go into this here patch of jungle. So we went down there and we walked our dogs across the clearin' and they picked up the track and into the jungle they go! To get to hunt on this ranch we had to bring 'em down two dogs. Well, I brought two real well-trained lion dogs and these two started ones, the started ones – a male and a female that I was gonna leave to the ranch for the hunt. This "Tigero" down there, a guy that the ranch had hired to shoot jaguars, and the way he hunted these jaguars was one of the cowboys'd find a kill. They'd tell him about it and he'd go to this kill and tie it solid to a tree right there were the ol' jaguar had it. It doesn't seem like these jaguars covered their kills like the lions do here. But anyway, he'd get about 15 foot away from that kill with a big tree at his back and sit there with his shotgun until this jaguar'd come in and start eatin' on this kill. He couldn't drag it off and when he was eatin' around on it and he'd expose his head real good, ol' Tigero would put a load of buckshot in its head. And that's the way he killed 'em! But he had a tiger dog – they call these jaguars "tigers" down there – so we had five dogs with the Tigero's dog. When they jumped this here jaguar in this thick jungle, there was a lot of bamboo and heavy vines that was all tangled up in the bamboo and jungle and, Christ, you had to hack with your machete to get clear. As soon as these two young dogs and the Tigero's dog got somewhere near that jaguar, it turned on 'em and growled and carried on and, hell, they quit it! They came back to me! They were the scaredest damn dogs I ever saw! They had their tails pulled up between their legs so tight it throwed a hump in their backs! And that's the way they walked. And this Tigero's dog, he had to get right between my damn legs! He was the scaredest one of the three.

I spend three hours in there, hackin' around – I'd hear a dog bayin' here and one over here and they'd be 50 feet apart. I'd try to hack in but I'd hack in there and the jaguar'd hear me and he'd run and then they'd stop him again. Three hours I was hackin' around in there tryin' to get a shot at this damn thing! I never ever saw 'im but I could hear 'im. While I'm a-hackin' away with this machete, I hit the ol' tiger dog right on top of the ear and cut a gash across there about an inch and a half wide; that machete was sharp! That ol' ear dropped down, hell, it was hangin' on the ground! I'm a little bit concerned about tellin' that damn Tigero about near choppin' his damn dog's ear off or killin' 'im with the machete. George said, "Aw, Ollie, that's no problem. They'll think the jaguar done it!"

Of course, after three hours this here blame jaguar run across the road. George had been sittin' there for three hours in a pickup in this opening where he could see all the way around there and get a shot if the jaguar came out, but he couldn't see where it went across the road. He run down there and this jaguar went right down to the edge of it and then he come right back and come out and went within 50 yards of where George had been a-sittin' for three hours waitin'! And there was some Venezuelans there puttin' up ensilage and they said he was a big ol' tom and he went in a grass pasture there. These hounds went in there and they run 'im outta there after awhile and run 'im into a banana grove. When they went into that banana grove these dogs was so hot they was just weavin' around, they couldn't hardly go any farther. George gathered 'em up and took 'em down and dumped 'em in a tank of water and cooled 'em off. And that was the end of that.

When the Venezuelans got there to see if we'd killed a jaguar they see this hound's ear a-hangin' and they say to the Tigero, "Look what that tiger done to your dog!" So that's what happened to the dog – the jaguar had cut his ear near off! They took him to the vet, who sewed 'im up and, hell, he got well. But I think he was a little more afraid of jaguars after that than he was before!

That pretty much ended our hunt. It was beginnin' to look like we weren't gonna get one. And hell, we had in a couple of weeks so we come back. It wasn't two weeks after we'd been back that they called George up and told 'im that a jaguar came in there and killed two calves. They took those two dogs I'd left down there and treed a female jaguar! They caught it! Of course, ol' Tigero went up there with his shotgun and shot it in the head. They sent the hide to George and we could see the buckshot holes where Tigero had shot it in the head. It was nice of them to do that. I guess they was happy with my dogs – hell, they should a-been! They caught 'em a jaguar! I don't know what they did after that. And that female was bred to this Abe dog of mine, which was one hell of a good lion dog! I'd a-liked to have one of those pups, 'cause I never did get a pup outta 'im.

Anyway, we come back from Venezuela and ol' George, first thing he does, he's gotta write to Goldwater. A letter. He says, "We went down there and took our guns and they confiscated 'em so I had to go see the General of the Army there. The general told us 'Well, hell, if you're huntin' jaguars I hope you kill several of 'em 'cause they're a menace down here. They're eatin'cattle! And if you're gonna hunt jaguar, you need your guns.' And he told 'im about the general tootin' on his whistle and the corporal fetchin' the guns and ammunition and gettin' a letter with permission for guns and huntin'. And George, he reminds Goldwater, he says, "You know, that attaché you got down there – I think you oughta replace him with a cowboy; somebody that knows how to get things done!"

Spotted Cats

I've had more trouble with spotted cats than anything else. The first time I hunted in Africa, we saw this here leopard run into a little bunch of trees, in a kind of savannah country all around with an occasional tree and grass. I think

I've told about that hunt. Anyway, that was just one of the damn problems I've had with leopards. Finally, on my fourth trip to Africa, I killed one! Everthing worked right 'cause I was with a guy then who wasn't afraid of 'em and knew how to hunt these damn leopards!

This was in South Africa. We found a place where a young giraffe had been killed. They had it pretty well eat up and he found some tracks around there of this big stud leopard. Sherry was with me and she shot a wart hog for bait and we tied it up in this tree, like where a leopard would pack it up in there. We built a blind back about 30 yards from it with the wind in our favor and everthin'. Then he tied a fish line to his bait, the wart hog, and he brings that in through our blind and then he hangs a handkerchief on this here damn line. So when a leopard come up there and starts eatin' on it, it would start that handkerchief to movin'. Damn, everthin' is quiet and along about 8:00 o'clock it's pitch dark. We'd put my rifle on a couple of forked sticks and sighted it in right on the bait where I could slip right in behind it. He told me, "Now, when you get your rifle on to where that bait is, you nudge me and I'll turn the light on". Well, when the time came, he turned the light on and seein' that damn leopard in the light, it looked like a damn cheetah to me! So I didn't shoot right off. And he said, "Shoot! Shoot!" So I shot and the ol' thing fell outta the tree, hit the ground – sounded like a lion a-hittin' the ground. But then the bastard jumped up and run! "Christ, Ollie," he says, "you've wounded that bastard! We've got problems!" It got out there about 75, 80 yards and, apparently it died in a leap, 'cause we heard it hit the ground. "Aw'" he says, "he's hit the ground." He turned to Sherry and says, "Give me your rifle!" Sherry says, "You're not gettin' my rifle!" He'd been lettin' us back one another up and didn't have a gun. He said, "That thing might not be dead! I want that rifle!" So Sherry says, "Well, you're not a-gonna have it!" "Well," he says, "I'm pretty sure it's dead." He finally convinced her to take the flashlight and get right behind him and he'd lead out with the rifle. I would be right behind her with my rifle and she'd be safe enough.

She'd decided it was better not to be up front of that little parade! We sneaked up there real careful and it's dead! It's a real good leopard 'cause we measured it out and weighed the thing the next morning and it was Number 10 in the record book, then, when we got the skull out. The thing weighed 147.5 pounds. So we done pretty good on that hunt, on the leopard.

In the meantime, I'd been wantin' to kill a cheetah. Ever place where I'd hunted or seen 'em, they was Royal Game; you couldn't shoot 'em. I also wanted a spotted hyena. I was havin' problems with this spotted hyena, too! I didn't get one a-them 'til my fourth hunt.

Then when Sherry and I made a world trip here in 2001, in Zimbabwe you could shoot a cheetah for $2,000. So I bought one. By golly, I hunted around there several days and they said they're real easy to kill, you'll see 'em, they'll just be a-sittin' in the grass. You'll have all the time in the world to get a rest and can shoot 'em. Cheetah are real easy! Well, we hunted several days and we didn't get it. This one morning Sherry got a stomach problem and she stayed in camp. At that time I was huntin' with one of their flunkies around there. We went out huntin cheetahs and there was a water hole there and we'd been by that water hole and we blew the varmint call and nothin' happened and we'd left. We went on to wildebeest. He just insisted that I kill this wildebeest. He says, "He's way up in the record book!" So I shot it and we took pictures of that but we can't put it in the truck. This kid and myself and two blacks – four of us couldn't get it loaded! So he gets on his radio and calls Sherry's guide. He finally got a-hold of 'im and he said that he'd be right out there to help load it. He come by this tank and we're 'bout a half a mile from this tank and he saw this cheetah there at the water! He drove on by and he got on his radio and called us and told us two cheetahs was there. He told my guy where he was at and to meet 'im there. We met 'im there and he drove off, maybe a half a mile, and I got in his truck and we went down to this water tank.

This cheetah just jumped outta the damn brush and started runnin' right straight down the road! So I raised up in the back of the vehicle and I got a runnin' shot at the thing, about 60 yards, and I just missed makin' a "Texas Heart Shot" by about a half inch. It went up through the pelvis, never broke a bone and come out in its flank. It run off in some brush so we went in there and it jumped out and I got another shot at it and I hit it too far back – I hit it through the stomach. Then it went a little ways in some brush and laid down. This guy says we gotta be real careful; this thing'll charge! We drove around in the vehicle where I could see it layin' there and it wasn't dead and I finished it off. I had my cheetah and of course, that made me real happy!

**Figure 25. Ollie's First Spotted Cat –
A South African Leopard**

They skinned it all out and got the skull out. Then a couple a-days after I killed it, this guy from Nevada, he's a taxidermist, he's an Official Measurer for Safari Club, he measured it up. And accordin' to his measure, the thing is Number Two in the record book! You know, anything in the Top Ten's gotta be done by a Master Measurer, and he's a Master Measurer! Fortunately. Measured it all up. Number

Two in the book. That's fine but, hell, I can't bring it back! Can't even bring the skull back! The United States says they're endangered species and I couldn't bring it in, so I didn't take it

Figure 26. The Leopard in Ollie's Trophy Room

And then Sherry settled up and this young guide, he charged her another $1,000 on her hunt because there was a cat involved! Damn, this Roger Whitall had promised me, he said, "The only thing it's gonna cost you on this hunt is if you kill a cheetah, it'll be $2,000. And if you see somethin' else that you wanna shoot, you shoot it for the trophy fee." That's fine. I shot this here Wildebeest on a trophy fee, $500. Then, when Sherry settled up, he charged her this extra $1000, which he shouldn't a-done. I didn't know it 'til after we'd left and she told me she'd had to pay another $1,000. I felt like I had to reimburse her for that, so the cheetah cost me $3,000.

When I got home, I didn't send it right in, and here just recently, Sherry thought that it outta be in the book. So she sent it in and I get the damn thing back from the Safari Club and they tell me that the Safari Club just recently, their Measuring Committee, is not puttin' anything in the book that you can't bring into the United States! So I got $3,000 spent and the Number Two damn cheetah and I can't even put it in the damn book! All I got is the memory and the pictures! So the other day I stopped by Jackie Parker's and got the Roland and Ward book out and I check it and its Number Two in the Roland and Ward! So now I think I got the address, I'm gonna see if I can get in the Roland and Ward book!

But this is the way my luck runs on spotted cats! I've had problems with jaguar, too! I've made three hunts on Old Mexico for jaguar and then George Parker and I went to Venezuela. The dogs had one caught in kind of an island of jungle, out in savannah country. But that's a whole story of its own and I told that already!

Safari 2001 – Around The World in 55 Days

This story was written by Sherry after we got back. She kept a journal all the time we were gone.

"Ollie and I had been talking about making another international hunt for years now. We had hunted South Africa in 1984, but for various reasons, we had been unable to schedule a trip until now.

I started to plan this trip in October 2000 by trying to contact the guide Ollie had used on two previous hunts in Australia. Peter Schultz was no longer in the business, so he referred us to an active guide he highly recommended, a man named Paul Convery. Paul sent us a video of his previous year's hunts and a lot of information about the hunts and facilities he could offer.

At first, we were primarily interested in the desert "varmint" hunts, but Paul had some interesting deer species available that neither Ollie nor I had ever hunted (or seen). We corresponded by email for several weeks and finally settled on a one-week deer hunt and a one-week desert hunt. We couldn't schedule the dates until we had attended the Safari Club International Convention in Las Vegas in January 2001 and got a definite date for a hunt with Roger Whittall Safaris in Zimbabwe. While at the convention, we planned to check out the New Zealand outfitters. Since we would be in that part of the world and neither of us had ever been in New Zealand, why not?

As a reference point, I asked Paul if he knew any good guides in New Zealand and what the price ranges were for an interesting hunt. He responded that, other than himself, he couldn't think of a soul. It turned out that Paul had lived in New Zealand for 11 years and had been a meat hunter for five years. He also had done a fair bit of guiding during that time. The New Zealand outfitters at the SCI Convention were terribly expensive and we didn't like their policy of pricing the trophy fees based on where the animal scored in the record book. So we made arrangements with Paul to hunt Himalayan Tahr and Chamois with a colleague of his who provided helicopter hunts in the Southern Alps of the South Island.

We had scheduled June 3rd through June 18th for the Zimbabwe hunt so we back scheduled the Australian and New Zealand hunts to start in early May. As a little "vacation" to finish off the trip, we planned one week in and around London before returning home.

Roger Whittall insisted that a .375 was the minimum caliber he would allow for a Cape Buffalo hunt (using solids), so Ollie found me one and loaded up 70 rounds of ammunition for the hunts. He put my 4X scope on it and sighted it in for me. I target shot enough rounds to get over being afraid of it. It was too big for most of the game I would be hunting, but I didn't want to take two guns. I planned to use Ollie's 7mm Mag whenever possible.

We left Tucson May 3, 2001. Today is my daughter Julie's birthday. That seems like an appropriate day to start an around-the-world trip. I checked my suitcase and backpack – I don't think I've forgotten anything important. I have one suitcase and the backpack. Ollie has one suitcase and the gun case. I think we are traveling pretty light for a long trip and three or four weather zones, but we have learned not to take more than we can manage by ourselves. Besides, on trips I never buy anything I have to dust or feed or might break on the way home.

Ollie's brother and sister-in-law, Dick and Betty Jo Barney, brought Ollie to Green Valley at 2:00 pm and Ollie, Damon (brother) and I left for the Phoenix airport just before 3:00 pm. Damon dropped us off and headed home.

We started checking in with American Airlines for the flight to Los Angeles, with baggage checked all the way to Adelaide, Australia, when we hit our first snag. We were scheduled to fly on American to LA, then on Quantas for all flights through Johannesburg, South Africa. It turns out that Quantas has some severe restrictions on the transport of firearms and ammunition. Our counter agent called the AA Help Desk to get the proper procedures. The AA Help Desk called the Quantas Help Desk, who said the normal procedure was notification one or two days prior to departure for the transport of ammunition. And guns. We waited about 30 minutes while this conversation was going on. It was finally decided that the guns could go but not the ammunition. Our agent called and had our two suitcases returned to the counter since she had already sent them through the system.

We were very polite and very patient and refused to go away. I told her that waiting two or three days was unacceptable, and leaving the ammo wasn't an option. Guns and ammo just go together. Our agent, bless her persistent little heart, decided that she really needed to solve this problem. So she called the Quantas Manager of Dangerous Goods in Sydney, Australia. After she got him on the phone, she said, "Please talk to this passenger; she has lots of paperwork." I talked to Dan, who asked what we were about and where we were. I assured him that we had less than five kilos of ammunition in each suitcase. He pulled up our records, verified our itinerary, and said, "I don't see any problem; give me three minutes and I will add the authorization to your locator code. You won't have any question about firearms after this." It took about five minutes after that. Everybody was happy and our retrieved luggage was sent back again, along with the gun case.

In LA, when we checked in, they took our pocketknives and my cigarette lighter and sent them in a sealed packet labeled as "Security" items to be retrieved at the luggage counter at Sydney.

That same night we backed away from the gate at 12:01 am, Quantas 108 LA to Sydney. These are very comfortable accommodations. They served a meal they called "dinner" about 1:00 am our time. This is going to be confusing. Ollie passed on dinner but I had to at least give it a try I was able to sleep or at least doze most of the time. Ollie did the same. We got breakfast about ten hours later. Wheels went down 14 hours 12 minutes after rotation in LA. I don't feel jet lagged. We just chased the night across the Pacific. Dawn broke about two hours from Sydney.

Second snag – no suitcase in Sydney for Ollie. A suitcase that looked just like Ollie's kept moving around the baggage carrousel, so we figured out what had happened. My suitcase and the guns made it OK, so we filed a baggage claim and went on to Adelaide. I need to call Quantas as soon as we get a hotel in Adelaide so they can deliver the suitcase. As soon as we arrived in Adelaide, I called Paul to find what hotel was closest to him. He insisted that we stay with him. They have a one-bedroom unit, with bath, on the lower level of their home. Ollie's suitcase was delivered there about 5:00 pm.

Since we crossed the International Date Line, we are now on May 6th. This is a "down day." We needed to loaf around and we did.

Next snag – the local bank wouldn't cash our Traveler's Checks. They felt they needed "recourse" in case of a problem. I pointed out the 800 number that the bank could call to verify that the checks were genuine and not stolen, but to no avail. I think they just didn't want to do it. We ended up chasing all over Adelaide to find the American Express office that cashed checks. It took three hours but we were patient and successful. We've traveled before.

We had a good lunch and left for the hunting camp in Water Valley about 1:00 pm. We got there in time to take an hour or so to look around the area nearest the camp.

This is our first day of hunting and we have seen more deer today that I have seen in all my years of hunting in Arizona and Mexico. Ollie agrees. I had one quick shot at a Red Stag that was running away from us, but missed. I could see by the look on Paul's face that he was thinking "This is going to be a long hunt."

Tomorrow we're going back to see if we can find the one I missed. Paul also got the go-ahead to take a water buffalo, so that is on the list for me. It would be nice to get one when we can recruit some help from the station hands. Those buffalo are really big boys.

That next day, after several hours of spotting and tracking red stag, we finally found one that Paul was happy with. It was another long shot and nearly dark, but that never bothered Ollie before. It didn't this time, either. He had a very awkward rest on the "bonnet" of the truck, but he still has the knack for getting a quick sight and shot. The stag is a very good representative of the species, certainly big enough to satisfy us, and we are all very happy with it.

On our next hunting day, after a long chase and a stalk through the brush, I got a look at a good fallow buck. It was down the hill and then up a bit on the other side; about 200 yards away. I was lying slightly downhill and had to use Paul's jacket as a rest to get the gun barrel high enough. He whistled, the deer stopped and I shot it. We now both feel much better about my shooting skills.

Ollie got a really nice chital stag. It wasn't too far from camp, either. It was a fairly long shot, but right on the button. As usual. Any animal within 300 yards is in serious danger from my Daddy.

That next day, after several hours of spotting and tracking Red Stag, we finally found one that Paul was happy with. It was another long shot and nearly dark, but that never bothered Ollie before. It didn't this time, either. He had a very awkward rest on the "bonnet" of the truck, but he still has the knack for getting a quick sight and shot. The stag is a very good representative of the species, certainly big enough to satisfy us, and we are all very happy with it.

Figure 27. Gareth (Paul's son) – the camp cook

We had enough time so we decided that we also wanted to hunt rusa deer and there are a lot of good ones. They are native to Indonesia and have been imported to Australia for years. They seem to thrive and prosper in this climate. Ollie got his first. They are still in velvet but it is very hard and makes the antlers look unusual.

I finally got a shot at one but hit it a little low. It was a hard enough hit to put the buck down so I got up to it quickly to finish the job. It has very hard velvet on the antlers – makes them look white in the scope.

Again, we are happy campers. This is very different hunting for us since there are so many animals, really good bucks, that Paul has to choose what he thinks is the best. The others are "rats." We saw bucks that looked good to us and Paul would say "Nah, that's a real rat." So on we would go.

This is our seventh day of hunting and we have tracked for hours again today, mostly from the truck. We're looking for a fallow buck for Ollie and a red stag for me. We finally started seeing lots of fallow deer and Ollie shot a good one. Paul wasn't as happy with it as he thought he would be, so when we found a better one he gave it to Ollie for his birthday. We had discovered that Ollie, Paul, Paul's wife Chris and his son Gareth all have birthdays on either the 23rd or 24th of January. Mine is in May, the same month as Paul's daughter. She's in London, so I'm all-alone with these Aquarians.

Figure 28. Ollie with Chital Buck

Anyway, the buck was moving at a slow trot about 300+ yards away. Part of the deal was that Ollie had to kill it with one shot. He had a good rest on the bonnet and hit it through the heart. The deer still ran 125 yards after it was hit and then dropped. Paul accused Ollie of showing off. Ollie told him that if he (Paul) wanted this stuff to stay alive, don't tell him to shoot! Paul can't wait to rag on younger hunters about this "Old Man of the Mountains."

Not long afterwards, we found a really good red stag with a dropped tine on the right. It was about the same size as the first one that I had missed, but had an interesting, atypical rack. The stag was about 200 yards uphill and facing me. I hit it right in the middle of the lower neck. It ran about 25 yards into heavy brush so we tracked it and I was able to finish it with a second shot. Paul had pointed the stag out to me and then turned away and plugged his ears. He claimed he could feel the muzzle blast on his butt. I accused him of being too sensitive. We are VERY happy campers now.

We went out again just before dark to look for a big chital buck for me (we had seen one the morning before in the area). We didn't get through the first gate away from camp before some bucks broke through the brush on the right. Paul told me to shoot the one on the left and I shot before he could plug his ears. That .375 with a muzzle break is a noisy puppy when it goes off close to your head. Paul's ears were ringing for hours. Maybe he's not so sensitive after all.

Figure 29. Paul and Ollie with Fallow Buck

Paul was very unhappy with himself because the buck had a broken "inner" and was not a typical shape. He thought he should have noticed that. Everything happened so fast that I don't know how he could have seen it. In any case, I like the size and shape of the antlers even if he doesn't. I killed it and it's mine.

Today is buffalo day. We found the big one we had been looking for all along. It was with two buddies. I shot him in just the right spot to bring him down and then was able to finish him with a second shot through the heart. We had to wait quite awhile before the other two moved far enough away that we could approach him. It took several hours to process him because it was so big and Paul wanted the cape. We were careful with the meat and Paul pulled out the back straps for himself and family. Ollie and I would have loved to make jerky out of the rest of the meat, but no time for that. The station hands got a lot of stew meat instead.

Figure 30. Sherry with Chital Buck

We packed up that evening and headed back to Adelaide. Gareth had tied my buffalo horns to the front grill of the truck. Most of the rest of the deer antlers were tied up on top of the truck. We looked pretty wild coming out of the bush. Ollie is a little deaf and Paul's truck is a diesel, so conversations were at a higher volume than usual. Paul would say something to Ollie in a normal tone and Ollie would ask him to repeat it. Finally Paul shouted: "The way we're yelling at each other, people are going to think we're married!" Ollie said that it was a good thing he couldn't hear everything Paul said because it would probably just piss him off.

It's hard to complain about 100% success for two hunters and five species, so we didn't. Ollie and I are having a great time.

Today is a quiet day. We all need some down time. Paul worked on the heads, getting them cleaned and boiled out. He'll ship them to us after we get home.

I caught up on the laundry. I also discovered that my ATM card works very well. I can trade plastic for Australian dollars with only a $2.00 ATM fee. That's a lot cheaper than paying a currency exchange rate. It kept telling me that I could have $1,000 AUS but would only give me $950. I, of all people, should know that one can't trust a computer.

This is the 14th of May and it's another quiet day. We had planned these in the schedule so Ollie and I could rest and Paul could work on the trophies.

After our "down" day, we drove north to the Timari Desert. It's in the northeast corner of South Australia, just south of the Simpson Desert in the Northern Territory. It's about a nine-hour drive. We saw a lot of country that looks like West Texas – miles and miles of ... miles and miles. When Ollie was here before, he hunted in the Simpson Desert.

We're staying at an old farmhouse and it's huge. It has six or seven bedrooms. The original walls are fieldstone and must be two or three feet thick. The temperature is so high here in the summer that they were needed just to survive. After sundown, it's like being in a cave. It's not all that bright during the day.

The station manager, Jason, is a young man who, with his wife Patsy and two-year-old son Wally, has been here for about six months. Paul didn't think she was a very good cook, but Ollie and I didn't have anything to complain about. Chris and Gareth spoil Paul because they are very good cooks. Gareth did all the cooking during the deer hunt in Water Valley and we never had a bad meal. However, I have never drunk so much coffee or eaten so much bread in my life. I may have to go home as excess baggage.

The average rainfall here is two to four inches but it hasn't rained yet this year. The livestock all look fat and healthy and we can't understand why – we don't see anything edible. Paul says they eat dirt with sand for dessert.

Our first hunting day here is camel day. Paul has been worried about this hunt because of the area we may have to cover to find them. Given our schedule (we have to be in Zimbabwe the 2nd of June), Paul could only allot three days to camels in order to leave time for wild donkeys and goats.

Jason went out early on his motorbike to see if some camels were still in the same general area where he had seen them earlier in the week. They were, so we headed out and found some in about one-and-a-half hours. Ollie and I each got one but they are so massive I couldn't find the right spot right away. I had to shoot two or three times before I finally downed it with a shot through the shoulder and one through the neck. This camel is the largest animal I have seen, other than an elephant. Ollie's camel had broken its jawbone and it had healed in a very unusual open position. It must have had to graze with its back teeth because there was no way it could close it's front teeth together. Paul said that the bull camels are very bad-tempered and aggressive and that the injury was probably a result of fighting.

We wandered around a lot since it's interesting country; it's a very sandy desert with a lot of scrub brush. On the way back we came across a herd of 12 to 15 camels, then later saw a small group of four or five.

Figure 31. Ollie with Camel

When we got back to the ranch house I showered and changed clothes. Clean clothes for my birthday tomorrow are a must. We left a day early. We're off to find the wild donkeys south of here.

Today is May 17, 2001. Today I am 59. That's awfully close to 60. I guess I'll learn to live with it.

We headed south this morning to find the wild donkeys. Paul hasn't hunted this area before, so he is worried about the details of the lodging and hunting. He can't get the kind of answer he wants from the Station Manager – DIRECT! Paul says that this is a national trait of Australians that *drives* him crazy (more like a short putt in my opinion). Ask a direct question: "How many?" Answer: "A few."

Figure 32. Ollie in the Outback (Timari Desert)

"Is that a couple?"

"Could be."

"Is a couple two or three?"

"About that."

"About two or about three?"

"More than a fair number, but less than a mob."

The cottage we're staying in is somewhat of a relic, but it has indoor plumbing with a flush toilet. All houses have rainwater tanks to augment well water. The central section of Australia is a huge basin; only a few rivers and streams actually run into the oceans. There must be a large aquifer under the basin, but it also must be deep. The rainfall around here is not much higher on average than where we hunted camels.

The Station Manager is Gordon, who lives here with his wife Lynn and daughter Ellen. Ellen takes school assignments over the short-wave radio and meets with her teacher from time to time. Next year she will be in eighth grade and will start boarding school in Adelaide until she finishes high school. Gordon, his brother and his uncle tend a station of 1,000 square miles. Many of the stations are that large, so local schools are not very practical.

Lynn and Ellen made a lovely dinner for us. Lynn had made a pineapple pie, so when she heard it was my birthday she put a candle on it for me. I had a birthday pie in the outback of Australia. That's a new experience.

Gordon's favorite joke: An outback farmer won the lottery; an enormous sum of money. When asked what he was going to do with all that money, he thought about it for a long while. Finally, he said; "I guess I'll just keep farming 'til it's all gone."

Paul isn't happy with Gordon's hunting vehicle. He will get things changed before he comes back here. Paul, Gareth and I are in the back on a bench. Ollie is in the front seat. There is a metal rack around the truck bed that is exactly the wrong height for a rifle rest – too high if sitting down and too low standing up. However, we are nothing if not flexible.

Again, we saw very little that looked edible but all the livestock looked fat and healthy. Gordon told me that it had rained once and grass actually grew for one summer, so the critters were just living on memories.

We saw a big kangaroo and stopped to take a shot
(Gordon had permits). Just as I was squeezing the
trigger, Ollie shot. We both hit it – thump, thump.
Paul said: "I can't believe that your own sweet daddy
poached that 'roo right out from under you!" It turned
out that Gordon, who was driving, told Ollie to shoot
at the same time Paul told me to. Ollie always had a
sensitive trigger finger.

Figure 33. Gordon, Paul, Gareth and Ollie at lunch break

We chased a large herd of donkeys for a long time
and finally got within range. Ollie, Gareth and I each
were able to kill two. I have great pictures of my "wild
black ass." Gordon had a lot of wild horses –
brumbies – that he would let us hunt but we
declined. Two donkeys were plenty.

We decided to move on this evening. That gives us
some extra time if we need it for the wild goat hunt.
We headed south again to find a motel somewhere
along the track. After stopping for diesel, the station
owner told Paul a shorter way to get to Pitcairn,
where we will hunt the goats. So, on we went. We
arrived about 9:00 pm and set up camp in the old

sheep shearer quarters. There are lots of small bedrooms with two twin beds in each one. There is a large, well-equipped kitchen and a refrigerator. There is also an old wood stove that was probably the original equipment for the kitchen. Also flush toilets (Ollie and I are getting picky in our dotage) just down the path from the rooms.

There are mobs of goats here. I shot one near the truck. Then Paul spotted a small mob of goats up on a hill about a half-mile away. We got closer and then went out to stalk them on foot. Ollie stayed in the truck since his knee was not going to allow that kind of hike. We climbed a steep hill and circled around behind them; it took nearly an hour and a half. I was winded – riding around in a truck for two weeks isn't very good training for this – but I recovered and was able to make some good shots. Three goats with four shots. I was using Ollie's 7 mag since I was conserving ammo for my .375

This is the prettiest country we have seen so far, although Water Valley is nearly the same. There are rolling hills, clumps of trees and scrub brush. The creek we go up and down has run once in the past ten years that Paul knows about. The station owner, Ross, said that they are in their sixth year of draught. He had to sell all his cattle three years ago. He now just runs sheep, and the goats are serious competition for what little feed there is.

When we got back to camp for lunch (we rarely miss a meal), Ross' wife Jean had made a big pot of soup and a bacon and egg pie for us. Dinner included a fantastic cheesecake with double cream. This is turning out to be a REALLY good hunt. Ollie laughs at me. He thinks my mother should have named my siblings and me "Scout" since we always seem to be looking for our next meal.

We fired up the donkey engine to heat water for showers. I was first. The water kinda slushed out of the showerhead and was just warm enough to stand next to and slosh around. I managed to get fairly clean and wash my hair. I was chilly but felt a LOT better. I guess we didn't wait long enough for the water to get hot because Paul was next and I had used up all the warm water. He was cold! He would have quit but didn't want me to think he was a wussy. Gareth decided to wait and Ollie opted to skip it altogether. After a couple of hours of spotlighting for foxes that evening, Gareth had a nice hot shower. Patience is a virtue.

The shearer's quarters are not used much anymore but are very comfortable.

Today is goat day again. Gareth spotted some big billies so we chased them until we got into range. Ollie did another one-shot kill. He's a tough act to follow. The bigger one had taken off so we went in wild pursuit until I could get a shot. It was still moving pretty fast and I had to shoot twice before I brought him down. I decided to keep the horns, since they were fairly big and well matched. I had forgotten how bad billy goats stink.

We went back to camp to pack up and head back to Adelaide. Paul can't believe how we have been able to find everything we were hunting for and finish early. Ollie keeps telling him what a lucky hunter he (Ollie) is. Paul seems to have the same charm, or animal magnetism or whatever it is that works. Some sort of pipeline to the Hunting Gods.

We weren't scheduled back until the 23rd so Ollie and I will have an extra day or two in Sydney. I can catch up on the laundry again and maybe find a dry cleaner. My sweater is in sad shape and our field jackets aren't any better. We took Paul, Chris and friend/taxidermy helper Jackie out to dinner at a great steak house. It was quite a change from the bush/outback.

On May 21st, Ollie and I flew to Sydney and arrived with all luggage and guns. I found an apartment hotel with a washer, dryer and a kitchenette. I found a small market only five minutes walk away that also was a dry cleaner drop-off. I bought all I could carry back and we're all set for the next three or four days. We had a big lunch on the plane, so a light dinner and early lights-out was the plan.

Today is laundry day. The machines are about half size so this is going to take most of the day. At least it is more convenient than a laundromat, which I never found. Maybe I should have just had everything dry cleaned. I need to find another ATM. Most places take MasterCard or VISA, but busses and taxis want cash. Ollie's knee is very sore today. We'll get out tomorrow and do some sightseeing. I'd like to see the harbor area and the opera house.

We're just tourists today. We took a taxi to the harbor area – it's called the Circular Quay – and caught a tour bus. The Red Explorer. They run all day and make 25 stops around the city and a ticket lets us get on and off a bus at any stop. We got off at the Hard Rock Café stop so I could buy a shirt. Since the busses run every 18 minutes, we just walked back to the stop and caught the next one that came along. It is an excellent way to see the city. The bus drivers are also the tour guides and know all about the places we go by.

We got off again at The Rocks, which is the first settled area; the first place the English landed in 1788. We went down to the waterfront and found a beachside restaurant. I had the lobster bisque and the bouillabaisse. Ollie had fried oysters. Mine must have been good because I got it on both of us. Everything was delicious, including the bread and beer. We like Foster's the best so far.

I skipped dinner and did some more laundry. I never did get all the soup stains out of my shirt. Oh well, it's old and I may leave it in Africa.

I called brother Damon this morning. There are 17 hours difference and he's a day behind us. It's May 24th 9:00 am Thursday morning here and May 23rd

4:00 pm Wednesday afternoon in Green Valley. He and Georgia haven't seen Cinco the cat for nearly a week and everybody is worried. All else seems to be OK.

We are still tourists today. Ollie and I took the Blue Explorer today and saw a different part of the city and harbor. It goes further north into the beach areas. On the way out of the harbor we saw the USS Kitty Hawk and one of its destroyer escorts moored at the navy docks. They must have come in during the night. The Kitty Hawk had a deck full of Tomcat fighters. We saw US sailors all over the city and I think every bar or pub had a "Welcome US Navy" sign on it. We had lunch at a sidewalk café across the street from the beach. Fish and chips and beer. Life is good! I bought a bunch of souvenir shirts for friends and grandkids so I had to buy a heavy-duty plastic bag for suitcase overflow. It's something I can check on the plane.

I found a letterbox and mailed postcards. I also found a corner bistro that had an Internet access machine (coin operated). I checked email and all is well. We loafed around today and I did a last load of laundry. This is it until we get to Zimbabwe. Nothing is officially dirty until we get there; only previously worn. There is daily laundry service at the Whittall hunting camps.

Today is May 26th and we flew to Christchurch, New Zealand and met Paul at the airport. There was no problem with the guns this time. I had sent the firearms permits in late March with a check for the fee. When we arrived, the police officer remembered the name and check because they couldn't process it. He sent me to the exchange window for cash. Money may talk but cash screams!

Paul had brought another hunter with him for this adventure. He's a young Australian man whom Paul had guided before. Terry seemed a pleasant sort of guy, so we think this will work out just fine. We found a hotel with shuttle service and went on our way.

The next day we took a four-and-a-half-hour train ride over some of the most spectacular scenery I have ever seen. We were on the Trans Alpine Railroad going from Christchurch to Greymouth over the Southern Alps. We were told that rain is measured in feet, not inches, in this part of New Zealand. There was lots of water in rivers, snow-covered mountaintops and long sandy beaches. In the lower elevations, it looked like rain forest. From the train, we boarded a minibus for a three-hour ride south to Fox Glacier, on the western coast of the South island. Paul couldn't remember the name of the hotel Chris had made reservations at, so the bus driver took us around to various ones until Paul found one he liked.

Our first hunting day, Ollie and I went together in the helicopter with Paul and pilot James. James can flat-ass fly a helicopter. He is also a hunter and the flying is so natural to him that he just hunts and the flying takes care of itself. We were close enough to the ground at times that I could see bird tracks in the snow. James has rotor clearance "feel" down to millimeters.

Figure 34. Ollie Boarding the Helicopter

These are the most rugged mountains I have ever seen. Everything is straight up or straight down with lots of brush and powdery snow. There are some rock falls at least 2,000 feet high or deep with huge icicles hanging off some of the ledges.

The hunting procedure is this: We fly around the 10,000 foot level of mountains that are just over 12,000 feet high and look for either tahr or chamois. When a good one is spotted, James will set down as close as he can on a ridge near the animal so the hunter can get out with Paul and try to get a shot. Sounds easy if you say it fast.

It turns out that James puts the right skid down of the edge of a ridge and Paul and I climb out on the skid and jump into butt-deep snow. The first leap from the chopper to the snow was an adrenalin *RUSH* I'll never forget!! (Part of the thrill was knowing that there was nothing under the other skid but 2000 feet of air. The other part was wondering how in holy hell I was going to get back.) I climbed part-way back up the skid to pull the rifle out from under the seat, then we hunkered down while the chopper pulled up and tried to keep the snow and ice from the rotor wash from clogging up the scope or rifle barrel. Next I had to flounder through the soft snow and try to get some sort of rest so I could take a shot at the tahr that was bounding down the mountain on the ridge across from us. I hit it twice and then it disappeared. James dropped back down immediately and picked us up in order to drop us off again on a ridge opposite from where we had last seen the bull.

I discovered how to get back in – I had to grab the skid and pull myself high enough out of the snow to get one foot on the skid, then reach up to open the door, push the rifle in under the seat, then climb the rest of the way back in and get the door closed. All while the chopper was wobbling just a little back and forth. I was determined to do this well. I was not going to give Paul a chance to talk about this chubby little old lady they had to leave on the mountain because she couldn't get back into the chopper.

Back to the hunt: Paul and I were just across a deep ravine from the tahr, who had run into some brush. I finally saw enough of him to get a good neck shot and killed him. James whipped back down, picked up Paul and they headed off to find a tahr for Ollie. While I waited for them to return, I moved around a little on the ridge. I moved slowly because it's hard to flounder around in the snow - one step is level and the next is hip-deep - and also because it's straight down on three sides and straight up on the fourth. Luckily for us, the weather was absolutely perfect. Cold at that altitude but no wind, snow, rain or fog. The sky was a deep blue. It was beautiful.

About 45 minutes later I saw the chopper coming back with a large bull tahr hanging on a rope between the skids. Ollie had made a very difficult uphill shot – one, as usual – and had gotten a very nice trophy. James hovered over my tahr and Paul got out to retrieve my trophy.

Paul had to pull the animal to a fairly clear spot, tie the rope on it and wait for James to put the chopper down low enough for him to hook the rope on the carry-ring. Low enough meant almost on Paul's head. Then Paul climbed back in and they came to get me. I lost my hat from the rotor wash this time, but there's no going back since it went over the edge.

After James found a flat place lower down the mountain for a photo op, we started out again looking for chamois. When a couple of good ones were spotted, James dropped the tahr and started looking for a good place to drop us. This time Paul, Ollie and I all got out – a thrill a minute!! It was just as exciting the third time as the first! We couldn't see the chamois after we were on the ground; they were across the ravine and straight up about 200 yards away in some heavy brush. We were looking into the sun, also. James immediately positioned the helicopter above and to the left of us so the chopper shadow would cover us. Finally one of the bucks stuck his head up a little and Ollie could see his head and part of his neck. Ollie made an absolutely incredible shot; he was lying on his back in the snow with the rifle nearly vertical and killed the chamois with one shot through the neck. Paul was nearly speechless with amazement. Ollie is his HERO!

Figure 35. Paul and Sherry with Himalayan Tahr

The second buck was in a brush cave and none of us could see him. So James picked Paul and me up and dropped us across the big ravine about 70 yards downhill and across a small ravine from where the chamois was. I fired twice, but too low; all we could see was his breath when he moved a little. Finally, we could see part of his face and Paul said, "Screw it, shoot him in the nose." So I did. He tumbled down the slope nearly to the big ravine and not too far from Ollie's buck.

James came in to pick Paul and me up, then Ollie, then back for the chamois. Paul had a tough time getting up to where they were because of the snow and ice on the steep slope. Then he had to wrestle them to a place where James could drop down low enough to pick them all up. We found a place for a photo op and went back after the tahr. Paul is getting a lot of exercise today!

We were all JAZZED! Four good animals in two-and-a-half-hours. And I was still on adrenalin high from the first jump! Ollie and I decided to have Paul do shoulder mounts on all four trophies.

After our successful day yesterday we had a quiet day. Paul went hunting with James and Terry, who was also successful on both tahr and chamois. Paul and Terry started skinning the six animals while Ollie and I supervised.

Figure 36. Ollie with Chamois

The next morning, Ollie and I rested while Paul and Terry went back to skinning. We were supposed to meet James at 1:00 pm but he called in early so we started out at noon. We still had one-and-a-half-hours of our agreed-upon six hours of chopper time. Paul wanted to get a tahr and I needed another chamois since my "nose shot" had gone down the side of the neck and ruined the cape.

I got out of the chopper with Paul when we spotted a good bull tahr. Paul got him with Ollie's 7 mag, but took two shots. Ollie is worried about Paul's teaching the rifle bad habits. Paul and I and the tahr were picked up in the usual manner. That's still pretty exciting, too.

We spotted some chamois so Paul and I jumped out again. Same rush!! I'm getting hooked on adrenalin. The animals were hiding in the brush and we floundered around in armpit-deep snow until I could finally see a little patch of hide. I took one shot, then gave the rifle to Paul, who wanted to get a chamois. He just kept looking into the brush and finally put the rifle down. He worked his way through the snow to the bushes and said, "You killed both of them with one shot! Is there no end to these Barneys?" He called me a greedy little girl! I told him I had to do something to keep up with my daddy.

Since we're leaving tomorrow we took the hides back to the motel and hung some of them up in the showers to let the water/fluids drain. I took a picture because it looked like we had killed and butchered someone in there.

Today, May 31st, is a travel day back to Christchurch. First the minibus, then the train and back to the same hotel. We hung up the skins in the showers again – another photo op. This time we had small suites with kitchenettes so we boiled out the heads, too. We kept all the draperies closed so the maids couldn't see what we were doing.

Our flight to Sydney is late morning, so I walked to the nearest store and bought 30 pounds of salt. Paul spread out a plastic tarp and re-salted the hides before we packed them back into heavy plastic bags (five of them). Paul borrowed the maid's vacuum cleaner so we could get rid of the mess (hide the evidence). We said that it's OK if they think we're trashy bastards, we just don't want them to know what we really did. Since Ollie and I were flying business class, we were able to check the five bags without paying excess baggage fees. Such a deal!! However, when we got to Sydney we lacked another firearms permit to re-enter the country. After considerable discussion, the senior Customs Agent asked if it would be OK if they just stored the guns overnight for us since we were just in transit to Johannesburg. We readily agreed.

We said goodbye to Paul at the airport – he was on his way to Adelaide. We'll miss him. This has been one of the greatest hunts either Ollie or I have had. The weather has been perfect everywhere, the company was the best and the hunting was 100% successful.

I had picked a hotel out of the Sydney Yellow Pages for an overnight stay because it claimed to be close to the airport. It wasn't. Not only that, it was in a tough part of town and turned out to be a backpacker hostel! So much for random searches. The room was clean and comfortable, if somewhat small. Only one of us could stand up at once but we managed OK. I'm sure we woke everyone up when we dragged our baggage downstairs at 4:30 am to catch a taxi to the airport. C'est la vie!

June 2nd and another travel day. We claimed our guns from Customs and checked in for our flight to Johannesburg. We all three wish Paul were going with us.

The plane was late in arriving; therefore it was late leaving. We have had so few delays in all the flights so far that we feel very fortunate. At this time we are 7 hours 25 minutes into a 14 hour 20 minute flight. HALLELUJAH!!!!! We're on the downhill run.

This is our last Quantas flight; we're on British Airways through London, then American from London to Tucson. Ollie has figured out that we will have flown 30,000+ miles by the time we get to Jo'burg.

We checked into the Intercontinental Hotel across the street from the airport. It's brand new with good staff people and restaurants. It's close to five star. This is the first hunting trip where I can take a hot bubble bath in a marble-floored bathroom. Life is really GOOD!

We took our second malaria tablet today. I guess we need to do this. It seems to make me a little dizzy. We fly to Harare today, June 3rd. We will be staying at Georgie Smith's B&B. I hope she meets us at the airport because I don't have her address.

Good News! Georgie and Anne Whittall both were at the airport to meet us. It was nice to see a familiar face. We paid out $30 US to get visas – gun permits were free. The economy seems to run on US currency. Even the government demands fees in dollars. We had tea in Georgie's garden and met her mother. She is quite a character. We had dinner and went to bed early.

Anne drove us to the Humani Ranch today. It takes four to five hours. The smog over Harare is the worst I have ever seen – even worse than what I saw in pictures of LA in the early fifties. Diesel fuel fumes, dust and wood smoke are the primary sources. We arrived at the Turgue River camp at 1:30 pm. We met our hunter, Clive Hallamore, whom we had met briefly in Las Vegas at the SCI Convention and his two trackers, Shortie and Piason. After lunch, we drove around and saw lots of game, but not what we are hunting.

Our first hunting day, we crossed the Turgue at dawn to the Bedford hunting area to look for Cape Buffalo. We spent most of the day driving the perimeter roads looking for tracks. Humani Ranch is one of 19 farms that joined together to form a hunting conservancy of one-million acres. Only the outer perimeter is fenced; all interior areas are unfenced. We found some fresh tracks in the afternoon and followed them into the jungle. We found four bulls (they're called "duggerboys") but all were immature males. That means that the boss is soft in the middle and will boil away leaving a big gap between the horns. So we let them go. It would have been a clear shot with a good rest.

Figure 37. Ollie and Georgie in Harare

The next day we walked all morning, went back to camp for lunch and walked all afternoon. We didn't see any buffalo. We had dinner with Roger and Anne Whittall at their house. It was a very pleasant evening. We met Daniel and Dee there. Daniel is an apprentice Professional Hunter. Dee works as general staff assisting all the hunting camps.

Our third hunting day, we found buffalo during our morning hike; one big bull in a small herd. We had been walking for about four hours, then started stalking the group. We crawled through grass, brush and buffalo shit for several hundred yards. Clive was waiting for the bull to move from behind thick brush when four game scouts walked over the hill and spooked the herd. There must have been 70 or 80 animals in the group. They flattened the jungle; it looked like someone was building a runway. We followed for hours but never caught up with them.

Hilton and Raye came to the camp for dinner. He's a PH for Roger working out of another camp. It was a nice evening. We had Wildebeest Wellington. Yum!

This hunt today (4th day) we found a large herd of buffalo. There were several hundred animals in groups of 30 to 50. We stalked one group for several hours but the biggest bull was immature. Paul would have called him a rat. We found another herd with a "shooter" but they spotted us and we had to freeze in place. Finally one of his wives or girlfriends warned the bull that he had better run, so they all took off.

Ollie went with Daniel today. He shot three Impala for camp meat. He also shot a civet cat during the evening spotlight run.

We stalked more buffalo on both morning and afternoon hunts. No shooters, though. Ollie went with Daniel again. He shot a monkey and a big dog baboon. I have seen mobs of impala, kudu, warthogs, baboons, some monkeys and lots of beautiful birds. No "shooter" buffalo.

Figure 38. Ollie in Clive's truck

We came across a king cobra today. An eagle had broken its neck and then started eating it from the tail. It was about 1/3 eaten but was still alive. Clive told me there are six varieties of cobra in Zim, two of them the spitting kind. If one spits, it aims for the eyes and is very accurate. The remedy is to wash out the venom with milk, water or urine (in order of preference). There is an acid in the venom that will cause blindness within 30 to 45 minutes. This might be more than I want to know. I also saw a puff adder.

More hunting, no buffalo, no cheetah. I saw nyala today from the camp veranda. We can see the opposite side of the river from camp. Lots of game comes down to graze and water. There is a troop of baboons that lives on the riverbank below our hut and another troop just across the river. When the troops aren't quarreling among themselves, they shout insults at the other troop.

More buffalo hunting today. We were driving down the Bedford perimeter road at 6:00 am when Piason saw buffalo across the river. We took off boots and socks and rolled up pant legs and waded the Turgue.

Shoes over the shoulder, rifle held overhead. The water was from ankle- to thigh-deep and was 120 yards wide. The water was cool but not cold. We climbed up the bank, dropped shoes and started stalking the buffalo through the reeds and grass. Clive had set up the shooting sticks (a tripod of sorts) but the big bull stayed behind the thickest bush. He was with three other bulls and a lot of other cows and calves.

They scented us and took off. We thought they had left the area but when we moved forward about 50 yards, they stampeded again. They thundered toward the jungle then suddenly turned towards the river. We ran barefoot through the underbrush to the river's edge and watched them going across the water about 300 yards downstream from us. They came up against a bluff and couldn't climb out so they turned left and ran up the river toward us. When they were exactly opposite us, 120 yards away, we were looking directly into the sun and couldn't see them anymore.

The lead cow stepped into a hole and went into water nearly over her head. She knew the calves couldn't make it so she turned to come back across the river. Four young bulls managed to climb out a less-steep bank and stay on the other side. The big bull and his four buddies stayed with the herd. When he was as close as I thought he would get, I took a shot. He was lunging through the water and I hit him too high on his back. He bled enough to leave a light blood trail.

We put on our boots and stalked the four bulls for the next ten hours through grass and brush higher than our heads. It was spooky. I walked about five yards behind Clive so we would both have a field of fire if the bull ever turned and charged us. After four hours, we caught up with the four bulls, which had split away from the herd, but the jungle was too thick to identify which one was mine. It was also impossible to get a clear shot. They ran and we followed again.

We found them once more, but the same thing happened. By now, I was hoping they would charge; at least I could get another shot. I think. The jungle was so dense in places that they could have been six feet away and we wouldn't have seen them.

Figure 39. Ollie and Big "Dog" Baboon

At near dark, we waded the river again and went back to camp. I was so disappointed in myself for making such a poor shot. I was also tired. A Diet Coke and a little water don't last all day.

June 12th and we went back to the same place we first saw the buffalo along the river and waded across. We zigzagged across the area where we last saw the four bulls, but no sign. They must have doubled back and crossed the river.

After lunch we started searching for tracks on the Bedford side of the river. We found some and followed for several hours. We were downwind and nearly walked into them before realizing they were there. We could hear them moving a little, we could even smell them, but couldn't see them. They were maybe ten or twelve feet away and didn't know we were there. Clive motioned for me to get my rifle ready to fire because if the nearest bull moved out onto the path we were on, we would have to flatten him. We had nowhere to go. Shortie and Piason, in front of us, started to kneel down so we could shoot over their heads. Shortie was just about to squat on his heels when we heard a SSSSSSSSSSSSST. We all went ooooooooooooooooooh and the buffalo stampeded off to our right. It was a large puff adder. We abandoned ship.

We followed the bulls for a while but it was getting late and we had a long way to go to get back to the truck. Shortie found some blood on a stalk where the bulls had been laying. On the way back to camp we saw five elephants, two cows with calves and one young bull. That evening Ollie went spotlighting. I went to bed.

I had an upset stomach the next morning, so Clive, Shortie and Piason went to see where the four bulls had gone. They found that the buffalo had crossed the river again to return to their normal feeding grounds close to the jungle. Ollie went out with Daniel and shot a huge wildebeest.

They called Clive for help and on his way to them he saw two cheetahs at a waterhole. He radioed Daniel to bring Ollie quick! They met and Ollie got into the back of Clive's truck and headed for the waterhole. It looked like both cats had left but suddenly one of them walked out and started running down the road ahead of the truck. Ollie had to do a "Texas Heart Shot" and missed a perfect shot by half an inch. The cheetah slowed down but kept moving. He had one more quick shot through the body that sent it down. He finished it with a third shot.

They came back to camp all JAZZED!!!! It was a big cat and they couldn't wait to measure it. It is seven feet one inch tip to tail and weighs between 115 and 120 pounds. It will easily make the book and so will the wildebeest. This is a real trophy day for Ollie. This makes the hunt for me.

Four new hunters and two more guides joined us in camp. We had roast warthog for dinner. Too much good stuff!

I feel better this morning; my appetite is back. We prowled around all morning, but no buffalo. We stalked a small group of waterbuck but didn't see anything worth shooting.

Figure 40. Ollie with Trophy Wildebeest

In the afternoon we drove the perimeter roads again. We started on the Turgue Camp side and were stalking a small herd of buffalo when we came across an elephant. It didn't scent us and kept on feeding. It broke off a tree branch bigger around than my thigh that spooked the buffalo into a full run, but only for a short distance. We followed and when we got close, Clive climbed a tree to find out where they had gone. When he got up high enough to see, he found that a young bull was looking straight up at him. The grass was so tall that all Clive could see was his face and horns. They really spooked then but my bull and his three buddies split away from the rest. We tracked them for several hours but the jungle was just too thick. Then we ran on to the elephant again and had to abandon ship.

We had impala roast for dinner, compliments of Mr. Barney.

We hunted hard all morning but again no luck. At near dark we went back to the river to try to catch the buffalo going to or from the water. Again, no luck. They didn't show before it was too dark to see.

We had impala stew for dinner. Everything is good.

Figure 41. Ollie, Piason, Shortie and Clive with World Record Cheetah

The next day we were at the river at first light but no buffalo were there. We hunted for several hours and ran across a really nice bushbuck. So I killed him. My first African trophy on this trip.

We saw a herd of buffalo on the way back to camp. We got out and stalked them for a fairly short distance and tried to get set up for a shot. They were moving too quickly by then, so I didn't even try. This has not been my lucky hunt. I'm really glad Ollie has gotten two record trophies.

This is the last hunting day, but Clive left for a hunt in the Upper Zambezi Valley. Roger had told us that this would happen when we booked the hunt. Ollie and I went out with Shortie and Leymon, another apprentice PH, looking for bush pig. We found tracks and sign but no pigs. We made another quick bush-pig hunt in the lagoon area. We saw no pigs but Ollie did shoot another big dog baboon. We left for Harare after an early lunch. Charlene, the wife of PH Peter who was with Clive, drove us there. We went back to Georgie's B&B and it felt like home.

Georgie took me shopping in Harare. I had to buy a big sports bag to replace the plastic one I had bought in Sydney. It held the entire suitcase overflow after I bought more souvenir shirts. It cost $700 Zim bucks. That's roughly $6.00 US. It's important to convert quickly before sticker shock takes over. Charlene came back to take us to the airport. She has the ranch minibus and it's a lot easier to haul the gun case around in it. We paid our $40 US Departure Tax and caught a one-hour earlier-than-scheduled flight to Johannesburg. Our flight to London leaves tonight about 8:00 pm and we can wait in the BA Lounge. This is a First Class leg so the service will be good.

This is an overnight flight to London and we landed a few minutes early. The seats reclined to an almost flat position, so I was able to rest. The recliners were a little short for Ollie but he made the best of it.

The suitcases and gun case had been marked with firearms tags for special handling. When we went for the baggage, we found the sports bag only. I went to BA Customer Service and there were two BA Special Baggage handlers with Ollie's suitcase and the gun case. My suitcase went somewhere else in the world. BA folk escorted us to British Customs where we learned that my information was wrong – Customs will NOT store firearms for short periods. After 45 minutes of "sorting" things out, Customs gave us two options: get an airline to store them or get a local, licensed firearms dealer to come get them, store them for a week, and them return them to us. Soooo, back I went to BA Customer Service and recounted my sad tale of woe. The BA agent called BA Security and they said..........No Problem! They came to Customs, picked up the guns and told us to have American Airlines notify them when we checked in for our flight to Chicago. I LOVE British Airways!! We could have had anything in the suitcases. Not one customs agent even looked at my backpack once we said that we had firearms. I filed a missing baggage claim and we headed for the train station.

The train to Paddington Station was fast; then we took a taxi to the hotel. It was the opening day of Parliament so traffic was worse than usual. The streets around Buckingham palace were closed. When we got to the hotel, a Comfort Inn, Damon was there to meet us. The rooms seem small but all three of us can stand up at the same time in the same room. Better than the backpacker's hostel in Sydney.

Today is June 21st and Ollie's and my first time in London. We took the Big Bus tours of London – all three of them. That is a really neat way to see the whole city. It took all day and we saw all the major attractions. We didn't walk much because both Ollie and Damon have bum knees. The weather couldn't be better. It is sunny and warm with a cool breeze. Damon never experienced this kind of weather is all his trips to London before, even when he stayed once for two months.

Today is Chunnel Day. We took a taxi to Waterloo Station and got on the Eurostar. Due to heavy train traffic, there were several delays along the way to the English Channel so the trip took a little longer than planned. It didn't matter to us. The "under Channel" time was 23 minutes and we estimated that we were going about 100 mph. We got off in Calais, France, and found that the station is out in the middle of nowhere. The dispatcher was kind enough to call a taxi for us and we went to a large mall where we had lunch. With lunch we had a French beer – it was no better than the New Zealand beer – basically swill. The "under Channel" time on the return trip was 21 minutes. The really fast times on the train are between Calais and Paris but we didn't want to take the time to go that far.

We are going to Scotland so this morning we took a taxi to King's Cross Station and caught the train to Edinburgh. I'm sure the driver cheated me on the change. I guess it's not a real trip until a cabbie shortchanges one.

The countryside is many different shades of green and brown with low, rolling hills. We passed five nuclear generating plants, one with 12 cooling towers. The train was going as fast as the Eurostar; it's 395 miles with six stops in just less than five hours. We arrived at the Waverly Station in Edinburgh and surprise! No taxis! There was a parade or march nearby and the cabs couldn't get down to the station. We walked to a nearby corner and finally found one.

We found a tour bus and rode it twice. The old city has some truly interesting features and monuments. It is much more gothic with spires and fretwork than London. We stayed at the Cairns (pronounced Kerns) Hotel. We walked around the corner and did a little pub crawling. We learned in London that pub food is probably the best available and the same is true here. Fish and chips and beer! At 11:00 pm it was still light enough outside that I could read my watch without turning on a lamp.

Ollie and Damon weren't up to a walking tour the next day so we ate breakfast at the hotel and went to the train station. We caught the 9:30 am train and arrived at 1:15 pm. That meant speeds were at least 100 mph along the way.

The weather continues to be perfect. In London, we went to "our" pub for a late lunch but there is no food service on Sunday. So we toughed it out with a couple of brews – Foster's on tap, of course. A nearby restaurant was open for dinner.

This is what cruise directors call a "leisure day." I need to sort out and repack all my stuff. I have lots of treasures now, mostly souvenir shirts. Remember the "no dust, no feed" policy! I would like to get the suitcase a little lighter, but I think it's hopeless. We met Paul Convery's daughter, Reanna, for dinner. She's a sweetheart, which we suspected she would be. Ollie didn't like dinner, also no surprise.

When we checked in with American Airlines, they told us that British Airways had delivered the gun case already properly tagged for Tucson via Chicago. Love BA! We left just a little late but landed in Chicago on time. US Customs cared not a whit about the guns but were very excited about our having been in a foot-and-mouth contamination zone (Zimbabwe). They routed us through the US Agriculture Station so our shoes could be scrubbed. Again, no one even looked at our suitcases. They didn't even check the serial numbers on the rifles! We must not look like smugglers.

The flight to Tucson was on time and Dick and Betty Jo Barney met us at the airport. This was a hard day for Ollie because of all the walking we had to do. We were both very tired since traveling West makes for a really long day.

June 27th and home again!

So the journey ends. We flew over 30,000 miles and traveled thousands more in busses, trains, and hunting vehicles. We saw some of the most beautiful landscapes in the world and met people that we want to see again and again. Ollie collected some world-class trophies and fulfilled a decades-long dream of hunting cheetah. I can't remember all of the people who told me that they wished so much to have been able to make this kind of trip with their fathers. I think I'm the luckiest woman on earth to have had this opportunity. If I hadn't taken a single trophy, it would have been worth everything it cost in both time and money. I wish all readers of this journal the same opportunity with someone they love."

Poland Hunt

Sherry and I wanted to hunt in Europe 'cause I'd hunted all the continents excepting Europe. We got hooked up with this Diane Hunting Club that pretty much has the control of all the huntin' in Europe. They priced out a hunt for us in Poland for October 2002 that sounded good; they named off all the animals they had to hunt there – they had mufflon, a small sheep, and they had these Japanese Sitka deer and they had these Russian boars. That's three animals that Sherry and I never shot so we bought the hunt. We knew when we bought it that it was just a token hunt that we could go over and have a hunt and say that we'd hunted Europe. That'd make all six of the continents for me.

I knew it was a token hunt 'cause they only had three animals we could shoot. They had three more over there that we'd already killed in other places in the world and we could shoot them on a trophy fee if they was better than anything we'd already killed. Which we intended to do. The problem was, when we got over there, these animals that they had to hunt was scattered all over Poland and their numbers was way down. They had the animals but they didn't have a big number to hunt and there was no such thing as pickin' a trophy. It turned out that we were real lucky if we could get a shot at anything; the game was terribly wild.

We had two camps we hunted out of; one of 'em was way down in the southwest part of Poland. They had the best variety of game there and then to shoot the Sitka deer, we had to go up on the north end, along the Baltic Sea. There's where they had the Sitka deer, they had red deer, and they had this roe deer. The season wasn't on for the roe, so we couldn't shoot one of them. I had the one opportunity in both of the huntin' areas to have shot one if I was a half-way decent shot and could a-killed it. Which I could have.

We started on the lower part of Poland and they had quite a number of hogs in there but I don't think they was Russian boars. I think, with all this farmland, they was bound to be mostly mixed up with the feral pigs. I could shoot them over in Australia; they're a whole lot less money and more of 'em and maybe even take out a big-headed boar. So we started huntin' there and Christ, the game is the wildest damn game I ever saw! The only reason I can figure for it bein' so rough is the fact that they were over-hunted. Because they had foresters workin' in there, lots of that forest they had loggin' and clearin' it out so they was seein' vehicles and people all the time that wasn't hasselin' 'em. But they'd hear a motor and, by god, they were gone! I hunted four days before I could get a shot at a mufflon. And it was down in this dark forest on a cloudy afternoon and it was spittin' a little snow and they had this mufflon ram there down below us. I could see it with my binoculars, it was standin' in between a couple of trees and I could see part of his shoulder and I could see most of his head. This Polish guide I had that don't speak a word of English – they have these tripods they shoot on because you can't sit down in that brush and see anything, you have to shoot off-hand and they furnish these tripods – and I slapped my rifle down on it and one of the three pods was hangin' in mid-air somewhere! So I only had two. I could see this ram down there, about 100 yards, maybe 110 yards, and it's wobblin' around and finally I got settled down enough and I squeezed off a shot. The animal just broke and run like it was a miss! I found out later that this guide thought I'd wounded it. He grabbed my rifle and he run down that 100 yards and he run about another 75 yards in the direction it took and he found it layin' there dead. Luckily, I killed that after four days a-huntin'.

Figure 42. Ollie in Poland with Mufflon Sheep

I hunted another day, and all the time we're tryin' to get a shot at a boar, which we never did get a shot at. Then we moved up to this upper hunting camp and the camp was fairly nice. I had to walk up 14 steps to get to the house and then to get up to the bedroom, I had another 18 steps. Then I had another 18 steps to go down to the bathroom and livin' room. With my bad legs and my havin' to go to the bathroom about three or four times a night, hell, in the two days we hunted there, I was wore out climbin' up and down stairs! Sherry got her Sitka deer there; somehow or another she got a good shot at one and killed it. My guide, he's hunted me out 'til after dark. And out in this field, I don't know whether they'd taken hay off it or what, it was dark, but it had a little skiff of snow on it. This animal out there, probably 150 yards, maybe even 200 yards, it was walkin' along and stoppin'. It isn't on my side of the vehicle, but you couldn't shoot out of 'em anyway, and he's sayin' "Shoot! Shoot!" So I got out and I got squared away and he's still a-sayin, "Shoot! Shoot!" I don't know, I looked at this thing with my Zeiss binoculars, and they're good binoculars, and I couldn't tell, I didn't know whether I was shootin' a farmer's calf or a Sitka deer or a boar or a red deer or what I was shootin'! But he's still a-sayin, "Shoot!" So I tried to get it in my scope and, hell, I couldn't see the crosshairs! But I could barely see my crosshairs on this snow. So I moved them crosshairs around to where I was right on the edge of this animal. So I figured if I move 'em over to where I can't see 'em, I should be on it. I did that and I squeezed off a shot and I heard the bullet hit! It was far enough I could hear it hit and this thing whirled and run about 50 yards and folded up.

This guide, he's a-hoppin' up and jumpin' up and down – I guess he was tryin' to congratulate me because he shook my hands two or three times, put his arm around me and said that I done a good job. So we drove off down there and looked around and we find this here Sitka deer, a nice one, probably weigh 140 pounds and I think that's about as big as they ever get, 140 to 160 pounds. And they're nearly black. It was shot through both lungs, a little farther back than I generally shoot one, but it killed it. Then we get into camp and we've got our interpreter there in camp and there's another couple of hunters there. They're a-jabberin' and a-talkin' and a-wavin' their arms and goin' on and then this interpreter tells me, "They tell me you're a real good shot, to be able to make that shot!" All I knew was I was damn lucky to get that shot! Let alone make it!

We hunted there for two days and they're tellin' us about all this game they got. And the reason we're not seein' it – it's all out in the forest. But we're drivin' around through all these forests all the time with a skiff of snow on the ground and on these loggin' roads, they're doin' some loggin'. They're doin' thinin' and they're cuttin' a lotta pulp wood, hardwood for flooring, and I never see a track on the snow! I know that game is not out in those trees, either. This guide would tell me something and the interpreter's sayin', "The game is out in the forest." I said, "You tell that hunter not to BS me, because by god, when I can't see tracks when I'm goin' out there in the snow, I know the animals are not there! Tell 'im one other thing: I've saw more game, killed more game than he's ever saw!" So there's a whole lot more jabberin' about that! And there's absolutely no pig sign up there a-tall. Where we hunted first, there was quite a lot of pig sign. But they didn't really know how to hunt 'em, you know, one-on-one. They're huntin' these European hunters and they hunt like Mexicans. With Mexicans, there's a minimum of six to a dozen of 'em in a hunt and they got, all over these farms and around these edges, these things they call tires or stands that run about 20, 25 foot high with a little cabin on 'em. They set these Europeans up in them around all over and wait for the game to come in and maybe get a shot at one. There's a dozen of 'em in a dozen tires, you know more'n likely, someone's gonna get a shot. And then they had stands that was just about four or five foot high and they had them up in the head of draws and little saddles in these little ol' hills all covered up with forest where the animals was a-stayin'. And apparently, after they got out of the stands in the morning – they go out and put 'em in these towers in the morning – and then they'd make a drive. That's the only way I could see they could be a-doin' it. I'm sure that's what they did. We was real, real lucky to have got two animals apiece, out of the three.

This last hunt up there, these two days, we had our two animals we could kill and the only thing next was a boar. We could never see a track of one of 'em or any sign of where they'd been a-rootin', so Sherry told our interpreter, "You just take us to town and we'll get a hotel and sightsee for a couple of days." "Well," he says, "I can do better than that! I'll take you home and you can stay right in my house! And I'll show you around." So that's what we did and damn, he had a real nice place for us to stay. And the bathroom right there – I only had to walk about 10 foot to get to it. We had to climb 15 steps to get up to the rooms. Christ, in that country, you climb a lotta stairs!

He showed us around and he had a younger brother there that was a history teacher in Poland. This town on the Baltic Sea there, Gdansk, used to be a big ship-building town. The brother could talk good English and he took us to a bunch of these old churches in some of the oldest part of town, original street and it's all blocked off and it's a quarter mile long or so. It's got all these shops along the edge where you could buy trinkets and spend money. This brother of his talked good English and I could hear most of what he said. I couldn't hear all of it but Sherry would interpret to me and we got along fine. We'd have a couple of drinks with our interpreter and his wife at night and she'd set us out some dinner.

Figure 43. Ollie with Sitka Stag

This guy was in his early fifties, I would guess, and he'd been over in the United States. He'd come over to Chicago to visit some of his relatives and he got a job and I think he said he worked for a house builder there for seven years. His car he drove, he bought it there and had it shipped back. When it was time, he took us down to the airport to get the plane to Warsaw. In Europe, apparently, with these heads, if you boil 'em out and dry 'em, you can haul 'em around in the airplanes, in the luggage. So, that's where we put our heads; in a pasteboard and then Sherry packed her dirty clothes around 'em 'cause we never had any place to do any laundry. We had a nice pasteboard box and we had to pack another piece of luggage. We flew into Warsaw and there we had a problem with our guns, to put 'em on British Air.

We went over with our guns and went clear to our huntin' camp, never checked 'em, just went right on through. No problems. We had a guy to pick us up and take us out to the huntin' camp and he grabbed the guns and we left. We got to Warsaw again and the papers was never stamped to where they'd come into Poland! So that created a damn problem and it went on, hell, we had a three-hour layover and it took all of that! First thing, we had to take our guns in and have 'em inspected; open 'em up, get the serial numbers and see that they're unloaded. They had to take all of our ammunition out, count ever round. They had to put them all in one suitcase. Then pretty soon, we had to have a paper that showed these guns and the amount of ammunition and the paper has to have our names and our phone numbers, most of our life history and passport numbers and Social Security numbers and they got that. Then they had to have it in duplicate! And they don't have copy machines there, so they gotta get another form and fill that out. And when they got that, they had to have it in triplicate! So we did it all over again.

Then they had what I figured was a corporal, Army guy, that was checkin' our guns and back there where they're checkin' our guns, in the floor, through the terrazzo there, there's a .45 bullet hole! I pointed that out to 'im and I asked 'im, course he knew what I was pointin' at, but he didn't understand English; he shook his head, he didn't take credit for it. I wonder what kind of excitement that started when they fired this .45 off there in the terminal! Finally, we had to board our airplane and when we get up to where we're gettin' on the airplane, they got the guns there, got 'em tagged. They give us the papers on the goddamn guns where they're goin' into London, but we didn't see the guns.

So we go into London. Then, they've got a problem. Finally, we're goin' in through Security and there's a girl there lookin' for Barney. That was the name that was on the gun tags. So I had to go down three flights of damn stairs down on the tarmac – there the guns are. I had to open 'em up and let 'em take the serial numbers, after waitin' for five minutes for Security to get there to do it. Then they rushed me back, by god, I'm holdin' up the airplane! I got through Security; I didn't even have to go through the checkers. I got on the plane and we get to Chicago and our guns is there. This officer that checked us through was a lady and she's a Polish lady. She found out we was from Poland and what were we doin' in Poland with guns? So we had to explain to her that we were huntin'. Well, what were we huntin'? I'm a-waitin' for the Agriculture people to get on us and confiscate our goddamn heads. She got our guns up there and I'm walkin' around there to open 'em up and I had to give her the key; I couldn't be in there. She'd open 'em and she'd close 'em and when she didn't get the case closed right I had to tell her she had to unlock 'em and get 'em closed up right. Then we had this cardboard box there. She wanted to know what that was, and that was where our trophies were. And Sherry, bless 'er, she can still think on her feet, says, "That's my laundry." Well, she did have her laundry packed in around 'em. Boy, she stamped that box and hell, we got back with our trophies and they never been inspected or anything! And our boots! You know, generally, they have to take them and spray 'em. When I put my boots in my suitcase, her horns hadn't fit in this box we had, but by springin' my suitcase a little bit, I could get 'em in over my boots. With all my dirty clothes and stuff around over 'em and all of our ammunition they put in there in Warsaw.

These Customs people, especially women, they're kinda finicky about goin' through your dirty clothes. So we got them all through, back home. If it hadn't been the guns she was worried about, she might a-wanted to check the dirty laundry. She said her parents had come from Poland and I guess guns over there is pretty dangerous after ol' Hitler killed about seven million of 'em there durin' World War II.

We got our guns back on the airplane and when we landed in Tucson, Sherry looked at her watch and she says, 'We've been 24 hours and five minutes since we left Warsaw!" And we had our guns and we had our trophies. And that's about the highlights of this here Polish hunt. But I can tell you with a straight face that I'm not goin' back to Poland and I have no desire to go back to Europe and look at all these old buildings; these thousands and masses of damn people! It amazes me why anyone ever wants to go to Europe! And why they ever go back the second time – they've got a curiosity that I don't have.

For the record, we hunted Poland for eight days, fired two shots each, got two animals each and was real lucky to get any shots at all! At the second camp, we was the first American hunters they'd ever saw; I hope we left a halfway decent impression on 'em.

Australia 2003

This story started in 2002 when I was in Reno with Sherry. And while we're there in Reno, I run onto this Steve, he's an Australian hunter. I got to talkin' to 'im and he's wantin' to sell me a buffalo hunt and I told 'im I didn't need a buffalo hunt. The only damn kinda huntin' I was interested in Australia would be a cullin' hunt. I've culled goats and I've culled these big kangaroos and I'd like to get a cullin' hunt on wild pigs. They're supposed to have four million wild pigs up there. And I've hunted Australia five times and I haven't saw a pig yet! I suppose they're there.

So I run onto this Steve up there and I was talkin' to him and he finally got a cullin' hunt lined up for me, it'd be donkeys and pigs. It was a $3,500 hunt for 10 days of huntin' donkeys and wild pigs. And right up at the last minute, the government went in there with helicopters; what they were doin' I have no idea, but they stopped our hunt in there. And he let me know that we wouldn't be a-huntin' there but he said he could come up with a cullin' hunt on dingoes, wallabies and a few buffalo. And that is the hunt we made.

There was the three of us left of the 4th day of August, went over to LA, got on the Quantas airplane and it was full. I'm really sure that this Quantas airplane was made for their flyin' around in the Orient for little people. People the size of myself and John Bessett and this Jerry Shaw didn't fit in too well. On the trip down and the trip back we had window seats and sittin' there right straight up, our shoulders touched. When I'd move, they'd overlap. And with our feet right on the floorboard, our knees was touchin' the seat in front. Invariably, we'd no more than get off the ground 'til the guy up in front would have to run his seat down. Then it got crowded. The stewardess would come along with their refreshments and we'd let our trays down to take on these refreshments and these gourmet meals that they serve that I don't like. Christ, you know, we didn't even have room to eat the damn stuff! And it was miserable, miserable!

By the time we got down to Brisbane where we had to unload our guns and go through inspections, this Jerry Shaw, we had to wait 'til the last baggage come through and his baggage is not there! So we take our rifles and our luggage over to go through customs and Jerry, he slowed that operation down. He had to tell the customs people that he'd lost his baggage and he'd lost all of clothes and all of his ammunition. He had to tell the customs everthing and really, all he had to do is just open up the rifle case and they check your gun permits and the serial numbers on the rifle. With ol' Jerry along, he had to explain everthing to these customs man, just killin' time! You know, instead of lettin' 'em do their business and go on. By the time we got through there, we'd missed our flight up to Darwin! Christ, then we had to go and make other arrangements to get to Darwin. We had to layover about two hours and then they put us on a plane that took us to Cairns. Then we unloaded there, had another couple hours layover, and then they flew us into Darwin. By then, we'd missed our flight to a little airport within an hour and a half from our huntin' camp. So we had to find a room and spend the night there in Darwin.

The next mornin' we got on this charter flight and it's a two-hour flight down to the little village, I don't know the name but it was mostly Aborigines there. They had a little store and the store charged three times as much in there as they did in other stores in the bigger towns. This pilot flew us down in an old, old airplane. I don't know what kind of a damn airplane it was but up front it had a seat for the pilot and a passenger and then they had four passenger seats in back. When I got inside that plane, I could see that this plane is pretty ancient! Anyway, it seemed to taxi real well and it got in the air and it flew good. While I'm a-sittin' up there, I'm a-lookin' at the instruments and they had the hours there. There was 76,000 plus a few more! While I'm comin' back in this same airplane, it's got the same amount of hours. So I asked the pilot, I says, "How many hours has this plane flew since your recorder on the hours broke down?" "Oh," he says, "about 5,500". The plane flew real well and run good but, god, the inside of it showed a lotta use, lotta wear and tear.

The first afternoon in the huntin' camp this Steve took us out. He found one of these here scrub bulls and he had Jerry shoot it for dingo bait. We drug it around all over the country and into this place where he'd had a horse in there for bait. It was all eat up and he cut this bull open and we went into camp. His wife's got a nice meal for us; we did eat good on this trip. Facilities in the camp was real good, nothing in the world to complain about. The next day we went up in an area where they had a bunch of wild horses. I'm not into killin' wild horses 'cause I saw down in mid-Australia, in central Australia they had good-lookin' quarter horse-type horses in there. The government, a number of years ago, shot a lotta of these here in-bred studs out of it and released some good stallions in there. These horses was good. I had the opportunity in a hunt or two before to shoot 'em and I wouldn't shoot 'em. I was reluctant to shoot these horses on Aborigine lands. After I saw 'em, I could shoot 'em 'cause they was little scrub horses and I think the average weight on 'em was probably around 700 pounds. And the stallions was probably, oh, I saw one or two that might a-went 800 pounds. I looked at their feet real careful and a double-ought horseshoe would be too big for most of 'em. I shot two or three horses that day and John and Jerry, they're up on the top and when I'd shoot one, they'd probably shoot four or five, which was all right.

**Figure 44. Ollie and Guide and
Termite Mounds in Australia**

The next day we went down to this Abo camp, had one old man there. He said he was a young man when the Japs was bombin' Darwin in World War II. His wife, she claimed she was a little girl back in those days. All these Aborigines we run across, they all talked English, nearly as good as the Australians talk it! She said she was a little girl when that went on. The night before, we'd killed about a year-and-a-half-old heifer and gutted it out and took it down to 'em and hell, this old man, he got his butcher knife out – no point on it – and hell, we could see he'd be forever skinnin' it, if he ever could skin it! So we skinned it out for 'im and he was real grateful for that. Well, as we come down there, there was three bulls a-hangin' around this Abo camp. There's four women there and this old man; they was occupyin' about three of the buildings. Then there was about three more that was vacant; real nice buildings, all metal up a-couple feet off the ground. I don't know when the Australian government built 'em for these Aborigines and what they cost, but I know a building of that type in this country would be around $75,000 or $80,000. They had outhouses and they had showers and they had a generator there and water tanks up off the ground, gravity flow to all these buildings. Water didn't go into the house, but outside the house they'd have a hydrant there. I got a few pictures of those Aborigines, a couple of the old ladies and this old man.

Figure 45. Ollie with his New Aborigine Friends

As we come in there, one of these bulls that they wanted killed is standin' out there about 100 yards, maybe 125. Steve told me to shoot it. I said, "Hell, let John and Jerry kill it 'cause John's only killed one buffalo and I've killed three and Jerry hasn't never killed one!" Christ, by the time they got the word to them, the thing went off into some real thick mango forest. There's water in there and, Christ, there's no way you could follow those buffalo in there. So we missed out on that and on the way back, Jerry was talkin' like he'd like to shoot a real good buffalo. He'd already passed up one that was as good as anything we'd shot. John wanted a decent buffalo and we run onto a good buffalo and hell, we was trackin' it around and tryin' to get it cut outta the main herd and get a decent shot at it. We finally got it cut out and Steve hollered at John, "Take 'im!" And John had one of Steve's loaner rifles, a .375, and the buffalo was runnin' out, a good 100 yards away, and John broke a shoulder on it. But it didn't slow 'im and he fired two more rounds at 'im and I think he probably shot 'im in the stomach, 'cause I see a bullet hole in the stomach. And then Jerry, in the meantime, he'd opened up. He was shootin' one of Steve's .426 or a .416, or some damn thing like that, a Remington and a good buffalo gun. John's outta ammunition - he just had three rounds in the gun – and this Paul, the one Steve had a-helpin' 'im, he hadn't put any ammunition in for the .375, so John, he couldn't do any more shootin' so Steve killed the buffalo, finished it off. After he finished it off and got there, ol' Jerry got to thinkin', well hell, he didn't want this bull! He didn't think it was big enough and besides, then he's givin' Steve this story that he thought it was a cullin' bull. That's the reason he was shootin'. Steve reminded him, he says, "You know we passed up all kinds of bulls that wasn't good as this; wasn't good enough for a trophy. We weren't shootin' 'em. When John took that bull and crippled it, you shouldn't a-been shootin'! Far as I'm concerned, it's your buffalo! I had to pay $500 for it so someone's gotta pay $500!" Well, Jerry didn't say he'd take it. I told Steve on the way back, I says, "Hell, if Jerry won't take this buffalo and I know John don't want it because when he kills a buffalo and it hangs up on his wall, he wants somethin' he's killed hisself. To stop any confusion or hard feelings, I'll pay you the $500." By the time we'd got back to camp, ol' Jerry come around and told me, "I fouled up, didn't I". I said, "Big Time! Anyone would know that the effort he was goin' through to get John this bull, that it wasn't a cullin' bull!" "Well," Jerry says, "I'm gonna take it." He talked too much, but he's a decent human being. He said that if he could find one, a real outstandin' one, he'd shoot it.

But John wanted one and then, I don't know, a day or two later, while we was huntin' horses, we run onto this extra-good bull and John killed it. And then Jerry told Steve, "If I can find somethin' bigger than the one John got, I'll take it!" And we run onto one! It looked like it was a lot better'n it was 'cause it was an old, old bull. Some of his teeth was even gone and he was in bad flesh. He wasn't as big by several hundred pounds as he would if he'd been in good flesh. Ol' Steve, he told Jerry, "Stalk down and shoot it. There's your bull!" Steve didn't give 'im time to change his mind. He killed it and when he measured it up, it's about a point and a half or two points bigger'n the one John got! Course, we used rough measurements and they only liked about a inch of bein' Gold Medal bulls! His was way up in the Silver and John's is way up in the Silver. They're both good, outstanding bulls. That pretty well took care of the buffalo hunts, because I didn't want one.

We made two more trips down there tryin' to find these bulls they wanted culled, because these women'd go out, there was some kind of a palm leaf they was collectin' to make baskets out of, and they would chase these women back to the house. That's the reason they wanted 'em culled. We never did get a chance to shoot 'em, just that one time when I could a-killed one. There was two of 'em out there that day.

Then we went back to our first cullin'. John and Jerry was doin' the bulk of the shootin', which was fine with me, because I really don't even like shootin' these scrub horses. They are a target. He took us into a place where he'd saw some pigs the week before and some donkeys. We went in and never found any of the pigs but we did run onto a herd of nine donkeys. I killed two and John and Jerry shot the other seven. I imagine John killed most of 'em – John's a good shot! He had a rifle he'd borrowed from one of his grandsons, a .308 Remington, goddamn; John was killin' them horses pretty well and fast! Steve told me, "Goddamn, I'd like to have that rifle John's a-shootin!" I says, "It's not the rifle! It's John! He can make any kind of ol' corker look good!" He had to take that rifle one day and go out finish off a horse that I'd wounded – shot it too far back – it was ready to die anyway. He told John, "If that rifle didn't belong to your grandson, I'd trade you out of it!" John said, "I'd like to trade it to you, but I can't do it."

Figure 46. John Bessett and Ollie with Water Buffalo

They had a few of these wallaby's in there and I shot one and John shot a couple and Jerry shot a couple of 'em and that was all we could. Then on the dingoes, I killed two dingoes, Jerry killed a couple and missed a couple, and John only ended up with one dingo. When we hunted in Australia in '88, John had killed a dingo. So we all just about even. I've killed three, John's killed two and Jerry's killed two.

About the last day and a half, we're prowlin' around findin' something to shoot and we found this bull that was crippled in the shoulder. Steve told me to cull 'im. I had a good broadside shot and I put a bullet in 'im, had to hit 'im in the heart 'cause he only run about 30 yards and folded up. I'd got another bullet behind his shoulder somewhere in his lung area and then he turned his rear end to us and I could get about a eight inch part of the buffalo to shoot in and break a shoulder and I plumb missed 'im! And all this time Jerry is a-shootin' at the rear end of 'im and I never could find a hole there but he said he'd hit 'im a time or two. But anyway, that was my buffalo.

Figure 47. Ollie and his Dingo

Then we went, the next to the last day, we went back in the area where ol' Steve had only been in it once, and a lot of the area he'd never been in. This Steve is a commercial helicopter pilot, too, and he'd flew all that area that he'd had and he said there was some tremendous bulls in there. And I know we was up there to look at these here sinker rocks that these Aborigines had and it was all posted "Sacred Land" and you couldn't pick up a rock or you couldn't pick a flower or you couldn't kill anything. And I know that ol' Steve is doing a little scoutin' mostly, and he knew I knew it, too, but I didn't say anything. It was all right with me, hell, it was all new country to me. On that hunt, we run onto one of these scrub bulls and Steve charges $250 to shoot 'em! And we got onto this one and he was just skin and bones, you know. He was in terrible shape. And Steve told Jerry, "Cull 'im! But shoot 'im in the head and put 'im out of his misery!" Christ, it took three shots in the head 'fore he killed 'im! He was shootin' it down in the jaw! He didn't know where the brains was in a horse; he didn't know where the brains was in a scrub bull or anything else! But like I told Steve, I said, "He's just a virgin at this huntin' and you expect almost anything then!" He learned a lot on this trip.

About the third day we had left, I was ridin' up front with Steve and I told ol' Steve that I was a little disappointed in Jerry 'cause he was a little pushy and talked a-way too much. But I says, "I'm glad I brought 'im along and give us somethin' to talk about. And it's makin' you a few extra dollars!" Steve, he just laughed. He never said anything bad about Jerry, but he had a way of keepin' 'im under control. Then he's tryin' to sell 'im a hunt in New Zealand! They've got some friends there; there's this young man, Paul, that came there from New Zealand a-huntin' with 'im. I guess he was puttin' 'im through a kind of a school to get a guide's license to hunt in New Zealand. And this kid's dad had a farm over there and a bunch of land and there was some pretty nice red deer in there. And he was tryin' to sell Jerry a hunt over there and this Paul would guide 'im over there. He'd get 'im a red deer and then he could get 'im a pilot and fly 'im up in the mountains and shoot a chamois and a Himalayan tahr. And then he said there's a world of rabbits over there to shoot and possums. I think he's got Jerry interested in it; he can't go next year, but the year after and his wife wants to go to New Zealand and he'll probably sell that hunt to 'im. He's goin' over to Africa next year. He's got three hunters and his son is gonna do some shootin'. A group of nine! I'm anxious to find out how this group of nine works over there. It's gonna be confusion like you can't believe. I hope they don't kill anybody!

Jerry was real careful with his gun but he did let it go off once pretty close to John's ear. He didn't hear much outta that ear for about three hours! I give Jerry, on his first trip, high marks. But to hunt with me again, he's gonna hafta learn not to ask too many questions and not talk so damn much!

And that's about the gist of this last Australian hunt; that makes five for me.

Argentina Hunt

Layne Brandt, his son Allen and I went to Argentina to hunt blackbuck in April, 2004. The Safari Club, they had their fund raiser and the outfitter down there give the Club three blackbucks and Layne bought 'em. I'd never been down there and I'd never shot a blackbuck so I told Layne, "Hell, I'd like to go with you if you'll let me shoot one of your three blackbucks." Well, he was agreeable to that.

We head off down there and I can tell you it's a long, damn long ways. We flew into Dallas-Fort Worth, then we flew to Miami, then we flew down to Buenos Aires, Argentina. It's quite a cattle country. We saw a lot of cattle, I thought inferior cattle, most of 'em was black and I don't like black cattle. The only thing I like black is black dogs. I've had good luck with them. Everthing else black, I've had problems with. This outfitter, he put us up in a pretty nice hotel there in Buenos Aires. I see marked on the towels and stuff that it was a three-star operation. That's a little better hotel than I'm used to stayin' in. Anyway, they treated us good down there. They talk Spanish and I talk a little Mexican so I had some problems with their Spanish. Then this outfitter, he had a couple of ladies there, real nice ladies, good-lookin' ladies, that he used for tour guides. He'd send a few of his hunters around to look at this Buenos Aires and I'll tell you, it's a town to look at. Buenos Aires, bein' in a poor country, I never realized that it would be as big as it is. Christ, I never did find out how many people's in it. Some people said there was 14 million and other people said there was 16 million. It looked like everbody but the poor people live in apartments 'cause this town is covered with high-rise buildings. These apartment buildings, near as I could count, run 15 stories or 20 stories high and then downtown some of their office buildings looked like they mighta been close to 40 stories high. There was more high-rise buildings than any place I've ever been before. I've flew over New York and I guess they got 'em higher down there and more of 'em but I never was down in their alleys where I could look at 'em.

The first hunt we had was blackbuck - it was down on this ranch where he had his blackbucks. We drove and it took about a little over two hours to get down there. We were there in the afternoon and we go out and the first field we come to – Layne was up in front with me and I wanted him to shoot – I didn't want to shoot the first blackbuck. But he gets out and this native they've got up front, he sees a couple of 'em out there, I don't know whether it's 150 or 200 yards, but it was quite a ways. Anyhow, he's a-sayin', "Shoot! Shoot!" and I'm a-waitin' for Layne to shoot. This one blackbuck is 'bout ready to walk behind some trees and he's sayin, "Shoot! He's good! Good!" So I shot, got a bullet in it a little too far back and it went in behind the trees and laid down. We get back in the vehicle and go down and got a gate to go down there and finish this off and take pictures.

Christ, this pasture is full of blackbucks! I'd never saw 'em in the wild before and the females is all kind of a blond color. The young bucks don't get black 'til they get mature, apparently. So we go to another field and a nice blackbuck run out there in front of us, run straight away from us. Allen is real anxious to kill one and he didn't wait for it to stop, he started shootin' at it a-runnin' and that didn't slow it down any. And he shot a horn off of it, right at the base of its skull. It started circlin' and he's still a-shootin at it and he run outta ammunition and he's gotta load up. By that time the thing is runnin' right straight towards us and he fired several more shots at it and it got up about 50 yards and he killed it. The guide let Layne off in one corner of another field and we went around to the other side. We kinda pushed the herd his way; he got a real clean look at one and dropped it with one shot. It's real good – all three of 'em we shot was good.

Figure 48. Ollie with his Blackbuck

This native and this outfitter, they started walkin' out in the field out there a couple hundred yards lookin' for the horn and I knew they'd never find it, but, hell, they walked right straight to it! Picked it up, brought it back! This native, he musta marked the spot or somethin' where Allen shot it off 'cause he walked right straight to it, picked it up.

Then we spent a night in another hotel. We spent five nights in hotels and one night in a ranch house. We went over to where they had their axis deer but here where the black antelope was, I saw better axis deer there than over where we was huntin'. Apparently, you weren't supposed to shoot 'em there on that ranch. I didn't wanna shoot one; I'd killed one in Australia, this axis deer, and then I decided, hell, this outfitter's been real good to us so maybe I'd better shoot one. We went over there in the afternoon and Allen, he shot a real nice one. Then Layne, he went off in the vehicle with the guide. Not long after Allen had killed his buck, Layne saw a really nice one and got it with one shot. I had to ride one of the horses. It looked like they had old McClellan army saddles there with three or four sheep hides over the top of 'em. And they had little ol' narrow stirrups; all I could get was my big toe in 'em. My big toe is not all that strong, you know? It was a little hard for me to get on the horse but I found a bank and I got on 'im. Here, I'm just a-sittin' up there just a-ridin' on my butt and I'm used to usin' my feet in the stirrups and puttin' weight in the stirrups and ridin' that way. Ridin' back to camp on these here sheep skins and no stirrups to put my feet in, I felt real damn awkward, to tell you the truth! They had me on a real damn nice horse; he reined well and he was well-behaved. Apparently he was gentle – he didn't throw me off or try to. We spent the night there and course this guy was wantin' me to shoot one so I go out with his native he's got there and we rode around a couple of hours. I saw one real nice one but he couldn't get me a shot at it. You know, my huntin' god is real good to me and she knew I didn't wanna kill one so she didn't let me kill one – saved me $1,400.

I was glad it was saved because we go back to town and we got these good-lookin' gals a-drivin' us around town and showin' us things I'm not interested in. I'm not interested in alleys and one-way traffic, but we did go down by the docks there and that was kinda interestin' to see these boats in there. Then they got a lotta elevated roads around there;

Christ, around where there's a lotta traffic. So we did a couple days of that, then we went up the river, the Tiger River, and somehow we got over into another river and come back a different way. That was a enjoyable trip. I enjoyed it. Then we went out on a ranch. The only question I could ask – I wanted to see their bulls. I'd saw all these here pot-bellied black cows and a few Herefords and finally, I told 'em, "I wanna see your bulls!" So they took us out; they had two bunches of bulls there. They had some two-year-olds and three-year-olds and then they told us about their breeding program. Twenty percent of their breedin' operation there on this ranch was artificial insemination. And as near as I could find out why they was artificial inseminatin' they was wantin' to keep the same blood. And keepin' the same blood there, they ended gettin' inbred cattle. They took us out in a pasture where they had 300 head of heifers. They liked these black cattle because they'd breed at 15 months. I'd asked about the cross breeds and no, they didn't like the cross breeds because they couldn't breed them 'til they was two-year-olds. I give this ranch manager the story that I liked the cross breeds; I realized that you didn't get a calf outta 'em for maybe six months later than you did the other, but when these Herefords and black cows get up to 10, 11 years old, they're wore out. These cross breed cows, hell, you can get a good calf outta 'em when they're 18, 20 years old. So you end up gettin' more calves out of a cross breed and they're generally heavier. But they'd been breedin' those cattle there for over a hundred years and they weren't changin'. They did say they had cross-breed cows further up north.

I looked at these 300 head of heifers out there and the first thing I noticed about them – they don't have any udders! Maybe there'd be one in 10 that had a little udder. If I was a-pickin' 'em, gonna buy 'em, those was the only ones I'd a-bought. He did say they'd had some problems with losin' new-born calves. That was their problem – they'd been foolin' around with this artificial insemination for the same blood for 15 years and they was just breedin' some cattle there, some cows that'd have a calf and wouldn't have any milk and the things'd starve to death. But they hadn't discovered that yet. I tried to find out who owned the ranch. Well, the granddad had homesteaded or got started there way back, I think it was 1891. Then his son took over and then this grandson had some along and he lived in town. I don't think he knew anything about ranchin'. So he was off on this tangent of artificial insemination and it looked to me like their cow operation was goin' downhill. I don't think I made any brownie points with 'em 'cause I asked questions and then I didn't like the answers. I finally just dummied up and quit askin' questions; I found out all I wanted to know.

Figure 49. Ollie and Friends in Buenos Aires

I had problems findin' out what the rainfall was down there. I know they get a lot of it. It's flat country, hell, it's flat and there's not many trees. You can actually see the curvature of the earth! I see drainage ditches around there, drainin' the water off. And then I tried to find out what the cow unit was, what the hell the cost of a cow unit was. They didn't understand that. Our interpreter was a nice young lady and she had absolutely no knowledge of agriculture; cattle or anything. And then her interpretations was a little different that I was a-gettin' from this ranch manager. This ranch manager, he said he thought they had around 48 inches of rain; our outfitter, he said 30, and our lady translator, she said that they got 200 mils of rain a year. With my knowledge of mils, that's less than eight inches of rain a year, so I know she's wrong!

Finally, we had two hard days a-huntin', some sightseein' and our experience on this ranch – and it must a-been a quite well-known ranch because that's where they took us. They were pretty well paid to let us wander around through it. Then it's time to come home. We got back a little quicker than we got down there because we flew straight from Buenos Aires to Dallas-Fort Worth and Dallas-Fort-Worth, after I think about a four-hour layover, to Tucson and we're back home! And I noticed how damn bleak this desert was; Christ, there's nothin' on it, no houses or anything. It sure didn't look like the country we were in, in Argentina. All green, all of this water; you could see rivers from the air.

All in all, it was a good trip and I'm a-workin' with this outfitter to put a hunt together for Sherry and I next year to go down and shoot three animals that we haven't shot. I can recommend this hunter we had. He was honest and he gives a fair price for stuff; he's not a-givin' it away. He does treat a man right. And that's my experience a-huntin' in Argentina!

Figure 50. Layne (top) and Allen Brandt with
Axis Deer in Argentina

Chapter Ten   Later Years

Southwestern Old Cowboys Association

One Saturday, this was in 2003, I went over to the Chiricahua Mountains to a meeting of this Old Cowboys Association. I had been once before with my good friend, Lloyd Harris. He wanted me to sign up so I got up there to the deal and I told 'em that I don't know whether I qualify or not. I said, "I owned a ranch one time." They said, "Well, hell, you could get in – you're old enough! And you're a lion hunter; you can get in on that. If you owned a ranch, you had to be a half-assed cowboy of some kind! And you're definitely old enough!" So they signed me up. This Lloyd Harris, he's up gettin' close to his nineties, and he had this couple there that he'd gotten acquainted with. The wife, Judy, would come in and clean his house all up once a week and check in with 'im every day. She'd take 'im shoppin' when he wanted to go and help 'im get his groceries. Her husband, Dennis Rogers, he was in construction, mostly dirt movin', and course, that's what Lloyd had done most of his life. So they had things to talk about. This couple really, really watched after 'im and took good care and about a year or two before he died, Lloyd told me one day, he says, "You know, I'm gonna make some changes in my will." I said, "Lloyd, it's none of my damn business, but I'll tell ya, this Judy is really been a godsend and a help for you. I don't think you oughta forget her." "Well," he says, "I'm not a-going to." And when he died, he willed everything he had to 'em!" He'd been married twice, never had any children and outlived both his wives. Anyway, he willed everything to them. I told Jackie Parker about it the other day and she'd known ol' Lloyd for years, back when she lived on the Bear Valley Ranch. "Goddamn," she says, "That's one of the nicest things I ever heard about anybody doin'"

He tells this story about his wife; she'd worked for the president of the Texaco Company for years, until he retired. And then she retired. He'd left her a bunch of Texaco stock.

Lloyd was tellin' me this story about the time he put in for a Texaco card and they rejected it! Sent it back; they didn't think he was qualified for one! And he says, "That kinda upset me! I called 'em up and got a-hold of someone there and told 'im I'd like to talk to someone on up the line somewhere. Not just some damn shoe clerk! I don't think you people know who I am!" He finally got a-hold of someone and he told him, "You know, I got six hundred shares of Texaco stock and you're tellin' me I'm not qualified for a card!" Well, in two days, he had a card! Special delivery!

So Dennis and I, we went over to this Southwestern Pioneers, Old Cowboys Association. We got up there where we signed in, paid our $5.00. Perkle, a vet who has worked here in Tucson and Green Valley most of his life, got to visitin' with us and Joe Goff, he showed up. I hadn't saw Joe Goff in years, but I'd hunted with 'im before. He told the story about that lion hunt (I told that story before, called it "Joe Goff") and he was pretty correct on everthing, but he didn't mention how slim the damn eatin' was! He did say that we eat part of that damn lion and fed the rest of it to the dogs. And then he told the crowd, he says, "You know, Ollie's caught three lions on my ranch. And I still owe 'im $1,500!" The bastard never did pay me a dime! And I told 'im, I said, "Well, hell, Joe, I'm glad you still owe me; you're not tryin' to beat me out of it!" And it happened a good 25 years ago!

He'd went to school with Dick, and Perkle had gone to school with Dick, and there was a couple of other guys who'd went and they was all wantin' to know how he's doin' and if he's still alive. Ol' Pickle, he saw some cigars in my pocket and says, "Ol' Joe Goff was tellin' me I'm older than you." I said, "No, goddamit, you're not older'n I am! The only thing older'n I am around here is these goddamn mountains! Might be an ol' crippled man or woman around here that's older, but you're damn sure not!" Turned out he's 78 and I was 84. Anyway, Ol' Perkle says, "It's them cigars that's kept you alive!" After I got away from 'im, I thought, "Jesus Christ, he probably wanted a cigar and I didn't offer 'im one!"

Made in the USA
Monee, IL
07 July 2026

56551275R00203